Conditionals and Prediction
Time, Knowledge, and Causation in Conditional Constructions

This book offers a new and in-depth analysis of English conditional sentences. In a wide-ranging discussion, Dancygier classifies conditional constructions according to time-reference and modality. She shows how the basic meaning parameters of conditionality, such as causation and logical sequence, correlate to formal parameters of the linguistic constructions which are used to express them.

Dancygier suggests that the function of prediction is central to the definition of conditionality, and that conditional sentences display certain formal features – verb forms, typical clause order, or intonation, each of which correlates to aspects of interpretation such as the type of reasoning involved, the role of causality, the use of contextual information, or the speaker's knowledge.

Although the analysis is based primarily on English, it provides a theoretical framework that can be extended cross-linguistically to a broad range of grammatical phenomena. It will be essential reading for scholars and students concerned with the role of conditionals in English and many other languages.

Barbara Dancygier is a Visiting Scholar at the University of California, Berkeley.

CAMBRIDGE STUDIES IN LINGUISTICS

General Editors: S. R. ANDERSON, J. BRESNAN, B. COMRIE,
W. DRESSLER, C. EWEN, R. HUDDLESTON, R. LASS, D. LIGHTFOOT,
J. LYONS, P. H. MATTHEWS, R. POSNER, S. ROMAINE, N. V. SMITH,
N. VINCENT

*Conditionals and prediction: time, knowledge,
and causation in conditional constructions*

CONDITIONALS AND PREDICTION

*Time, Knowledge, and Causation
in Conditional Constructions*

BARBARA DANCYGIER

CAMBRIDGE
UNIVERSITY PRESS

PUBLISHED BY THE PRESS SYNDICATE OF THE UNIVERSITY OF CAMBRIDGE
The Pitt Building, Trumpington Street, Cambridge CB2 1RP, United Kingdom

CAMBRIDGE UNIVERSITY PRESS
The Edinburgh Building, Cambridge CB2 2RU, United Kingdom
http://www.cup.cam.ac.uk
40 West 20th Street, New York, NY 10011-4211, USA
http://www.cup.org
10 Stamford Road, Oakleigh, Melbourne 3166, Australia

First published 1998

Printed in the United Kingdom at the University Press, Cambridge

Typeset in 10/13 Semitica   [SE]

A catalogue record for this book is available from the British Library

ISBN 0 521 59151 1 hardback

Contents

Acknowledgments

Writing this book took a long a time and could not be either begun or completed without the help, inspiration, and moral support of many people. I would like to thank them all here.

I have to start with the late Professor Olgierd Adrian Wojtasiewicz, who knew I had to become a linguist even before I discovered it myself and who never stopped encouraging me to keep on. I also want to thank Keith Mitchell, who first taught me that grammar has meaning and has been a great friend and an inspiration all along. This book also owes its existence to Basia Szymańska, the discussions with whom opened my eyes to the awe-inspiring beauty and complexity of conditionals.

So I started to work on this project, but the more I thought about it, the more lost I was. I could not have maintained the courage to keep on, if I had not met Eve Sweetser and gotten to know her work. I learned many important things from her, about conditionals, naturally, but also about scholarship, about working together, and about being a partner and a friend. Eve also introduced me to the linguistic community of the University of California at Berkeley, where I had a chance to work for the last few years. Among the people I met during my stay at Berkeley I would like to thank Chuck Fillmore first of all – for being an intellectual inspiration and a gentle critic, and for undeserved kindness in difficult moments. I am also grateful to Elizabeth Closs Traugott for her interest in my work and for most inspiring discussions.

Many thanks go also to all the people who, at various stages of the project, took time to listen to me or give their comments, and, overall, provided justification for taking conditionals seriously. The list is too long to be given in full, but I would like to mention Johann Van der Auwera, Bernard Comrie, Paul Kay, Derek Herforth, George Lakoff, Suzanne Fleischman, Debby Schiffrin, Sarah Taub, Adele Goldberg, Seiko Yamaguchi, Ewa Mioduszewska, Gilles Fauconnier, and Mark Turner. Needless to say, if this book is still full of flaws, it is because I myself failed to do a good job.

It is known that book-writers need their families more than others, just so they can remain sane. I was very lucky in this respect. I am grateful to my husband, Jacek, and my son, Szymek, for reminding me every day that life is much more varied and exciting than conditionals can ever be. I also want to thank my mother for her trust in me and for all the help she provided.

Last, but not least, I want to thank Peet's Coffee of Berkeley. Theirs is the best coffee in the universe and its magic quality of "turning caffeine into ideas" (thank you, Mark Turner, for the phrasing!) has probably made Berkeley what it is. I was glad to enjoy it while I needed it most.

1 *Conditionals as a category*

1.1 Constructions, conventional meaning, and the grammar of conditionals

This book is an attempt to provide a description of a certain fragment of the grammar of English, namely, conditional sentences. By "conditional," I will mean primarily the sentences so labeled by grammarians (rather than logicians): complex sentences, composed of the main clause (sometimes also called *q*, or the apodosis) and a subordinate clause (*p*, or the protasis). The subordinate clause is introduced by a conjunction, the least marked of English conditional conjunctions being *if*.

The analysis of conditionals attempted here will focus on providing an explanation of how aspects of conditional form give rise to a variety of meanings that conditional sentences express. That is, following the framework of cognitive linguistics, I will not treat the "grammar" as an autonomous formal description of linguistic structure, but rather as a representation of the speaker's knowledge of linguistic convention. In the cognitive approach (advocated by Fillmore 1977, 1982, Lakoff and Johnson 1980, Langacker 1987, 1991a, 1991b, Lakoff 1987, Fillmore, Kay, and O'Connor 1988, Fillmore and Kay 1994, and many others), it is not possible to speak of grammar in isolation from meaning, on the contrary, grammar is meaningful and essentially symbolic in nature. In Langacker's Cognitive Grammar, for example, lexicon, morphology, and syntax form "a continuum of symbolic units serving to structure conceptual content for expressive purposes" (Langacker 1987: 35). In Construction Grammar (Fillmore 1988, Fillmore, Kay, and O'Connor 1988, Fillmore and Kay 1994) each grammatical construction (whether lexical or syntactic) has a semantic and/or pragmatic interpretation as part of its description. In cognitive approaches every aspect of the structure and wording of a given sentence is thus considered to make a contribution to its overall interpretation in ways that are governed by linguistic convention. In this work I will attempt to describe how various aspects of the form of conditionals (including the choice of the

1

conjunction, verb morphology, intonation, and clause order) map onto various aspects of their interpretation.

Conditionals pose a number of questions. Their logical structure has been a puzzle to philosophers since Aristotle. They have been used as a testing ground for some of the most influential theories in the philosophy of language, such as, for instance, the theory of implicature. Their linguistic form also seems to escape elegant, uniform descriptions and they have been an object of interest to research in a whole range of fields, including syntax, semantics, pragmatics, discourse, language acquisition, history of language, language universals, and language teaching. This is because conditionals have an imposing variety of forms, and a still more overwhelming variety of interpretations. They are an area of language use where the interaction of form, meaning, and context is exceptionally complex and fascinating.

Attempts at unified accounts of conditional meaning have generally been easy targets for criticism precisely because the misleadingly simple *if p, q* structure can receive a great number of widely divergent interpretations. I would like to mention just two examples from two disciplines which have tried to describe conditionals. On the one hand, we have seen a long history of speculation among philosophers about the criteria for the truth of a conditional. The earliest truth-conditional treatment which involves material implication ran into trouble not only because of well-publicized paradoxes, but most importantly, perhaps, because it could not offer an even remotely convincing account of all conditionals. For example, the so-called indicative ones clearly required a different treatment from the so-called subjunctive, or (as many logicians call them) counterfactual ones. Since material implication means that a conditional is false when *p* is true but *q* is false, we might be able to account for truth values in examples such as *If a bird has wings, it can fly*; but we can already see difficulties looming even in cases with future reference (not yet "true"), and worse ones for "counterfactuals" like *If pigs had wings, they could fly* (how do we even evaluate the truth of a conditional where *p* is presumed to be false?). The more recent and more broadly accepted possible worlds solution, at least in one of its versions (Lewis 1976, 1979), acknowledges that a different interpretation is required for indicative and subjunctive conditionals. One might note here that both of the philosophical (or logical) solutions focus on the truth-conditional meaning of conditional sentences, practically disregarding differences in linguistic form. Thus, the assumption seems to be that *if p, q* is indeed a sufficient formal description of a conditional – it just needs to be paired with a similarly transparent logical formula.

On the other hand, there exists an equally longstanding tradition of describing conditionals in pedagogic grammars. These accounts (e.g. Eckersley and Eckersley 1960, Graver 1971, among hundreds of others) are centered around revealing formal differences among three major types of sentences, such as:

(1)   If I catch/caught/had caught the 11.30 train, I will get/would get/would have gotten to the meeting on time.

The description focuses on the verb forms used in such sentences, while the analysis of meaning is reduced to an absolute minimum: grammars usually mention that different forms may mark temporal reference and reality versus unreality of the condition. No examples of conditionals which have other, less regular verb forms are mentioned. In this model, then, the patterns of forms are the main concern, while other data or arrays of interpretation are not addressed.

Interestingly, a similar focus on the patterns of verb forms is characteristic of some approaches whose objective is primarily the description of syntax, viewed as an autonomous language system. For example, Hornstein (1990) proposes an account of well-formedness of sentences based on what he calls "the syntax of tense." The account is based on Reichenbach's theory of tense and offers a formalism which is designed to filter out ill-formed tense configurations. It makes specific claims about the grammatical tense configurations in conditionals, but treats them strictly in formal terms. That is, the principles proposed are meant to obtain regardless of the actual interpretation of sentences, and to account for possible and impossible pairings of verb forms in *p* and *q* clauses independently of the semantic, pragmatic, and contextual factors involved. Thus Hornstein's analysis (which will be reported in some detail in chapter 2) attempts to reduce the study of conditionals to the study of their form.

The two approaches mentioned are thus trying to describe conditionals either from the point of view of their (logical) meanings or from the point of view of the forms used. It is doubtful, however, that we could obtain a unified analysis by combining the two descriptions into one. First of all, the impression is that different sets of sentences are in fact being interpreted. For example, logicians' favorite examples, such as *If all men are mortal, then Socrates is mortal* are not considered relevant by the analysts interested in form (like Hornstein) because they fail to show the sort of tense-sequencing manifested in examples like (1). At the same time, some sentences that might be interesting from both a logical and a formal point of view will escape a linguistically revealing analysis because they are too bizarre to be readily contextualized (consider Goodman's famous *If the match had been scratched, it would not have been dry*). It seems implausible that we can hope to obtain a unified and linguistically sound account of conditionals by combining approaches that have different goals in analyzing at least partially complementary sets of data; on the other hand, single-framework accounts often fail either by disregarding part of the data and providing an account only of certain "central" cases, or by stretching a single analysis beyond credibility to account for the outlying areas of data.

"One solution fits all" kind of approaches are not common among linguists, because a linguistic analysis cannot fail to notice the significant differences between types of conditionals. Therefore we have seen many interesting proposals which address specific formally distinguished types, uses, or interpretations of conditional sentences (Haiman 1978, 1986, Haegeman and Wekker 1984, Funk 1985, Akatsuka 1986, Van der Auwera 1986, Fillenbaum 1986, König 1986, to mention but a few). There have also been attempts to offer broad guidelines as to what an analysis of conditionals should be sensitive to (Traugott 1985, Comrie 1986). Finally, purely descriptive grammars have become more open to data beyond the realm earlier ruled by language pedagogy – for example, Quirk, Greenbaum, Leech, and Svartvik (1985) use a much broader data base than the one reflected in the earlier 1972 edition of what appears to be the most comprehensive description of the English language. Consequently, we have now been given studies of conditionals which describe the variety of interpretations possible and recognize more of the complex ways in which conditional interpretations are arrived at.

However, in spite of their obvious merit and many fascinating insights into the nature of conditionality, these works have not created a unified analysis of the form and meaning of conditionals. In fact, it is still possible that many of the accounts offered do not even share a common view of what a "conditional" is. What has not emerged from all the impressive work and what is missing is a concept of a conditional as a category. So the crucial question now seems to be not so much "what differences are there?", because much has been said about them, but rather, "what is it that these various conditionals share over and above the notorious *if p, q*?" If we can identify a common function of the *if p, q* formal structure, it will then be possible to examine the ways in which interpretations of actual conditionals are based on that common function, in combination with the meanings contributed by other formal elements (verb forms, clause order, etc.) and with contextual factors. Divergent meanings of conditionals need not be attributed to divergence in the meaning or function of *if p, q* itself.

In this approach it is not satisfactory to simply document the various meanings of conditionals. Instead, we have to show how they are motivated compositionally. So we have to find out which formal aspects of conditionals are relevant to which aspects of their interpretation. In other words, we need to discover the parameters of conditional meaning as well as the parameters of conditional form and see how they correlate. It is through this type of analysis that we can discover what different conditionals share in their meaning and their form and thus reveal both the similarities and the differences. In order to do that, we need to not only identify those aspects of the form of conditional sentences that contribute to interpretation but also be able to specify the aspects of the interpretation each formal distinction is connected with. The description will thus cover the role of the component clauses and the conjunction, but will also look for other exponents of grammatically relevant meaning – morphological clues, function words, word and clause order, etc. It will also have to consider the significance of these formal exponents in context.

The grammatical description outlined above will thus view a conditional sentence as an example of a ***construction***, as defined and exemplified in works such as Fillmore 1986, 1988, Fillmore, Kay, and O'Connor 1988, Fillmore 1990a, 1990b, Fillmore and Kay 1994, Goldberg 1994, Shibatani and Thompson 1996. A construction is described as a conventional pattern of linguistic structure which is paired with features of interpretation. A construction may thus be specified with respect to lexical, morphological, or syntactic properties, but it will also be provided with semantic and/or pragmatic features of interpretation. The structural part of a construction may involve an assembly of patterns found elsewhere in the language, but in any particular construction the selected patterns are associated with special meaning (semantic, pragmatic, or both). The way in which constructions receive their interpretations is not fully compositional, but the non-predictable semantic and pragmatic information is in fact associated with the formal features of the construction in a conventional way. Therefore, a description of a construction involves an explanation of how its lexical and structural features are mapped onto aspects of interpretation in ways that may be construction-specific.

I will argue that conditionals can be best described within such a framework. Their meaning is determined by a number of form–meaning correlations which are construction-specific. For example, their verb forms signal important aspects of the interpretation (such as the type of reasoning involved, or the speaker's and the hearer's knowledge which constitutes the background for the reasoning), but they do so in ways that affect the whole construction, rather than one clause, and which are specific to conditionals. Furthermore, conditionals in fact represent not a single construction but a set of related constructions, involving a central category (which has a further set of specific constructional characteristics) and other peripheral categories (which inherit only the general conditional construction, and derive the rest of their form from the grammar of English at large). The relatively rich constructional specification of the central category of conditionals (constraints on verb forms and on pairings of verbs between *p* and *q*, clause order, etc.) is accompanied by a richer and more precise specification of the function of such conditionals; the meaning of the other formal components constrains and adds to the meaning of the general construction. For the types of conditionals with fewer formal specifications, there is a corresponding lack of constraint on the interpretation of the conditional relationship, whose nature will therefore be contextually determined. The constructional approach allows one to identify the formal correlates of conditionality and show how they are assembled to foster a particular type of interpretation.

The analysis of conditionals undertaken here will thus focus on describing what various aspects of conditional form conventionally contribute to interpretation. Conventional meaning includes aspects of interpretation which have been variously labeled as semantic or pragmatic by previous analysts, but which appear to be regularly attached to forms by linguistic convention. It attaches to forms on various levels of linguistic structure: morphemes, phrases, as well as whole constructions. Thus, the fact that the protasis of a conditional construction can be interpreted as a comment on the speech act in the apodosis (Van der Auwera 1986, Sweetser 1984, 1990), or on the choice of linguistic expression used there (Dancygier 1992), is a conventionally established option for interpretation, though it would not be included in the semantics of the construction under a narrowly truth-conditional definition of semantics. Nevertheless, as I will try to show, such interpretations arise in constructions which can be distinguished by some formal parameters, independently of being contextualized in some special way. To sum up, I will review features of conditional form, such as the use of lexical items (first of all, the conjunction *if*), morphology (the verb forms), and structure (clause order and intonation), from the point of view of what they conventionally contribute to the interpretation of conditional constructions. The aspects of interpretation motivated in this way may be semantic and/or pragmatic in nature, and they will affect the overall interpretation of the construction, rather than any of the particular expressions used.

Two recent works on conditionals address the issues raised above at least partially. Sweetser (1990) reveals a dimension of conditional interpretation which shows that conditionals are used as wholes to conduct specific types of reasoning. That is, they cannot be viewed as logically or syntactically governed combinations of randomly selected clauses. They are more accurately described as constructions in which the clauses are connected by specific types of relations. The nature of the relations, in turn, depends on the cognitive domain in which the assumptions expressed by *p* and *q* are considered: in the

content domain causal relations hold between the described events and situations, in the ***epistemic*** domain the construction links premises and conclusions, in the ***speech act*** domain *p*'s are used as comments on the speech acts performed in *q*'s. The use of conditionals in the three domains is exemplified in (2), (3), and (4):[1]

(2)   If Mary goes, John will go.
        (The event of Mary's going might bring about or enable the event of John's going.)
(3)   If John went to that party, (then) he was trying to infuriate Miriam.
        (If I know that John went to the party, then I conclude that he went to infuriate Miriam.)
(4)   If I haven't already asked you to do so, please sign the guest book before you go.
        (For the purposes of our interaction, let us consider that I make the following request if I didn't previously make it.)

Sweetser shows that ambiguity and semantic change of various other expressions (verbs of perception, modals, conjunctions) result from their being interpreted in these cognitive domains; what is more, the domains themselves are linked via a metaphor which motivates extensions of meaning from the physical into the mental and social domains. The approach not only reveals a fascinating dimension of the interpretation of conditionals, but also, or perhaps first of all, shows that different meanings can and should be analyzed as growing one out of the other. That is, in an analysis of a given ambiguous form it is not enough to say what the differences are, one also has to be able to express generalizations about the relationship between the meanings of polysemous or polyfunctional forms. Sweetser treats the general *if p, q* construction as having a general semantics, which is (in the sense of Horn [1985, 1989]) pragmatically ambiguous between content, epistemic, and speech-act level interpretations of the conditional relationship.

Another recent study of conditionals (Fillmore 1990a) analyzes the verb forms in conditional sentences as indicative of two aspects of their interpretation: temporal reference and ***epistemic stance.*** For example, the present tense form *catch* in (1) above is indicative of neutral epistemic stance towards a future event, while *caught* signals ***negative epistemic stance*** to it. The third form, *had caught,* is here used to express negative stance towards a past event. In this way, Fillmore accounts for a great variety of conditional sentences, showing important form–function correlations. Fillmore thus treats conditionals as constructions, in which the choice of a verb form in one clause is related

---

[1] All examples and glosses from Sweetser 1990.

to the choice made in the other in a way which is dictated by the overall interpretation of the construction in terms of time and epistemic background, rather than by any strict rules of well-formedness. For example, the choice of "present" and "future" verb forms in the clauses of *If I catch the 11.30 train, I will get to the meeting on time* are not made independently; but the dependence is not based on some formal constraint on sequence of verb forms. Rather, the pairing itself is connected constructionally to a given variety of conditional interpretations. In Fillmore's analysis the verb forms are thus treated as contributing to the construction's interpretation in a regular, conventionalized way. The analysis offered in this book has profited a great deal from the insights offered by Fillmore's work, although the actual contributions of conditional verb forms are here described differently.

There is, however, yet another dimension of analysis to be considered. In a project which seeks to show how interpretations are arrived at, it is important to be able to account for inferential mechanisms which guide interlocutors in their choice of the best form of expression and in interpreting utterances against the contexts in which they are used. There is indeed a rich tradition of frameworks offering explanations of the nature of inferential aspects of interpretation, the origins of which go back to the Gricean theory of implicature. Grice's (1975) original proposal of the interpretive maxims of Quantity, Quality, Relation, and Manner was a major advance in our understanding of the relation of form-specific conventional meaning to contextually conveyed meaning. In particular, it allowed linguists to see that there were regularities to be observed in contextual interpretation, as well as in "grammar" *per se.* Grice's treatment of *or* remains a classic example of an analysis which successfully combines a general (or minimally specified) semantics with further interpretive constraints to account for unexpected variation in actual interpretation of a form; *or* does not **mean** exclusive *or*, but **implicates** the exclusive interpretation. (Why would a speaker say *or* if she meant that *and* was a possibility?)

The original seminal concept of implicature stimulated a growth of new ideas in at least two directions: on the one hand, many analyses focused on the possible ways of distinguishing propositional and non-propositional meaning, and on the other hand, attempts were made to revise or expand the set of maxims first proposed by Grice. For example, R. Lakoff (1973) proposes a special set of maxims of politeness (e.g. "Don't impose," "Give options," "Make interlocutor feel good"), while other analysts formulate more general principles of inference, which often involve questioning the validity of particular Gricean maxims. In the latter area, particularly interesting proposals were

made by Horn (1984), who reduces the Gricean maxims to two principles: the
Q principle (related to Maxim of Quantity), and the R principle (related to the
Maxim of Relation) and shows how inferences based on these give rise to
implicata.

An approach which revises the Gricean idea in perhaps the most interesting
way is the theory of relevance (Sperber and Wilson 1986), which reduces the set
of maxims to just one principle – the Principle of Relevance – and offers an
explicit account of inferential processes involved in interpreting utterances.
The relevance-theoretic approach claims that utterances come with a guarantee
of their optimal relevance, which means that they present the message to the
hearer in the way which ensures maximal communicative gain (in Sperber and
Wilson's terms, maximal contextual effect) and at the same time minimizes the
hearer's processing effort. Hearers are thus assumed to conduct their search for
the most relevant interpretation by weighing what was said against what they
already know, and (as is argued in Sperber and Wilson [1993]) inferential processes are involved at all levels of interpretation, including the possibility of
inferential enrichment of logical form.

What the theory of relevance offers, then, is the most elaborate account of
inferential aspects of interpretation, set against a special understanding of the
nature and role of context. In most pragmatic theories to date the context is a
given, and therefore an interpretation of an utterance is arrived at by eliminating
the ambiguities which are incompatible with the context and supplying contextually derived information where the utterance is vague or indeterminate. In
Sperber and Wilson's theory, the context is dynamically built in the process of
arriving at the optimally relevant interpretation and does not have to be limited
to the immediate location and history of the particular speech event. The
context, therefore, is not only what the interlocutors have said in the exchange
or the immediately surrounding situation, it is all the knowledge the participants bring to bear for the purposes of the interaction. As will be seen throughout this book, such a treatment of context helps to explain how more
pragmatically complex relations between protases and apodoses are constructed and understood.

A proper understanding of inference and context is necessary in accounting
for important aspects of conditional interpretations. However, there remains the
question of the relationship between the aspects of interpretation arrived at via
inference, and the rest of the meaning. In a number of theories, the theory of relevance included, it is assumed that pairing the truth-conditional meaning with
what is inferred against the context is sufficient to explain the meaning of all
utterances. In the constructional approach advocated by Fillmore and Kay,

however, important aspects of meaning of constructions are seen as conventionally associated with certain aspects of their form, in ways which are independent from the interaction of truth-conditional meaning and context. As was shown in Fillmore and Kay (1994), constructions may have a pragmatic force which does not arise from general strategies of inference and which is conventionally associated with the morphosyntactic properties of the construction. Work in Construction Grammar has focused on the aspects of meaning, "semantic" or "pragmatic," which conventionally attach to a construction. This, however, does not rule out the possibility that interpreting a construction involves recovering both the conventional aspects of meaning and those arising via non-linguistically motivated inference. In fact, I will claim that conditionals are best accounted for if both aspects of their interpretation are treated as equally important. Therefore, I will rely on the constructional approach in looking for meaning correlates of aspects of conditional form, and on the inference-in-context approach (following workers in Relevance Theory) in accounting for contextually determined aspects of conditional interpretations.

To sum up, the description of conditionals to be proposed in this book will be based on several assumptions:

- that it is possible to offer a general and motivated account of the full range of conditional constructions;
- that the description must centrally address form–meaning correlations;
- that among the various uses of a construction some are more central while others more peripheral;
- that the peripheral uses of the construction bear some resemblance to the core;
- that the more central the use of the construction the greater the reliance on conventional meaning; and
- the more peripheral the use of the construction the greater the reliance on the (dynamically constructed) context.

1.2   Basic parameters of conditionality

It is necessary, in describing conditionals, to choose a set of descriptive parameters. In my choice, I have been particularly influenced by the work of Comrie (1986) and Fillmore (1990a). Comrie's proposed set of parameters for the description of conditionals is richer, and therefore more useful, than more parsimonious delineations of conditionality. He accepts a material implication account of conditionals, but also proposes a list of formal and interpretational parameters which provide guidelines for analyzing conditionals in any language. Among the proposed descriptive dimensions there are some which have to do with the form of a conditional construction (clause order, markers of the protasis and the apodosis), and those that relate to the interpretation (the type of link between *p* and *q*, hypotheticality, temporal reference). Also, as Comrie argues, the description has to address the question of the way in which various aspects of interpretation arise in the construction. For example, in Comrie's analysis some aspects of constructional meaning traditionally associated with the form of the conditional (like counterfactuality) are claimed to arise through implicature.

The description to be offered in this book will try to characterize conditional constructions in English along major parameters of form and interpretation, very much like the parameters proposed by Comrie. The sections below will give a brief description of the parameters chosen.

1.2.1   The *if p, (then) q* frame: its aspects and varieties

The first requirement of a more general analysis of conditionals is a definition of the category to be analyzed. For precisely what class of forms are we seeking a motivated treatment? In the first paragraph above I suggested that the broadest definition should see conditionals as complex sentences composed of two clauses: the main clause and the subordinate clause. The subordinate clause is also introduced with a conditional conjunction *if*. This definition seems to be most appropriate from the point of view of the task undertaken here: it provides a general specification of a broad formal class. *If p, q* covers a range including the most common conditional sentence types; it likewise shows a wide variety of interpretations, which have proven difficult for analysts to bring together. There are other constructions which have conditional meaning, but a different form – for example, coordinate constructions with imperatives, as in *Say one more word and I'll kill you*. These constructions have repeatedly been claimed to be (at least partly) derived from conditionals or to be conditionals in disguise (e.g. Lawler 1975, Bolinger 1977, Lakoff 1972a, Fraser 1969, 1971). They do undoubtedly have an interpretation which resembles that of many conditionals, but they will be treated here as independent constructions. There is, of course, an interesting question to consider: how is it possible for two different constructions to share an area of interpretation? I will touch upon the question in the last chapter and point out some features that certain conditionals share with coordinate imperative constructions, but the assumption throughout the book will be that the standard example of a conditional has two clauses and a conditional conjunction.

Of course, there are many varieties of conditionals within this very broad formula. First of all, different types of sentences can serve as main clauses of conditionals: declaratives, questions and imperatives can all be used as *q*'s. Second, both protases and apodoses can be used in an elliptical form in appropriate contexts (e.g. *If not now, then maybe next week*). Also, there are conjunctions other than *if* which are conditional as well, for example *unless*, and *if* itself can appear in combinations with *only* or *even*. Finally, there is the conjunction *then*, which often introduces main clauses of conditional constructions, but is usually not necessary. All these variations within the pattern influence the interpretation of the conditional, but treating the *if p, q* structure as the broadest syntactic frame allows one to see the ways in which other added formal elements affect the interpretation of the general construction.

The *if p, q* formula represents the basic conditional construction in another respect as well. It instantiates the clause order which has been found to be most typical (if not universal) in conditional sentences (see Greenberg 1963, Comrie 1986, Ford and Thompson 1986, Ford 1993). One might think that the "subordinate clause–main clause" order is a feature of a larger class of sentences (perhaps sentences with adverbial clauses), not just of conditionals, but a recent study of clause order in adverbial sentences (Ford 1993) does not support the suggestion. Ford has shown that temporal, conditional, and causal clauses have very different patterns of sentence organization. Temporal clauses are most often pre-verbal and sometimes sentence-initial, *because*-clauses are predominantly sentence-final, while *if*-clauses are most commonly initial. As Ford claims, these generalizations can be explained by general rules of discourse organization and by the specific semantic and discourse functions of the adverbial clauses under scrutiny. This means that in order to understand how conditionals are used we have to understand how the initial or final position of the *if*-clause affects the general interpretation of the sentence as well as of the relationship between the protasis and the apodosis. What is more, conditionals seem to also allow a configuration where the *if*-clause is actually inside the main clause, as in *My significant other, if that's the expression to use these days, has just bought me a diamond ring*. Ford's corpus did not contain any such sentences, but they seem acceptable, even if not very common. The clause order, then, is yet another parameter to be considered by the descriptive grammarian.

As I noted above, recent work (Sweetser 1990) has shown that overall interpretations of conditionals can be seen in terms of different cognitive domains in which the assumptions[2] expressed by *p* and *q* are related. Thus Sweetser distinguishes the *content* domain, the *epistemic* domain, and the *speech act* domain. The relations linking *p* and *q* are construed differently, depending on the domain in which the conditional relationship applies. Thus, clauses in the content domain are linked causally; in the epistemic domain the protasis expresses a premise and the apodosis a conclusion; in the speech act domain protases express conditions which render speech acts in the apodoses relevant and felicitous. As I have argued elsewhere (Dancygier 1986, 1992, 1993) the clauses of an *if p, q* construction can also be linked metatextually, with the apodosis performing its usual assertive function, and with the protasis providing a comment on some aspect of the linguistic form of the apodosis. In some earlier works (Dancygier 1990, 1993) I have also tried to show that these interpretations correlate with some formal parameters of conditional constructions: verb forms, clause order, and intonation. Thus the nature of the relationship between *p* and *q* will be assumed to be one of the essential aspects of constructional meaning.

Contrary to many other accounts of conditionals, I will not assume that there are infinitely many types of protasis/apodosis relations and that they can be explained against the context and the speaker's or hearer's beliefs only. The relations I have found fall into several classes and rely on the nature of the cognitive domain as well as on the context, but are also correlated with some formal exponents. I will argue, therefore, that the type of relation between *p* and *q* is an important, if not essential, element of constructional meaning and that many other formal distinctions are related to this aspect of interpretation. In fact, the correlations between the conditional construction's form and the cognitive domain in which it is interpreted have been documented in German: Köpcke and Panther (1989) discovered word order differences between content conditionals and conditionals in other domains.

Furthermore, the interpretation of the relation between *p* and *q* is crucial to

---

[2] Throughout the text I will use the term "assumption" to refer to *p* and *q* on any level other than their syntactic form. Even though the term may suggest a strong commitment on the part of the speaker (perhaps close to "belief"), which is often inappropriate in the case of conditionals, it still seems useful for several reasons – it is less concerned with truth or falsehood than "proposition" and at the same time less specific and objective than "content" or "meaning." The problem is that *p* and *q* appear in conditionals with varying degrees of commitment on the part of the speaker, and are brought into the construction for different purposes; also, there are many ways in which they are grounded in the speaker's knowledge and the context of the utterance. It is important, however, that the term we use recognize the fact that *p* and *q* are entertained (or considered) by a specific speaker, who nevertheless considers them with a varying degree of commitment. Still, they are provisionally "assumed" for the sake of the reasoning process the conditional is involved in carrying out.

the interpretation of the whole construction, because in a prototypical conditional the connection between the assumptions in the two clauses is what is actually being asserted (in the speech act sense of the word assertion). That is, a sentence such as *If it gets colder, we'll turn the heating on*, which is interpreted in the content domain, does not in any way commit the speaker to the belief that it will get colder or that the heating will be turned on. It does, however, communicate the belief that the change in temperature will result in turning the heating on. In other words, what is asserted is the causal connection between *p* and *q*, not the clauses themselves. As it has already been suggested, there may be several ways in which *p* and *q* are connected, but in each case the type of connection will play a central role in the interpretation of the construction.

1.2.2   The role of *if*: constructional meaning, non-assertiveness, and mental spaces

The most controversial aspect of conditional constructions is the contribution of *if* itself to the meaning of the utterance as a whole. The semantic development and content of conditional markers is in itself an interesting issue (see Traugott 1985). But in the majority of analyses of conditionality, *if* is seen as the primary exponent of conditional meaning in English.

In classical analyses offered by philosophers, *if* takes all the weight in accounting for the semantics of the construction. The meaning attributed to conditionals in these studies is most often seen as truth-conditional.[3] However, numerous studies have claimed that material implication is not an adequate representation of the semantics of conditionals. It has been shown that assigning positive truth value to sentences with false antecedents leads to numerous paradoxes and that logically correct reasonings are often intuitively unacceptable (in the simplest case, saying *If you submit your thesis this month, we'll consider your application* is never interpreted to mean that failure to submit the thesis will also result in the application being considered, though such an interpretation is logically correct), that material implication cannot be used in interpreting *if* compounds such as *even if* and *only if*, etc. The list of such problems is indeed long and impressive.

Even with a richer theory than the purely truth-conditional ones, it remains difficult to evaluate the degree to which an analysis of *if* as a logical connective can account for the actual processes of arriving at particular interpretations of particular conditionals in particular contexts. One significant attempt at clar-

---

[3] For a broad overview of both truth-functional and other logico-philosophical approaches see Jackson 1987 and 1991.

ifying the relationship between truth-conditional meaning and interpretation has been made by Smith and Smith (1988). In the paper the authors review the major paradoxes of material implication to demonstrate that the truth-conditional account can be saved if it is paired with the theory of relevance.[4] In other words, Smith and Smith argue that material implication is indeed the only semantic tool one needs in analyzing conditionals. The paradoxes are resolved by demonstrating how the theory of relevance accounts for the fact that some logically consistent interpretations are not accepted as communicatively useful or that some sentences are never said. Let us look at two (out of many) examples discussed by Smith and Smith (1988).

The first one has to do with conditionals with false antecedents, which, as Smith and Smith put it, have "been . . . a perennial problem for traditional semantic treatments" (1988: 325). The problem consists in the fact that the truth table for material implication treats conditional sentences as true not only when both clauses are true, but also when the antecedent is false. Thus, Smith and Smith's example, given here as (5):

(5)   If you mow the lawn, I'll give you $5.

can be logically interpreted to mean that the addressee may get the money if he mows the lawn, and also if he doesn't. In actual communication, however, the sentence is interpreted in such a way that mowing will be paid for, while failure to mow will not be paid for. The relevance-theoretic account of this is as follows: utterances come with a guarantee of optimal relevance, that is, the speaker formulates them in such a way as to minimize the hearer's processing effort and to maximize contextual implications (what the hearer will get out of the utterance). If the speaker were ready to pay whether the mowing is done or not (*p* or ***not p***), she would have simply said that she would give the hearer $5 (*q*), and spare him the effort of processing the *if*-clause. Since the speaker chooses to mention the mowing, she also implies a "no work, no pay" belief. Thus, as Smith and Smith put it, "the putatively undesirable reading . . . doesn't emerge" (1988: 333).

The repair offered by Smith and Smith is certainly convincing. Why would the speaker mention *p* if it were not to be processed as a background to *q*? One might also add that considering both *p* and ***not p*** as valid with *q* being true would probably result in the speaker saying *Whether you mow the lawn or not, I'll give you $5*, rather than just *q*. Such a repair, though, is still faithful to the principle of relevance. However, a number of crucial questions remain

---

[4] An earlier version of the argument can be found in Smith 1983.

unanswered by the claims that *if* is a logical connective, that this is all the semantics we will ever have, and that only the interpretations reasonable to the hearer will come up. First of all, how do linguistic clues given in the sentences help the hearer arrive at the interpretation, or how does it happen that some patterns of form welcome some interpretations but exclude others? How does it happen, for instance, that (5) welcomes a causal interpretation similar to (2) (*If Mary goes, John will go*), but is not likely to be understood as a conclusion, along with (3) (*If John went to that party, he was trying to infuriate Miriam*)? How does the hearer assign a future interpretation to the protasis of (5), but not to the protasis of *If you mow the lawn, you get pollen in your hair*? How does the hearer know that the protasis of (3) refers to the past, while the protasis of *If John went to the party, he would see Miriam there* does not? There are many such questions that have remained largely unanswered so far and a satisfactory account of conditionals requires that such answers be provided. Let us consider another example from Smith and Smith (1988) – the famous pair of sentences first discussed by Adams (1970):

(6)   If Oswald did not kill Kennedy, then someone else did.
(7)   If Oswald had not killed Kennedy, then someone else would have.

Apparently the fact that (6) is commonly interpreted as true and (7) as false has made many philosophers claim that material implication can perhaps account for some conditionals (like 6), but not for all (not for 7).

Smith and Smith point out that both (6) and (7) can receive different truth values if they are processed against a different set of assumptions than the ones invoked by standard analyses. Thus, if the hearer believes Kennedy to be still alive, (6) becomes false. Similarly, if the hearer believes that Oswald participated in a conspiracy of assassins, (7) becomes true. Many logical accounts of conditionals have certainly failed to see how conditional interpretations are rooted in the speaker's and the hearer's beliefs, which may or may not be shared. The fact that conditionals can often be interpreted in more than one way also needs to be more broadly recognized. But there are still further questions to be asked and answered. How does the hearer know that the most immediately plausible interpretation of (6) is one which attributes to the speaker the assumption (which the hearer does not have to share) that Oswald did not kill Kennedy, while in the case of (7) the probable underlying assumption is that he did? The answer is widely known – the hearer's primary clues are different verb forms. But in that case, we need some account of how verb morphology can be conventionally interpreted in this way, especially since not every case of Past/Past Perfect contrast invokes such differences (*I bought my ticket before I bought yours* versus *I had bought my ticket before I bought yours* does not imply any difference in underlying assumptions). Also, why cannot one say **If Oswald didn't kill Kennedy, then someone else would have* or **If Oswald hadn't killed Kennedy, then someone else did*?

Answers to such questions cannot be offered if we insist on treating *if* solely as a logical connective, and give all the responsibility for any non-logical interpretation to contextual ("pragmatic") factors. In particular, such an approach cannot account for the role of particular form/meaning mappings in building the interpretation of the whole construction (Dancygier 1993, Sweetser 1996b). It is necessary that we treat conditionals as wholes – as constructions – rather than analyzing independent propositions against a truth table and context. Once we accept *if*'s role as a lexical exponent of a specific meaning in a construction it builds, we will see how its contribution to the interpretation is different from what is motivated by clause order configurations or verb forms. As I will try to show, verb forms are in fact the best indicators of intended interpretations of conditionals (which gives special weight to all the questions raised above with respect to [5], [6], and [7]). They are crucial exponents of various aspects of conventional meaning expressed by the constructions. But they cannot be considered independently of the use of *if*, because the meanings in question arise on the constructional level, not in verb phrases or even clauses themselves: "past" verb forms take on "counterfactual" readings specifically in conditional formal contexts.

Another question one can pose is this: in exactly what sense does the interpretation of (5) rely on the protasis and the apodosis being interpreted as true (putting their potential falsehood aside for the moment)? The sentence performs a speech act of the type that Fillenbaum (1986) calls an inducement. The speaker is trying to get the hearer to do *p* by offering the reward described in *q*. The hearer can say "no," or bargain for a better reward, etc. At no point in the saying or interpreting of (5) is it clear that *p* or *q* are true or even that they are judged primarily with respect to factuality. What is more, the speaker may say (5) even if she expects the hearer not to accept the offer – it is then still valid for the hearer to believe that *p* will result in *q*. Finally, if the offer is accepted, the hearer and the speaker have each accepted certain obligations – to mow the lawn, and to pay, respectively. But this is not part of the interpretation of (5) and these are still beliefs about the future, not verifiable assertions.

What seems to be the case is that conditionals like (5) do not overtly express the speaker's beliefs about *p* or *q* being true as independent assumptions. In fact, the analysis of different types of conditionals offered by Akatsuka (1986) shows that the concepts of "truth" and "falsity" in conditionals may be context-dependent and depends crucially on the speaker's and the hearer's viewpoint. In the examples she looks at, such as *If you are the Pope, I'm the Empress of China* (presumably an attested example of a response to a caller identifying himself as the Pope), the addressee seems to believe *p* to be true, while the speaker makes it clear that she believes it to be false. As Akatsuka points out, examples like these shift the question of the truth or falsity of conditional clauses to a different level of analysis.

I will assume, then, that the clauses of a conditional should not be treated as assertions of true or false propositions. I will also argue that the fact that participant clauses of conditionals are not asserted in the traditional sense, or at least not interpreted as factual, seems to be attributable solely to the presence of *if*. Whatever its interpretation as a logical connective, *if* in natural languages is an exponent of a special status of the assumption in its scope. The status is probably best described with reference to Searle's (1969) definition of the speech act of asserting. In Searle's description, to assert (affirm, or state) an assumption counts as an expression of the speaker's belief. The felicity conditions for the speech act of asserting (as stated in Searle 1969 and 1979) require that the speaker have evidence to support her belief and actually believe the assumption to be true, and that the hearer not be known to share the same belief (needs to be told or reminded about it). Searle stresses repeatedly that assertion is an act, which counts as the speaker's commitment to the truth of a proposition, but should be sharply distinguished from the proposition itself. In what follows I will argue that *if* functions as an instruction for the hearer to treat the assumption in its scope as not being asserted in the usual way.

Treating assertions as speech acts opens up the issue of how utterances come to be interpreted that way. While there may be few formal exponents of the act of asserting (indeed, even declarative/indicative utterance forms are often seen as neutral, rather than as marking a declarative function), non-assertive utterances are often distinguished formally; in particular, the grammatical category of mood can be interpreted along these lines, as imperatives and questions (and conditional mood in languages that have one) are used to express assumptions which the speaker is not treating as factual. In the case of *if*-clauses, however, the form of the clause is often declarative, and, consequently, one might predict that conditionals without special forms like conditional mood should be interpreted by the hearer as reflecting the speaker's belief about a certain state of affairs.

However, what the presence of *if* seems to signal is that at least some of the felicity conditions for asserting do not hold: the speaker does not have enough grounds for asserting *p* as a factual statement and may in fact not believe *p* to be true. It is a well-known fact that conditional protases are often interpreted as "contrary to fact" (on a regular basis in sentences that have often been called "counterfactual," but also in sentences with indicative forms, such as the so-called "indicative counterfactuals" of the type *If he is a college professor, I am the Easter Bunny*). It is also well known that many conditionals refer to the future, and therefore cannot be interpreted as assertive. But there is also a large class of conditional sentences whose protases have been labeled as "given," either because they are assumed in context to be true or because they are actively asserted in preceding discourse. For example, the speaker of *If (as you say) John left for France last week, we need another interpreter* does not necessarily express any doubt at all about the truth of the protasis, but may be fully accepting the truth of the interlocutor's claim, even if she does not mark that full acceptance with a non-conditional form. I will try to show, however, that even in such cases the presence of *if* requires an interpretation under which the assumption in its scope does not count as an act of asserting (it repeats the hearer's preceding assertion, thus violating one of the felicity conditions, and does not always count as an expression of the speaker's belief). Taking *if* as a marker of non-assertion does not mean that speakers always have the same reasons for not engaging in full assertion. Indeed, other components of the sentence form are likely to reflect the aspects of the speaker's own beliefs (positive, negative, or neutral) about the content, and about the hearer's beliefs, which motivate the use of a non-assertive form. Thus the ways in which conditionals receive non-assertive interpretations may vary, but the role of *if* as a signal of non-assertive meanings remains constant.

The contrast between the truth of a proposition and an assertion of a statement is also used by Horn in his work on negation (1985, 1989), which will be addressed in some detail in section 3.5.1. His analysis of the pragmatic ambiguity of negation is based on the work of Grice (1967) and Dummett (1973) which recognizes a use of negation which signals the speaker's refusal to assert a proposition, rather than her assertion of its falsehood. Thus, in Horn's terms, a sentence like *The cake isn't good, it's divine!* uses negation to mark **unassertability**, not falsehood, since the speaker does not intend to deny a positive evaluation of the cake, but rather refuses to describe its qualities with the word proposed. As Horn says, the notion of assertability "must be taken as elliptical for something like 'felicitously assertable' or 'appropriately assertable'" (1989: 379), which relates it to the Searlean act of asserting recalled above. When an assumption needs to be entertained or considered, but cannot be asserted felicitously, it will be presented as **unassertable**. In chapter 3, conditional protases will be analyzed in terms of reasons the speakers have to present assumptions in the scope of *if*; they will be treated as non-assertive, within a framework of unassertability like that used by Horn.

As the discussion so far suggests, the type of analysis attempted here, which will look at conditionals as constructions and explore form–meaning mappings that give rise to a variety of related, but different interpretations, is incompatible with a framework which treats *if* primarily as a logical connective. As I noted above, it is also not sufficient to enrich a truth-conditional type of semantics with an account of inferential processes guiding hearers in their search for interpretations, although an understanding of such processes is of course indispensable. What is needed is an approach which helps us see a variety of ways in which language forms themselves participate in the construction of meaningful discourse. At one level (so far referred to as constructional) this requires that we document the meanings that linguistic elements (be they lexical, morphological, or syntactic) carry by virtue of linguistic conventions. At another level, though, this means exploring the ways in which linguistic communication is involved in building extra-linguistic cognitive structure. The framework which offers a paradigm for describing the latter has been offered by Fauconnier (1985/1994 and 1996) in his theory of ***mental spaces***.

Mental spaces are "constructs distinct from linguistic structures but built up in any discourse according to guidelines provided by the linguistic expressions." (Fauconnier 1985: 16). For example, a speaker may build up an understanding of some state of affairs (present or non-present, realis or irrealis), or of other structured domains such as depictions (pictures, plays) or frames (interaction in a restaurant, for example). The hearer is guided by the speaker's language to set up mental constructs parallel to those of the speaker, and also to move from one mental space to another. Thus certain expressions, called spacebuilders, establish new spaces or refer back to the spaces that have already been established. A variety of expressions can perform the space-building function: *in the picture, in 1950, in my opinion, probably, X believes*, etc. All such expressions set up a mental space which is included in its parent space (in the simplest case, the speaker's conceived reality space), and in each case there is a pragmatic connector linking the new space and the parent space (or, more specifically, elements in the two spaces). For example, a sentence such as *In that movie, Clint Eastwood is a villain*, the expression *in that movie* sets up a "movie" space, embedded in the reality space, and the two spaces are connected by pragmatic connectors going from actors to characters they represent. This allows the name of an actor to be used to refer to a character played by that actor.

Mental spaces can be set up with respect to various domains: time, geographical space, domain of activity. A specific type of mental space, however, is also built by linguistic expressions such as *if*: in this case, *if p* structures a mental space in which *q* holds as well. The kind of space set up by *if* is hypothetical in the broad sense of the word, that is, the space builder itself does not pre-determine whether the space will be counterfactual (in the logician's sense) or not. The particular relation between the parent (reality) space and the conditional space being set up will be constrained lexically or grammatically (by specialized verb morphology), but the actual interpretation of spaces as compatible or incompatible is not a matter of language only, but primarily of the structure of the spaces, as they are built and negotiated in discourse.

The view of space construction offered by Fauconnier is different from, among others, the "possible worlds" approach, in that new mental spaces are structured only locally and partially; the needs of particular discourse determine how much of the parent space is inherited by the new space. That is, a conditional space can be constructed by simply adding *p* to the reality space, and all the relevant local structure of reality space is inherited. There is no specific linguistic algorithm for building hypothetical spaces out of the reality space (though there may be linguistic constraints on such construction), and pragmatics will constrain the kinds of dependencies between the two spaces. But in each case the structuring will serve particular communicative goals, rather than setting up a world for the evaluation of truth values. As Fauconnier argues, there is no point in trying to evaluate the truth of sentences like *If Napoleon had been the son of Alexander, he would have been Macedonian* or *If Napoleon had been the son of Alexander, Alexander would have been Corsican*, because there is no "absolute" truth when only some facts and laws are imported into the hypothetical space, and those that are imported are selected to carry out a specific reasoning. The general point Fauconnier is making in this argument is that whether there is a possible world in which these sentences are true or not has no bearing on their linguistic status, that is, on the fact that sentences like these are easy to construct, process, and use. In other words, the algorithm for arriving at the truth conditions of a conditional sentence should not be confused with its semantics (in the broad sense of the word).

Fauconnier's approach, as formulated in Fauconnier (1996), takes a view of linguistic semantics which opposes the traditional truth-conditional accounts in important ways. As he puts it: "as discourse unfolds and mental spaces are set up, the recovery of meaning fundamentally depends on the capacity to induce shared structures, map them from space to space, and extend the mappings so that additional structure is introduced and exported" (1996: 67). This view of construction of meaning assumes the availability of various aspects of the speaker's and hearer's knowledge at any stage of interpretation, and sees the knowledge (which includes linguistic knowledge) as structured by cognitive constructs of various types: frames (e.g. Fillmore 1982 and 1985) and idealized cognitive models (Lakoff 1987), as well as cultural models and folk theories (Holland and Quinn 1987). It also invites the use of current context and discourse structure as new cognitive structure is built, rather than strictly distinguishing between pre-pragmatic (truth-conditional?) and pragmatic aspects of interpretation. There is, in this framework, no way of establishing a pre-pragmatic "meaning," since conventional aspects of the meanings of morphemes and constructions are in essence all communicative prompts towards pragmatic construction of spaces. Their compositional interpretation depends on the construction process at hand, as well as on the conventions of the grammar.

Structure is transferred across spaces in a variety of ways. Fauconnier describes a number of mechanisms for this transfer of structure, generally referred to as Spreading. For example, mental space construction involves creating counterparts of entities present in the parent space (via the so-called Access Principle). That is, in the now classic example first mentioned by Jackendoff (1975), *In Len's painting, the girl with blue eyes has green eyes*, the "picture" space creates a green-eyed counterpart of the blue-eyed girl from the reality space. Fauconnier's point here is that the linguistic expression describing the painter's model can be used to identify the image in the picture, that is, counterparts can be accessed across spaces via pragmatic connectors such as the "image" connector in this case.

Other Spreading mechanisms involve inheritance of structure from the parent space to the child space and projection of semantic frames along with transferred counterparts. For example, a sentence such as *If I had caught the 11.30 train, I would have gotten to the meeting on time* (first given in [1] above) sets up a conditional space which has a counterpart of the subject referred to as *I* and preserves a wide range of relations, frames, and other mental constructs involved. That is, it still assumes that catching this particular train was sufficient to get the subject to the meeting on time, while missing it meant being late, that being late to meetings is undesirable, that the subject's presence at the meeting was expected, that trains run according to set schedules, etc. The space is different from the reality space only in one explicit respect – that in the reality space the subject missed the train and was late to the meeting, while in the new space the opposite is the case. So building this new space does not involve situations beyond what is particularly mentioned as the space is set up – it does not, for instance, consider the situation whereby the subject caught the desired train but then got stuck between stations because of power failure or engaged in an animated discussion with another passenger and got off one station later, in each case being late to the meeting or missing it altogether.

At the most general level, *if* is thus a space builder for conditional (hypothetical) spaces. As Fauconnier argues, the particular type of space structuring will be determined by the use of linguistic form, but also by the pragmatic constraints on the particular discourse. In this project I will thus try to show how this type of space structuring is constrained by linguistically relevant facts. For example, at the level of linguistic structure, *if* itself plays a specific role as a lexical exponent of the conditional constructions in which the protases and apodoses are interpreted non-assertively. Other aspects of the constructions, such as, among others, verb morphology, will specify the space construction as taking place to serve specific types of reasonings in various cognitive domains (for specific correlations between mental space building and conditional form see Sweetser 1996a, 1996b, Dancygier and Sweetser 1996). The analysis of the speaker's and hearer's assumptions and their use of contextual clues will show how pragmatic factors constrain the nature of space structuring. Also, a look at clause order and intonation will reveal how conditional spaces function in a broader discourse setting. In other words, the analysis undertaken here has the goal of reviewing all the linguistically relevant parameters of conditional space construction.

To sum up, *if* has been argued to have three functions. At the most general level, it is a linguistic exponent of the mental process of space construction – it is a space builder for conditional spaces. As a lexical item, it is a marker of non-assertiveness and its presence in front of an assumption indicates that the speaker has reasons to present this assumption as unassertable. At the constructional level, *if* introduces one of the clauses of a conditional construction, which presents the assumptions *p* and *q* as connected in a given cognitive domain and uses an array of specific conventional form–meaning mappings to determine all aspects of the construction's meaning.

The analysis postulated in the chapters to follow will address all the aspects of conditional interpretations mentioned above. In chapter 2 I will discuss verb forms; choice of verb form is the formal parameter which plays the most significant role in indicating such aspects of the construction's meanings as time, speaker's background assumptions, type of distancing, etc. Verb forms will be claimed to fall into two major classes: predictive ones, where the modal verb *will* is used to mark predictive meaning, and non-predictive ones, where other verbs are used. The proposed solution will be compared with other current descriptions of the use of verbs in conditionals. Chapter 3 will describe types of protasis/apodosis relations in greater detail. I will consider sequentiality and causality, as well as inferential, speech act, and metatextual relations. In chapter 4 I will address the question of the speaker's beliefs about the content, and about the hearer's knowledge state; I will show how these beliefs influence the choice of formal construction, and correlate with types of p/q relations. The next two chapters will consider in some detail how the form of the clauses and their order contribute to interpretation, and how other conjunctions interact with conditional meaning (I will consider *unless* and *even if* in greater detail). Finally, in chapter 7 I will review some of the main claims of the book to propose an account of prototypical conditionality. I will then try to use the proposed prototype to offer some explanation of how conditional meanings may arise in the absence of explicit expressions of conditionality. In particular, I will look at some conjunction-less conditionals (e.g. conditionals with inversion in the protasis) and at some constructions (e.g. coordinate imperative sentences) which acquire conditional meaning in spite of non-conditional form.

Conditionals will thus emerge as a cognitive category in the sense described by Berlin and Kay (1969), Rosch (1977, 1978), and Lakoff (1987). Different sub-types of conditionals may be "better" or "worse" examples of the category, in the sense of being more or less central members; and various sub-types may be more connected by common resemblance to more central cases than by resemblance to each other. The divergent meanings and interpretations of conditional structure nonetheless stem from a common core.

My goal is to systematically lay out the particular form–meaning mappings relevant to the description of conditional constructions. Such a description of parameters of conditionality should offer an understanding of how conditionals can be viewed as a category. In particular, it will allow me to distinguish the central case as well as study the mechanisms relating the less central uses to the prototype.

2 Prediction and distance: time and modality in conditional clauses

Verb forms in the clauses of conditional sentences are commonly seen as an important aspect of the overall characterization of conditionals. However, most analysts' interest has centered on subjunctive and "counterfactual" sentences, where they signal the speaker's negative commitment to the proposition. The unmarked, indicative verb phrases in conditionals are consequently assumed to be interpretable along with straightforward, non-conditional indicative declaratives. Consequently, sentence (1) below is usually claimed to belong to a different class of conditionals than (2) and (3). The analysis advocated below assumes that all verb forms in conditionals contribute in a significant way to the overall interpretation of the construction, and, in particular, reveal the specific nature of the non-factuality of the assumption in the scope of *if* and of the relation between *p* and *q*. With respect to these criteria the sentences exemplified in (1)–(3) will be claimed to form a uniform class, which I will refer to as ***predictive conditionals***:

(1)   If it rains, the match will be canceled.
(2)   If it rained, the match would be canceled.
(3)   If it had rained, the match would have been canceled.

Predictive conditionals such as (1)–(3) will be discussed in the sections to follow with respect to their temporal interpretation and type of modality, as well as the kind of unassertiveness signaled and the relation between the assumptions in *p* and *q*. I will also argue that the verb forms used in other, "non-predictive" conditional constructions (such as *If it's raining now, let's cancel the match,* or *If it rained yesterday, I'm sure the match was canceled*) are interpreted along the same lines, although such conditionals have additional dimensions of freedom involved in their interpretation. I will begin, however, with a review of the existing accounts of verb morphology in conditionals.

2.1 Verb forms in conditional constructions

The forms of verb phrases used in the *if*-clauses and main clauses of conditional sentences are usually seen as surface devices encoding first of all the type of condition and the speaker's beliefs. Their temporal reference is not always univocal, so the overall temporal interpretation of conditional sentences is often arrived at on the basis of other lexical indicators (like time adverbials) and the context. Even in the approaches which focus on the description of English verb phrases and their meanings (Joos 1964, Palmer 1965, Leech 1971) the use of verb forms in conditional sentences is largely seen as an integral part of the overall characterization of the *if*-construction. In fact, analyses of the meaning of tense and modality in conditionals are most commonly offered only in the cases where the form of the verb phrase deviates from what is considered a rule (e.g. if *will* is used in the protasis, see Haegeman and Wekker 1984, Close 1980, Comrie 1986).

The actual form of the verb in conditionals receives differing amount of attention, depending on the general assumptions of the analyst. I will briefly review some of the more common ways of approaching verb forms.

The crucial assumption to be considered is whether conditionals use verb forms in their own specific way, or whether they are more effectively described in terms of devices generally available in the grammatical system. Pedagogical grammars (e.g. Ward 1954, Eckersley and Eckersley 1960, Graver 1971) usually present conditionals as complex sentences with adverbial clauses, which require separate description because they use patterns of verb forms which are particular to these constructions. The number of patterns described is extremely varied (from three – in a majority of foreign language textbooks – to ten in Ward 1954). The three patterns which are considered essential and are never left out are exemplified in (1)–(3) above (*If it rains/rained/had rained, the match will be/would be/would have been canceled*).

The related patterns of verb forms exemplified in (1) to (3) constitute the core of pedagogical descriptions of grammar. Such an approach to teaching is well justified: it simplifies the learners' task by providing them with a pattern and drawing their attention to the cases where overgeneralization errors can potentially appear. Other patterns exemplified in pedagogical grammars represent less common *if*-constructions, e.g. "general truth" sentences like *If you heat ice, it melts*, or variants of the constructions (1)–(3) with imperative consequents (e.g. *If it rains, cancel the match*), with different modals (*should* and *were to*), with inversion (e.g. *Had it rained, the match would have been canceled*), etc.

Interestingly enough, though, pedagogically oriented descriptions often disregard the existence of *if* sentences in which the use of verb does not require learning specific forms, such as *If Bernie is a linguist, he surely knows several languages* (Eckersley and Eckersley's grammar [1960] is a notable exception). They apparently assume that learners will be able to understand and produce such sentences based on some combination of their knowledge of general English grammar and (possibly) their native language's structures. Also, very few textbooks stress whatever is systematic in the choice of Past, Past Perfect, or *would* forms in conditionals and in other constructions, like *I wish . . ., It's time . . .*, etc. For example, it is uncommon for textbooks of English to relate the use of the form *were* in conditionals such as *If I were you, I would apply* and in sentences with *wish* such as *I wish I were you.* At the same time, the peculiarity of the use of verb forms in conditionals is often underemphasized by applying familiar terms whenever possible. Hence the use of basic terms such as Present (Simple), Past (Simple), and Past Perfect for the respective protases of (1), (2), and (3), and calling the *will* + *V* of (1) Future tense. The problem arises with the apodoses of (2) and (3), as there is no standard terminology here – they are thus called Conditional (tense), or Future (Perfect) in the Past, or the constituents of their verb phrases are simply enumerated.

The assumption behind the approaches with broader descriptive goals is that the use of verb forms in conditionals is related to similar uses of the same forms elsewhere (see, for example, Zandvoort 1962, Joos 1964, Palmer 1965, Leech 1971, Quirk, Greenbaum, Leech, and Svartvik 1972, 1985, Leech and Svartvik 1975). The particular semantics of *if* sentences is thus found in the overall *if p, q* construction and its interpretation, not in the use of verb forms. Consequently, in grammars such as Quirk, Greenbaum, Leech, and Svartvik (1985) sentences like (1) above (*If it rains, the match will be canceled*) are not seen as requiring separate discussion. They are treated on a par with sentences such as (4)–(6), which are also seen as expressing so-called "open" conditions, that is, conditions which, in the speaker's knowledge, may or may not be fulfilled:

(4)   If he had a cold last week, he couldn't come to your talk.
(5)   If she is giving the baby a bath, I'll call back later.
(6)   If I have met him, I didn't recognize him.

In (4) through (6) the verb phrases in both clauses are constructed and interpreted in the same way as in similar independent sentences. One can thus conclude, from their treating (1) along the same lines, that Quirk, Greenbaum, Leech, and Svartvik (1985) do not consider the shift from *will* + *V* to Present tense to be meaningful.

In sentences like (2) and (3), the verb phrases are seen as expressing hypothetical meaning in direct connection with time reference. The verb forms used are presented in table 1 below, adapted from Quirk, Greenbaum, Leech, and Svartvik (1985: 1092):

Table 1

	Conditional clause	Main clause
Present/Future	*Hypothetical Past*	*Past Modal*
Past	*Hypothetical Past Perfective*	*Past Perfective Modal*

The same means of expressing hypothetical meaning can be found outside conditional sentences as well (Quirk, Greenbaum, Leech, and Svartvik 1985: 1010, Leech 1971). The emerging distinction is thus between a variety of non-hypothetical forms on the one hand, and a set of hypothetical forms on the other, with the latter appearing in hypothetical conditionals according to a certain pattern, and in other hypothetical constructions (*I wish I hadn't called, I'd rather you didn't call me 'honey'*) according to other rules.

What the two approaches outlined seem to share is the view that *if*-clauses, being a type of adverbial clause, constitute a part of their main clauses. Clauses introduced by *if* and not presenting a situation on which the situation in the main clause is contingent are either disregarded (as in most pedagogical approaches) or seen as essentially different (Quirk, Greenbaum, Leech, and Svartvik call protases like *If I may be quite frank with you* . . . or *If you remember your history lesson* . . . "indirect conditions"). Also, both approaches distinguish the same two types of hypothetical constructions (as in [2] and [3]). They differ, however, in their treatment of sentences like (1), which are classified either with (2) and (3), or with (4)–(6).

Terminology itself is a problem in the literature on conditionals: there is quite significant variation in the use of terms to refer to verb forms, in particular. *Rains* (as in [1]) is uniformly referred to as Present tense (or *V-s*), while *will be canceled* is sometimes labeled Future tense and at other times simply *will* + *V*. In (2), its verb *rained* is variously termed Past (tense), Hypothetical Past, Present Subjunctive, or *V-ed*, while its main clause verb – *would be canceled* – Past Modal, Conditional, or *would* + *V*. Finally, *had rained* in (3) is called Past Perfect, Past Past, Hypothetical Past Perfective, Past Subjunctive, or *have* + *V-en*, while *would have been canceled* – Past Perfective Modal, Conditional Perfect, or *would have* + *V-en*.

Some of these terms, as we have seen, are associated with the two approaches outlined above. Apparently purely descriptive terms like *will* + *V* or *have* + *V-en* are often applied in analyses meant to be unbiased. In general, the literature reflects the difficulty analysts have had in deciding how to treat uses of verb forms in conditionals which are formally identical to tense forms, but may not carry the same temporal reference – e.g. the apparently future reference of the present *rains* in (1), or (more worrisome) the future reference of the "past" *rained* in (2).

The third approach to be noted is represented by the majority of philosophical writings on conditionals (Stalnaker 1968 and Lewis 1973 are central to more recent discussions in this tradition). In these analyses the distinctions used are based on a selected aspect of the global interpretation of conditionals. Verb forms, even if considered somehow indicative of the interpretation, are not subject to interpretation themselves.

There are two main terminological distinctions used. In classical philosophical writings one finds a classification of conditionals with respect to the attitude of the speaker towards the fulfillment of the condition. The speaker may not express any opinion (*realis*), she may see the fulfillment of the condition as possible (*potentialis*), or as impossible (*irrealis*). Sentences classified as *realis* can be exemplified as in (7):

(7)   If two and two make four, then two is an even number.

Sentence (1) above is a case of *potentialis*, while sentences (2) and (3) are *irrealis*. It seems, then, that the distinction resembles the one within the descriptive approaches in being motivated by hypotheticality of some conditionals, but non-hypothetical ones are further divided on the basis of other criteria.

More recent philosophical and logical writings have concentrated, broadly speaking, on the truth values of conditionals and their constituent clauses (for example Chisholm 1949, Anderson 1951, Downing 1959, Stalnaker 1968, Lewis 1973, 1981, Harper, Stalnaker, and Pearce 1981, Ellis 1984, Jackson 1987, 1991). They also do not make reference to verb forms, and the emerging division between indicative and counterfactual conditionals (with the third term, subjunctive, being used either independently, to refer to sentences like [2], or abandoned in favor of a purely binary classification) is not really applicable to any descriptively oriented analysis. Verb forms are not used as a criterion, although the fact that counterfactual sentences (like [3]) are indeed marked differently from other types is certainly used in the analysis.

To conclude, all current approaches to the analysis of conditionals, whether they admit verb forms as a criterion or not, contrast sentences using so-called hypothetical forms (and having a hypothetical interpretation) with a much less uniform body of non-hypothetical conditionals. I will argue for a different type of classification.

2.2   What do verb forms indicate?

In all of the three approaches outlined above, the choice of verb forms in conditional sentences is seen as guided by two factors jointly: the type of condition in
the subordinate clause and the temporal reference of the construction. The only
work that argues for a purely temporal interpretation of these forms is that by
Dudman (1984), but it is universally admitted, at least for hypothetical sentences, that actual time reference is different from that indicated by the verb
phrase. This is partly true of (1), which refers to the future by use of a Present
form in the *if* clause; it is also true of (2), which has a present or future reference,
but not past, even though its *if*-clause verb is Past, and of (3), which uses Past
Perfect in the protasis without reference to a pre-past situation. The use of the
Present in (1) is not given much attention: it is treated as a peculiarity of the
English language, rather than as an important formal aspect of the representation of conditionality, that future reference in *if*-clauses is expressed through the
Present. The time/tense discrepancy in (2) and (3) is interpreted as indicative of
hypothetical meaning, in the sense postulated by Leech (1971), and the verb
forms used are called hypothetical themselves. The two sets of hypothetical
forms are associated with time in the manner indicated in table 1 above. As for
the sentences without "special" forms, such as (4)–(7) above, their temporal
reference is not mentioned, because the tense forms used seem to indicate time
in the same way as they do outside conditionals.

As for the non-temporal classification of the condition, two main types are
distinguished almost universally: **open** and **hypothetical**. The former (also
called **real, factual, neutral**) do not make any predictions about the fulfillment
or non-fulfillment of the condition, while the latter (also termed **closed,
unreal, rejected, non-factual, counterfactual**) express the speaker's negative
belief as to the fulfillment of the condition. Open conditions are most typically
future in their time reference (see [1]). Descriptive grammars, with Huddleston
1984 and Quirk, Greenbaum, Leech, and Svartvik 1972 and 1985 being the
most comprehensive ones, say very little about non-future open conditionals
(like [4]–[7]), but admit their existence, whether explicitly or implicitly. In
foreign language textbooks, on the other hand, futurate conditionals are
usually treated as sole representatives of the class, apparently because they are
the ones that require learning of a special verb pattern, while others are
assumed to be predictable from other facts of English grammar. Hypothetical
conditionals are presented as referring to varied periods of time, with the
variety resulting in each case in a somewhat different understanding of the
hypotheticality. In future sentences the fulfillment of the condition is seen as

contrary to expectation, in the present ones as contrary to assumption, and in the past ones as contrary to fact.

The interpretation outlined above is pervasive in all writings about conditional sentences, even though there is variation in the terms used. A closer look at language use, however, suggests that the open/hypothetical division is not sufficiently motivated in its present form, and that the time reference in conditionals is, on the one hand, more varied than it is believed to be and, on the other hand, less clearly connected to the verb forms used.

2.2.1   Time reference in hypothetical and open sentences

In the present section I will be concerned with the question of how systematically temporal reference is established for the two proposed classes of *if . . . then* constructions. I will first consider the two subclasses of hypothetical sentences, then "open" conditionals will be reviewed.

Under the standard interpretation, hypothetical conditionals are said to appear in basically two patterns, given in table 1 above. The first pattern is capable of representing either the *future* or the *present*, as in (8) and (9) respectively:

(8)   If you drove to the city on Monday, you would avoid the weekend traffic.
(9)   If I had my car here, I could drive you to the station.

The sentences are said to express a negative belief of the speaker, such that she does not expect the hearer to drive to the city on Monday, or believes that her car is not available at the moment of speech. Similarly in (2) above, which has future reference, the speaker does not expect rain and therefore thinks the match will be held.

The question arises how temporal reference is established in each case. Sentence (8) contains explicit information about the time not being "now" – the expression *on Monday* cannot be used to indicate the present. But even without the adverb of time (as in *If you drove to the city across the other bridge . . .*), or with *now* (*If you drove to the city now . . .*) the verb cannot be interpreted as referring to the present moment. A true present interpretation requires the progressive form as in *If you were driving to the city now, you would avoid the weekend traffic.*

The explanation (as suggested by Dancygier and Mioduszewska 1983, Fillmore 1990a) seems to be that the verbs in (2) and (8) are not state verbs. The stative interpretation is inherent in verbs like *have, be, know, understand,* etc., hence (9) is typically understood as present. However, hypothetical sentences with state verbs can also be used with future reference, especially with explicit indicators of futurity:

(10)   If he had the photographs with him at the party tommorrow, I could finally see his grandson.

Presumably, then, the choice between the future and the present as temporal reference of conditionals depends on a variety of factors, but it is not clearly indicated by the verb form. As a matter of fact, there is a possibility that neither of these two is meant. In a sentence like (11):

(11)   If I lived in Italy, I would eat pasta every day.

the speaker is imagining Italy to be her (presently construed) country of permanent residence. But she is not specifically considering living there at the moment of speech or moving there in the future. One can assume that for such cases the time span understood as "state at present," which invariably encroaches on both the past and the future, is rather broad. Also, there are sentences where the "state at present" would have to be broadened infinitely:

(12)   If water boiled at 200°C, making tea would take twice as long.

The speaker of (12) is not restricting the image of water coming to a boil at a different temperature to the speech event she is participating in, and leaving its characteristics unchanged the rest of the past and the future. Rather, she is imagining water to have different properties, regardless of time.

The above remarks should make it clear that the temporal interpretation of hypothetical conditions using the Past in the protasis and *would* + *V* in the apodosis is dictated by a variety of factors and cannot be seen as univocally present or future. It does not seem to be possible to explain the actual interpretation solely in terms of the verb forms used. The verb forms are thus indicative of a type of hypothetical meaning which restricts the temporal range to exclude the past, but is not temporal itself.

A well-motivated temporal interpretation of the second set of hypothetical forms is also difficult to find. They have traditionally been seen as having a past reference, so that a sentence like (3) was claimed to make a reference to a situation in the past, such that it did not rain and the match was held. However, sentences with the same forms as (3) can be used to refer to the present or the future:[1]

---

[1] Fillmore (1990a) does not include sentences like (14) and (15) in his analysis, saying that they do not occur in his speech. As a result, his interpretation of their verb forms is counterfactual and restricted to non-futurate temporal reference.

(13)   If your mother had been here now, she would have been in tears.
(14)   If John had come to the party tomorrow, he would have met you.
(15)   If I hadn't been seeing my doctor tomorrow, we could have had lunch
        together.

Sentence (13) refers to the present situation at the point of speech and is temporally equivalent to *If your mother were here now, she would be in tears.* A sentence
like (14) could be used in the situation where the speaker knows that John was
going to come to the party, but has just learnt that he will definitely not come (he
had an accident and is in hospital, badly injured). Example (15), on the other hand,
is a refusal to accept an invitation for the next day. In these sentences, then, verb
forms leave room for *all* types of temporal interpretation: past, present, and future.

In the majority of cases hypothetical forms are used according to patterns presented in table 1. In some sentences, however, the two patterns are mixed, as in:

(16)   Tom wouldn't be so hungry if he had eaten a proper breakfast.
(17)   If Ann had a better memory for faces, she would have recognized you.

Sentence (16) talks about the present consequences of a past action, so it is
interpreted as mixed between Past and Present; in (17) a general (not strictly
Present) feature of Ann's character is mentioned with reference to her past
behaviour. But it is possible to interpret these (and similar) sentences differently, for example (16) could describe Tom's habitual behavior (as in *Tom
wouldn't be so hungry by noon every day if he had eaten a proper breakfast*),
while many sentences with verb form patterns identical to (17) are used to reject
possible future developments (as in the case of *If Chris had missed another
meeting, he would have been fired*, said on seeing Chris entering the conference
room). It seems, then, that mixed sentences pose the same problems in establishing time reference as non-mixed ones.

Existing descriptive accounts say very little about the verb forms used in so-
called open conditionals, or about their temporal reference, usually restricting
the presentation to examples, while pedagogical descriptions concentrate on
sentences like (1). The class of open conditionals is an extremely varied one: this
much is clear, despite the many descriptions which have defined it on different
grounds and by different names. As a first attempt, the best unbiased definition
of its scope would need to include all conditionals except hypothetical ones.

But this approach has evident limitations. First of all, "open" forms are not
uniform in their treatment of time. For example, there are two groups of "open"
if-clauses referring to the future, each using a different verb form:[2]

---

[2] In this section I disregard the volitional and "insistence" uses of *will* after *if*, which I consider to
be strictly modal (e.g. *If you will look after the luggage, I'll find a cab, If you will sit and watch TV
all night, what can you expect?*).

(18)   If he won't arrive before nine, there is no point in ordering for him.
(19)   If he doesn't arrive before nine, we'll have the meal without him.

Both (18) and (19) have protases referring to the future, but (19) is a more common version of expressing futurity in a conditional construction. It will probably not be argued that the *p*'s of the two sentences, or the sentences as wholes, can be interpreted in the same way, yet they are both classified as "open."

The second problem is that we ought to be able to account for the difference in uses of the same tense. In the protasis of (19) the present tense is used to refer to the future, while in that of (20) it refers to the present. And yet, both sentences count as "open" and no further explanation of the difference is offered.

(20)   If she is in the lobby, the plane arrived early.

We have thus seen that with regard to time reference, the open/hypothetical distinction offers a rather confusing classification of conditional sentences and will not be useful in our attempt to map the verb forms used in conditionals onto their temporal interpretation. This is not surprising in view of the fact that the distinction was postulated primarily with respect to the concept of the speaker's attitude towards the fulfillment of the condition. This issue will be discussed in the next section.

2.2.2   The fulfillment of the condition

Apart from the contrast between hypothetical and non-hypothetical verb forms, the open/hypothetical opposition is also grounded in a twofold distinction among types of conditions: open conditionals are seen as neutral with respect to the fulfillment of the condition, and hypothetical ones are said to present it as contrary to expectation, assumption, or fact, depending on time reference. In recent work by Fillmore (1990a, 1990b) hypothetical forms are described as representing the speaker's negative epistemic stance – negative belief about the actuality of *p*, and, in some cases, of *q*.

In the existing literature, future hypothetical sentences such as (15) (*If I hadn't been seeing my doctor tomorrow, we could have had lunch together*) are given very little attention, and are usually excluded from philosophical considerations, while the past ones, called counterfactual, and the present ones, sometimes called subjunctive and sometimes also counterfactual, constitute the core of philosophical dispute (e.g. Chisholm 1949, Anderson 1951, Lewis 1973). These are seen as presenting the situation as contrary to the present or past fact.

However, the point has been made more and more often (Karttunen and

Peters 1979, Barwise 1986, Comrie 1986) that counterfactuality is not part of the meaning of these sentences, but is only implicated and can consequently be canceled. Thus examples like (21) and (22) are said to be interpreted non-counterfactually as a result of the cancellations provided by embedded clauses.[3] That is, it is claimed that the sentences first implicate that fusion did not result and that Mary is not allergic to penicillin, and then cancel the implicature:

(21)   If fusion had resulted, there would have been the reaction that we did in fact see.
(22)   If Mary were allergic to penicillin, she would have exactly the symptoms she is showing.

The result of the cancellations is that the protases are now unlikely to be interpreted counterfactually and are open to interpretations such that the fusion occurred and that Mary is allergic to penicillin. These interpretations can again be challenged by further comments, such as *but in fact we know that fusion did not occur/Mary is not allergic to penicillin*, which can be appended to (21) and (22) without contradiction. The difficulty with such examples is that they mention contradictory pieces of evidence. On the one hand the speaker implies that she has evidence suggesting that **not p** (no fusion, not allergic), by the use of hypothetical verb forms. There is no reason to suppose that this evidence is ignored at any stage in her reasoning, or is negated by the coming cancellation. On the other hand, the speaker is confronted with evidence suggesting that p (there was fusion, Mary is allergic to penicillin), which is given in factual clauses embedded in q. The sentence does not resolve a contradiction, so it cannot be interpreted either counterfactually or factually. It seems, then, that hypothetical sentences are not unambiguously counterfactual, but the "knowledge to the contrary" signaled through hypothetical verb forms is part of what is being communicated, and cannot be "canceled." It can, however, be considered along with other pieces of evidence, and the question of whether p is true or not may remain unresolved.

There is also the problem of future hypothetical sentences, which are glossed as "contrary to expectation," and sometimes as "improbable," or "unlikely." Such explanations are perhaps adequate (though not necessarily satisfactory) for sentences like (2) (*If it rained, the match would be canceled*), but they do not seem convincing in the cases of (14) (*If John had come to the party tomorrow, he would have met you*) and (15) (*If I hadn't been seeing my doctor tomorrow, we could have had lunch together*). (14) could be appropriately uttered when the speaker knows that, being in hospital with a serious injury, John cannot appear at

---

[3] I quote examples (21) and (22) after Karttunen and Peters (1979) and Ferguson (personal communication), respectively.

the party, while (15) could be felicitously read as a refusal to meet the hearer for lunch because of other established obligations. In both cases the convictions expressed are stronger than "contrary to expectation" or "unlikely." Part of the explanation may be that (2), as opposed to (14) and (15) uses the "weaker," less remote set of hypothetical verb forms. It seems to be clear from all the examples above that the "stronger" set of forms, as used in (14) and (15), does not necessarily denote pastness, but does express a stronger negative commitment on the part of the speaker. Nevertheless, the speaker's negative attitude is not adequately described by glosses such as "contrary to fact/expectation."

Similar difficulties arise in defining the class of "open" conditionals. A common way to describe them is to say that their protases present conditions towards which the speaker's attitude is *neutral* – i.e., that she has no specific opinion on whether the condition will or will not be fulfilled. However, the protases of (18), (19), and (20) are certainly not neutral to the same extent or in the same way: the expectation that X will not come before nine is clearly stronger in (18) than in (19). Also, one can think of examples, however rare they may be, where the position of the speaker is apparently not neutral at all (despite the "neutral" verb form), as in:

(23)   If John wins in the election, it'll be a shock.

Such interpretations can arise if contextual assumptions (independent of the conditional form) make *p* sound highly improbable rather than neutral – news gives the public a shock when a different development was expected. Other, more macabre examples of this type are given by Dudman (1984). His sentence *If Grannie attends the rally, it will be as a ghost*, said of a dead Grannie and a rally scheduled for tomorrow, considers the only conceivable – not in any way neutral – possibility of a deceased person's participation in a social event. The speaker can, of course, entertain any assumption and examine the consequences which the event considered might bring about. And of course an assumption as bizarre as the possibility of a dead person attending a rally can lead only to a restricted number of (possibly also bizarre) predictions. But this does not mean that, from the point of view of the speaker, the condition of Grannie's attending the rally "may or may not be fulfilled/be a real event," etc., as many descriptions of neutral or open conditions claim (see, e.g., Eckersley and Eckersley 1960, Leech and Svartvik 1975/1994). However, any reinterpretation of "neutral" will fail when we attempt to extend it from (19) and (23) to (18) and (20), where the truth of the protasis' content might well be presumed by the speaker in the context, and the apodosis is not predicted.

An interesting re-definition of the terms discussed above is offered by Funk

(1985), who reserves the term "open conditionals" for sentences referring to non-manifested, unverifiable events, that is, for conditionals with future reference, whether hypothetical or not. Consequently, all other sentences will in Funk's classification be "closed" – including counterfactuals, as well as sentences like (20) (which we have so far considered "open"). His proposal gives the terms "open" and "closed" a much more specific meaning, but basically a temporal one, for all conditionals are considered either futurate ("open"), or non-futurate ("closed"), and the verifiability criterion follows from the temporal description in a straightforward manner. Although Funk notes that the meaning of *if* in "open" and "closed" conditionals can be interpreted respectively as "if it happens that" and "if it is true that," it is not clear what the status of these differences is, and, furthermore, neither of these interpretations of *if* seems applicable to hypothetical conditionals, which are also divided into "open" and "closed" ones. Other distinctive features used in Funk's classification are "$+/-$Real" and "$-$Real", the former label being used for cases where reality of the condition is neither affirmed nor denied (neutral), and the latter for cases where the reality of the condition is denied. In this part of the classification, apparently, Funk is using the concept of "neutral" conditions in the sense described and criticized above.

My claim is, then, that the division into "neutral" or "open" versus "unreal" or "closed" conditionals is not sufficiently useful to be maintained, because of its misleading representation of temporal reference and its unclear stand on the nature of the two types of conditions. I will argue for a different distinction, which should give us a more accurate account of the use of verb forms in conditionals. The class of *predictive* conditionals will include the former futurate open conditionals (e.g. [2], [19], and [23]) and the "unreal" ones, which I will refer to as *hypothetical* or *distanced predictive conditionals*. The *nonpredictive* class, on the other hand, will cover all conditionals not marked with backshifted verb forms, a special set of verbal patterns which will be discussed in the following section. They are a varied class, admittedly (including examples such as [4]–[6], [7], [18], and [20]), but they can be convincingly distinguished as a class on the basis of the parameters postulated in the introduction.

2.3   Backshift in conditional constructions

The main criterion in classifying *if*-constructions with respect to the use of the verb forms is the presence or absence of *backshift*. The term "backshift" should be applicable to every case of language use such that the time marked in the verb phrase is earlier than the time actually referred to. For example, the use of *rained* in the protasis of (2) indicates the past, but in fact refers to the future, and similar backshifted use marks all the verb forms in (2) and (3). In the accounts reviewed above the criterion of backshift is also used (though not explicitly invoked), but it is considered to be restricted to the cases of hypothetical Past, hypothetical Past Perfect and hypothetical uses of verb phrases with *would* characteristic of conditionals such as (2) and (3). I will argue, however, that the protasis of (1) also qualifies here – the form *rains* refers to the future, but indicates the present. This also means that not every case of backshift in conditionals is hypothetical in meaning.

Backshifted use of verb forms is a special, and yet most common case of what Fleischman (1989) calls a basic linguistic metaphor of temporal distance, which consists in expressing various kinds of non-temporal distance by using a temporally more distant form. The extension marked is in most cases that of non-actuality ("distance" from reality or belief), but also of speaker subjectivity and evidential distance. Among the instances of the metaphor that Fleischman mentions there is a case of marking non-actuality by means of the future (which we could call a "fore-shift"), but the majority of examples are examples of backshift and concern uses of the past marking various cases of non-actuality: counterfactuality, lack of commitment, politeness (social "distance"), and reference to imaginary worlds. Not surprisingly, these are the most common interpretations of hypothetical forms in conditionals.

The variety of meanings expressed through backshifted uses of the past is well documented in James (1982), which deals with all forms used in hypothetical conditionals, but also with wishes (particularly contrasts such as *I wish I was/were there* versus *I hope I am/will be there*), requests, expressions such as *as though, let's suppose, imagine*, etc. However, Present tense *if*-clauses of futurate open conditionals are not considered instances of the distance metaphor, and consequently no connection is claimed to exist between the backshift in these clauses and in hypothetical *if*-clauses. On the other hand, both Fleischman and James are concerned with the difference between the distancing expressed in the *if*-clauses and that of the main clauses, and claim the apodosis to be more hypothetical than the protasis, as a result of its being an imagined result of an already imagined situation.[4]

---

[4] One could note that the suggestion about a "double" application of the metaphor in apodoses of hypothetical conditionals does not find confirmation in the data from languages like Polish and Russian. Russian is one of the languages James quotes in support of her solution, but she apparently misinterprets the data by concentrating on the verb phrase only. In Russian and Polish hypotheticality (conditional mood) is marked with a morpheme (-*by*), which attaches to the past tense form of the verb or to the conjunction, but not to both. Both clauses of a hypothetical conditional in Russian and Polish are marked for hypotheticality in the same way – but in the clause containing the conjunction the hypotheticality marker is morphologically a part of the conjunction.

I would like to argue for a different position on backshift in conditionals. First of all, backshift is what distinguishes predictive conditionals from non-predictive ones. Certain conditional constructions conventionally make use of backshifted verb forms – as do certain other constructions (e.g. complements of *wish*), and the contrast between backshifted and non-backshifted verb forms is a crucial one in distinguishing between different classes of conditionals, whose conditional relationship is to be interpreted in different ways. Sentences like (1)–(3) differ from other conditional constructions in that they are representative of two kinds of patterns. First, they all have non-modal verb phrases in their protases, and they all have the same type of modal in their apodoses. Second, as we go down the list represented by (1)–(3), the verb forms in both clauses indicate going further back into the past, although this is not matched by the actual temporal interpretation. Thus, in the protases we find the forms *rains*, *rained*, and *had rained*, while in the apodoses – *will be, would be*, and *would have been* respectively. The choice of verb forms seems to be systematic, then, but the distance marked in each case (with the exception of the apodosis of [1], which is not backshifted) seems to be concerned with unassertability rather than time. I thus want to suggest that (1)–(3) should be seen as representative of two kinds of backshift: the modal-erasing backshift in the *if*-clause, which I will call *if-backshift*, and the backshift affecting (2) and (3) as wholes, which I will call *hypothetical*, since the verb forms used there are called "hypothetical" in some widely known descriptions of English (Quirk, Greenbaum, Leech, and Svartvik 1972, 1985, Leech 1971). A sentence like (2) will be said to have **weak** hypothetical verb forms, while one like (3) employs **strong** hypothetical verb forms. The nature of the two forms of backshift is different, though one complements the other in interpretation.

The fact that sentences like (1), (2), and (3) are somehow related to one another has formed the core of all pedagogical descriptions of English. Recently, a new interpretation was offered by Dudman (1984), who describes them all as instances of what he calls "projectively parsed sentences," which encode judgments arrived at by imagining developments. Dudman's account is based on three major assumptions. First, projectively parsed sentences may or may not contain *if*-clauses, but even if they do, the *if*-clauses constitute a part of the overall message – a projective judgment – and have no independent status of their own. Thus Dudman rejects all analyses which consider *if*-clauses as logical antecedents, having their own truth value, or even as descriptions of situations on which the situations described in the main clauses are contingent. They cannot be considered outside the situation they are part of. The second assumption of Dudman's approach is that the essence and constitutive feature of a projectively parsed sentence is that it refers to a fantasy. The speaker of (1), (2), and (3) is thinking steadily futurewards, imagining developments, and assuming the course of history only up to a given point. The third major claim Dudman makes is that what the verb forms in projectively parsed sentences encode is the temporal boundary between history and fantasy. Verb phrases of *if*-clauses encode the starting point of the fantasy, called the change-over point, which is the point of speech for the Present in (1), a point past with respect to the point of speech for the Past in (2), and a point past with respect to another past point for the Past Perfect in (3). As for the main clauses, their verbs encode the point of view, that is a temporal point from which the speaker starts imagining developments and at which actual historical developments give way to the fantasy. The point of view is thus the same as the change-over point, but, since projective sentences may not contain *if*-clauses, the two encodings are independent.

Dudman's interpretation has several major advantages. It presents the three types of sentences in question as similar in interpretation, in the communicative purposes they serve, and in the types of meanings their verb phrases encode. These three temporal/projective frames are thus naturally distinguished from other sentences containing *if*-clauses and yet encoding essentially different kinds of messages (e.g. sentences such as *If Socrates is a man, Socrates is mortal*, which are also non-predictive in my analysis).

There are some points in Dudman's account, though, which raise some doubts. The idea of a point of view, or the change-over point, at the point of speech is clear – the point is a well-defined one for any communicative event; also, it marks the boundary between history and fantasy in a natural way, for the past (until now) is known, while the future (after now) is not. As regards the point of view which is past or "before past," though, it is much more difficult to specify, on the one hand, and more difficult to justify on the other.

What Dudman is essentially saying is that the fantasy which projective sentences express has to start before the projected occurrence of the imagined situation. In the case of a future fantasy the most natural point of view is that at the point of speech, because one does not know history beyond that point, hence imagination has to take over. The justification for the Past or Past Past point of view for other futurate sentences (which employ morphologically Past or Past Past forms) is much less clear. What fact has to be erased from history to justify the choice of verb forms in (10) (*If he had had the photographs with him at the party tomorrow, I could finally see his grandson*)? Is it necessary for the speaker of (10) to know of some aspect of the situation at present which would be an impediment to the man's having the photographs at the party and which would have to be erased from history to allow the imagined situation to take place? Such an interpretation does not seem necessary. The speaker may have not talked to the man about the photographs; the man may not even be aware of her wish to see them. She is apparently imagining a situation which she wishes for, but which is beyond her influence. I am not convinced that accounting for this requires a past point of view and that the fantasy consists in attributing the speaker with some way of influencing the man's behavior (and in particular, his past behavior).

Another troublesome example is (15) (*If I hadn't been seeing my doctor tomorrow, we could have had lunch together*). One might of course claim that the fantasy has to erase the past fact of my making an appointment, hence it has to start "before past." But the sentence is not really concerned with the moment of making the appointment, but with the speaker's decision to keep it – which is marked in the progressive used in the protasis relating the sentence to *I'm seeing my doctor tomorrow*. It is not that Dudman's interpretation is inadequate, because there must have been a point in the past when the appointment was made, but there seems to be no need to reach so far back into the past in order to arrive at the interpretation of the sentence.

The difficulties are more acute with some sentences having present reference. Dudman's interpretation may be adequate for (9), which possibly requires reaching back to the moment when the speaker arrived without the car, but is less convincing for (13) (*If your mother had been here now, she would have been in tears*), especially if we compare it with *If your mother were here now, she would be in tears*, because in both cases the mother is absent at the moment of speech, and though, admittedly, this state of affairs has its inception or roots in the past, reaching back into "before past," which would be the case for (13) as it stands, does not seem temporally justified. Also, the contrast between the two versions of (13) does not seem to be a temporal one. Dudman argues further that the choice of the change-over point can be dictated by how much of durable aspects of history – like people's personalities – are accepted in the fantasy. But there does not seem to be much difference in the speaker's assessment of the mother's propensity to burst into tears, or whatever else is involved, in the choice of one or the other hypothetical pattern. Also, Dudman seems here to be arguing against his own assumption that the change-over point marks the abandonment of history in favor of fantasy.

The remarks above raise the question whether the change-over point, or the point of view, can legitimately be called a point. The purpose it serves is to include or exclude facts in the past and the present and it is in fact located where Dudman suggests not because the point is temporally salient, but because the fact in question has to be covered by fantasy. In other words, when the change-over point is "before past," it means that there is a fact in the past which will be covered by fantasy, and not that any time interval before the past point in question is relevant to the interpretation. What Dudman is in fact talking about is the speaker's knowledge of some facts about the present and the past which is ignored or explicitly rejected for the purposes of the fantasy. These points do not have to be temporally located, and what the speaker seems to be marking in the verb forms is precisely the clash between what she knows and what she talks about – between the assumptions she holds and the ones she communicates.

Finally, as Dudman himself at least tangentially notes, the type of temporal interpretation that he offers is difficult to apply to "mixed" sentences like (16) (*Tom wouldn't be so hungry if he had eaten a proper breakfast*) and (17) (*If Ann had a better memory for faces, she would have recognized you*), for in these the change-over point does not seem to be equal to the point of view. Dudman's suggestion that the same point is presented as "before past" in one clause, and as "past" in the other in fact goes against his own assumption about the verb form encoding time in a straightforward manner. Similar remarks can be raised in connection with conditionals expressing "general truths" like (12) (*If water boiled at 200°C, making tea would take twice as long*), the atemporal, or omni-temporal interpretation of which is encoded similarly to the cases interpretable as Present. I suggested above that these are in fact special cases of the Present, but certainly this is a Present which has the whole of the past as part of it, not prior to it. There is no change-over point here, therefore the entire past and present would be seen as different from the real ones.

The discussion above shows that many of the difficulties that Dudman's analysis runs into are caused by the notion of the change-over point. In his interpretation, real events develop until a certain moment, and then "fantasy" takes over. As I argued above, the term "fantasy" is not helpful for a number of reasons, but the crucial difficulty is apparently in trying to clearly separate reality from what the conditional describes. The problem is, as Fauconnier (1985, 1996) observes, that conditionals are not meant to be so far removed from reality. As I tried to show in chapter 1, following Fauconnier's work, they build mental spaces which inherit much of the structure of the speaker's reality space; where the conditional space is incompatible with the reality space, the sentence itself tells us in what way it is incompatible. It builds a mental space in which *p* and *q* hold, and the co-existence of *p* and *q* may be the only difference between "reality" and the conditional space. But there is no way to strictly correlate this difference with the temporal sequence of events, although a broad (and, as I will show, by no means necessary) correlation with pastness or futurity may become important in the interpretation. However, this will depend on the particular space set-up, not on sequential ordering of real and imagined events.

Dudman's interpretation of conditionals makes a very interesting contribution to our understanding of the constructions. It tries to account for formal patterns in a new way and seeks to explain form–meaning correlations. The problems that it faces are primarily due to the underlying assumption that the main aspect of conditional interpretations revealed in the verb forms is ***temporal*** in nature. As I have shown in the previous sections, temporal reference of verb forms in conditionals is often difficult to establish, and in the absence of time adverbials the context often remains as the sole source of information. Being rooted in the interpretation of time, Dudman's account leaves some questions unanswered. In the sections to follow I will advocate an analysis of backshifted conditional constructions which links verb form use with degrees and types of unassertability, rather than with temporal reference *per se*.

2.4   Prediction and distance: two types of conditional backshift

One of the main points in which I want to oppose the dominant views on interpretation of conditionals is the question of "what they are about." In the majority of accounts they are seen, on a par with other sentences, as representing states of affairs or events in the world. In many approaches these states and events are considered qualifiable in terms of truth and falsehood. It is further noticed that some conditionals represent non-facts in the actual world, and the conclusion is drawn that they are facts in some other, possible world. Another group of analyses is concerned with the way in which the proposition represented by the main clause is contingent upon that represented by the *if*-clause. Dudman's account stands in opposition to all these (crudely summarized) analyses in that it interprets a major category of conditionals – which he calls projective – as being representative of a fantasy. The fantasy, as Dudman claims, is about the actual world, not a possible one, since, in his approach, possible worlds semantics is an inadequate tool in describing conditionals and all that is needed is an appropriate interpretation of temporal relations. With a proper understanding of time, says Dudman, the boundary betwen fact and fiction is clearly marked.

In the approach advocated here conditionals are seen as representative of neither fact nor fantasy. Instead, they build mental spaces in which the assumptions of *p* and *q* hold, and new conditional spaces built that way inherit much of the structure of the base, "reality space," Also, *if*-clauses of conditional constructions do not represent facts, and are not assertions about states of affairs. As I claimed in chapter 1, every *if*-clause presents an assumption which can be asserted under the right set of circumstances, but is not asserted in this particular utterance by the particular speaker. The reasons for which the content of the clause is presented as not asserted are epistemic in nature, that is, they derive from the assumptions the speaker holds. The particular aspect of the speaker's knowledge which renders the assumption in the *if*-clause non-asserted is encoded, among other things, in the verb forms used. At the same time, they do not represent a fantasy in Dudman's sense, as they are grounded in the reality (mental) space, and build upon the current knowledge of the speaker as well as on what the speaker expects the hearer to know.

As I proposed above, there are two types of backshift in conditionals, which mark two different ways in which the content of a conditional can be presented as unassertable. The *if*-backshift, which is the topic of next section, is explicable against a proper understanding of the form that it contrasts with as a default representative of future reference – that is, the modal *will*. Being the least specific expression of futurity, it is still marked with modality, which can most adequately be called ***predictive***.

2.4.1   *Predictive modality and conditional protases*

There does not seem to be any controversy about sentences like (1) being interpreted as future, both in the protasis and in the apodosis. And it is perhaps the norm, rather than an oddity, cross-linguistically, to find future forms used in both protases and apodoses of conditionals like (1). In English, the future interpretation of the apodosis can clearly be attributed to the presence of *will*, which is a standard, "colorless" expression of futurity. However, as Huddleston (1984) and Palmer (1965, 1974) claim, when *will* is used in its unmarkedly future meaning, it is still used modally, not just temporally. The modality has not been clearly specified. For instance, Palmer 1965 lists "future" among other modalities *will* is capable of expressing, while Huddleston (1984) presents a broader argument, attempting to identify the kind of modality involved. He admits that it is intuitively close to epistemic modalities, but also points to the fact that it is not subjective, and thus different from them.

The most adequate way to describe the use of *will* in sentences like (1) seems to be offered by the term "prediction." The term seems to be a convenient and appropriate one here, even though it has been used (for instance by Leech 1971, Quirk, Greenbaum, Leech, and Svartvik 1972) to refer to other, clearly epistemic uses of *will*, where the speaker is evaluating a situation at present or making a prediction about timeless rules and habitual actions (consider saying *That will be the postman* on hearing the door bell ring, or a statement like *Oil will float on water*). The main difference between the epistemic prediction advocated by Leech (1971) and Quirk, Greenbaum, Leech, and Svartvik (1972) and the prediction I am arguing for is the period of time they refer to, for the genuinely epistemic predictive uses do not concern the future in the sense that they do not evaluate situations in the future. They can, however, be seen as somehow reaching out into the future, because the confirmation of epistemic predictions, especially those made on the basis of the situation at the moment of speech, will only occur in the future – the speaker will know if the person ringing the bell was the postman when she answers the door. The reference to the present in *That will be the postman*, on the other hand, is achieved perhaps not so much by the use of *will*, as by the deictic pronoun *that*, and we should note that discussions of this type of modality invariably repeat the structure *That will be X* as a paradigm example. As for the "habitual" (so-called) epistemic prediction, it does refer, albeit implicitly, to future (and perhaps past or present) events.

The prediction expressed by the most common uses of *will* represents future events and thus the evaluation of its validity will also take place in the future, and not necessarily the immediate future. This "strictly future" prediction found in statements such as *The match will be canceled* is different from epistemic or habitual prediction in its temporal aspect, but is also similar to them in that it presents the speaker as making the prediction on some sound epistemic basis. In the account of *will*-future offered, for example, by Joos (1964), *will* is seen as a kind of commitment on the part of speaker that she has sufficient grounds for saying what she does and takes a kind of responsibility for the statement made. Swan (1980) also seems to be using the term "prediction" in a similar sense.

The idea of predictive modality as making somehow reliable statements about the future seems to stand in some disagreement with a widely held belief that the future is entirely unpredictable and uncontrollable. This is in fact a view that not only philosophers, but also ordinary language-users express upon conscious consideration of the question. In everyday language use, however, *will*-statements about the future are treated as well-founded and are not approached with suspicion.

The question is why predictive *will*-statements are treated with trust. Apparently, it is because predictions, as opposed to acts of imagination, day dreaming, etc., are assumed to have an appropriate basis in reality – they are like factual beliefs in that the speaker making a prediction is taken to have grounds for making it. The grounds that she may have cannot be described as knowledge of the type one has about the past, but rather as an extrapolation from knowledge possessed at present. This, in turn, is not only the knowledge of facts, but also of typical relations between cause and effect. Thus, for instance, knowing that it is just before five o'clock, that it is raining and that tennis matches are canceled when it rains allows one to make a prediction that the match which was scheduled for five o'clock will be canceled. The prediction does not amount to a "knowledge of the future," and is not equivalent to assertion, but it is an assumption which the speaker communicates as well-grounded and presents with a similar amount of confidence. What she predicts is rooted in the knowledge of the present, and arrived at as the knowledge of consequences the present state of affairs may bring about via the knowledge of causal chains.

The speaker making a *will*-prediction must have grounds for making it and is often taken as accountable for its validity. In other words, predictions concerning the future are treated in discourse in a way similar to statements of present or past facts – with one provision. Predictions about the future are treated as reliable, except in the cases which Dudman (1984) calls "abhorrent developments" – disastrous, uncontrollable events which may prevent things from developing as expected. In fact, the trust language-users have in predictions and the ease with which they overlook possible "abhorrent developments" seem to follow from the nature of mental space construction, since, as Fauconnier (1985, 1996) has shown, "child" mental spaces inherit the structure of the parent space unless the transfer is blocked by factors inherent to the new space. That is, if we are structuring a future space around a predicted event, we are not including "abhorrent developments" in its structure, because they are neither imported from the base space, nor brought about by the event we are predicting. In other words, such events would require independent space set-up, which would not be predictive (because it would not be based in the present reality space), and would thus be expressed differently. Interestingly enough, the convention whereby "abhorrent developments" are ignored in typical predictive reasonings is exploited in sentences like *If I'm still alive tomorrow, I'll call you.* In a context in which the speaker's life is not known to be threatened the protasis cannot be informatively interpreted literally, as a condition under which *q* will occur, for this really adds no relevant information to the prediction *I'll call you* within the cultural context. The protasis is there to implicate that no impediments of a less frightful nature can prevent the speaker from calling – which makes the obligation to call sound very strong.

The above view of prediction contradicts the analyses which treat all non-factual statements equally. Dudman (1984), for instance, classifies both *will*-future statements and the so-called counterfactual ones (like [2] and [3] above) as instances of "fantasy." This does not seem to be an adequate description of *will*-statements, for the process of arriving at these is not only rational, but also reality-based.

So far we have considered *will*-predictions in simple sentences like *The match will be canceled*. It may be the case, however, that the speaker wants to make a prediction about a situation which is not fully licensed by her present knowledge. For instance, she wants to consider a tennis match which is scheduled for the next day, and think of it in the context of unfavorable weather conditions. Her epistemic state at the moment of speech differs from the one that licensed the prediction discussed above in that she has no well-justified assumptions about the weather tomorrow at five (the weather forecast is insufficient, not surprisingly). This is where the future is truly uncontrollable. The speaker may choose to make her prediction nevertheless, but she has to signal it to the hearer that one of the assumptions she is using is not known at present and not itself predictable – she thus has to eliminate the marker of prediction, that is *will*. Thus in a sentence like (1) the assumption in the protasis is an assumption which is not itself subject to prediction, but is used, along with other relevant assumptions, in arriving at the prediction in the apodosis. With the marker of predictive modality not present in the verb phrase, the verb can only be marked with the remaining category – that of the Present tense. The temporal reference has not changed, however, and if the same assumption were to be communicated as an independent statement, it would constitute a prediction and would have to be marked with *will*, or another modal indicating the speaker's attitude towards the future event.

As Derek Herforth has pointed out to me, the fact that prediction is not in any sense a part of *p* may be demonstrated by adding a predictive expression to it without causing redundancy. It is thus acceptable to say *If it rains, and I predict it will, the match will be canceled*. At the same time an additional predictive expression in *q* renders the sentence unacceptably redundant: **If it rains, the match will be canceled, and I predict it will*. What is more, as Palmer (1983) notes, conditional protases are not used with *may* and *must* in their epistemic use, which shares many features with prediction. It is unacceptable, says Palmer, to say *If it *may/*must rain, I'll take an umbrella*. My explanation of the restriction is that protases of predictive conditionals present assumptions which are not subject to evaluation against the speaker's current knowledge. On the other hand, the predictive modality expressed in the apodosis seems to be an integral part of this type of conditional construction. As Palmer (1979) shows, other expressions of futurity, such as *going to*, are extremely rare in main clauses of conditionals, and when they appear there, they are highly marked. To conclude, the use of verb forms in futurate predictive conditionals supports the constructional meaning of such sentences. What we are dealing with here are not two clauses combined at random, but elements of a construction, formally marked so as to best represent the meaning of that construction.

I claim, then, that assumptions expressed in protases are not themselves predicted, but brought up in order to make predictions. This explains the interpretation of sentences like (23) (*If John wins in the election, it will be a shock*), which seemed to pose problems for previous analyses. If the context of (23) is, as we can guess, that John is not expected (by the speaker and/or the public) to be the winner, then bringing up an assumption about his success calls for a somewhat special kind of prediction. The prediction will have to reconcile the old assumption and the newly added one and take into account the conflict between the expectations preceding the election and the unexpected result. But the assumption in the protasis (about John's victory) is not itself predicted, and thus in order to make the prediction in the apodosis the speaker does not have to make assumptions about the fulfillment or non-fulfillment of the condition.

It should now be clear why the elimination of modality, which I called *if*-backshift, appears also in temporal clauses. In a sentence like *When the lights go out, the performance will start* the speaker is also making a prediction in the main clause, but the assumption in the *when*-clause is background to the prediction and not predicted itself. The difference between *if-* and *when*-clauses in this case is that an *if*-clause informs the hearer about an additional assumption which is not known to the speaker but used in arriving at the prediction, while the *when*-clause presents a similar assumption (also assumed, not predicted) to set the temporal parameter of the prediction.

I also want to argue that the backshift from future to present in the protasis is always a signal of a predictive statement in the apodosis – even if the surface form of the apodosis does not contain *will*. There are essentially two variants of such predictive sentences: in one case the apodosis does not contain any verb form that would indicate the future, in the other the apodosis uses a modal other than *will*, but with future reference. In the former case the statement in q does not concern a state of affairs in the future, but is nevertheless essentially futurate. For instance, in (24):

(24)   If the leaves wither in a day or two, you added too much fertilizer.

the assumption in p licenses a conclusion which will, however, only be drawn in the future, upon p becoming true. One can say that q is a prediction of a conclusion, which can be recovered in paraphrases like . . . *you will know that you added too much fertilizer.* Similarly, in (25):

(25) If he attacks me, I've got a gun.

the apodosis leaves out the prediction of danger which the actual form of *q* is meant to refute. In other words, the interpretation of (25) involves an implicated prediction of danger inherent in an attack, and *q* is specifically meant to cancel the implicature. Interestingly enough, the sentence is equally acceptable and has the same interpretation with *even if* instead of *if*. This should not, however, be surprising, given the element of "unexpectedness" usually attributed to *even*, as (25) can be loosely paraphrased as "If he attacks me, you may expect me to be in danger, but (even though you expect this) I will be safe, because I've got a gun."

The cases of sentences with apodoses in which other modals are used instead of *will* are much more common. It is not unusual that future events are talked about with less confidence than *will*-predictions express. In those instances modal forms like *can, may, could,* or *might* are often used: *If it rains, they can/may/might/could cancel the field trip.* The sentences are still predictive at least in the sense that they talk about possible future developments on the basis of newly postulated, but not predicted assumptions. The predictions are made with less conviction, however.

As I noted above, sentences like (2) and (3) are essentially like (1) in that they also lack the marker of predictive modality in their protases and that their apodoses are predictive. However, they are additionally marked with hypothetical backshift, which affects both clauses. The effect of hypothetical backshift will be considered in the next section.

2.4.2   Hypothetical backshift

The most general description of the nature of hypothetical forms is that they mark an imagined situation. But this is too broad a definition, since, as we know, statements about the future can also be seen as describing imagined situations, and yet they are usually formulated with non-hypothetical modal *will*. Also, we should note that hypothetical backshift occurs commonly outside conditionals. For instance, it is obligatory after the expression *I wish*, it often marks sequence of tenses in reported statements, it is also widely used to indicate politeness, as in the expressions such as *I would like . . ., Could you, please . . .?, Would you mind . . .?*, etc. What all these uses seem to share is the expression of **distance** (in the sense of Fleischman 1989), such that the speaker feels the need to distance herself from the assumption in question and does not commit herself to the statement. The reasons for marking the distance in the verb form are different in each case: negative expectation of the speaker, evidential or temporal "distance," or giving the hearer an opportunity to express a negative attitude. But in all these cases the hypothetical forms present the speaker as distancing herself from the content of the clause.

In hypothetical conditionals such as (2) or (3), the speaker is presenting two situations in two clauses, and both clauses are marked as hypothetical. However, the distancing imposed does not affect the structure of the predictive statement: the protasis is still modal-less, because it is not itself predicted, while in the apodosis distance is added onto the same predictive modal *will*. The result is "Past" and "Past of Past" forms in the protases, and *would* (*will* + Past) and *would have* (*will* + Past of Past) in the apodoses. Thus the protases of (2) and (3) can only be entertained as hypotheses, because, as the verb forms indicate, the speaker holds or entertains other assumptions which contradict the assumption given in *p*. As a result, the predictions in the apodoses of (2) and (3) are far less strongly made. They are predictions, essentially in the sense established above for sentence (1), but hypothetical backshift warns the hearer that they are different from non-distanced predictions, because the speaker had to set aside some part of her knowledge to be able to arrive at them. In other words, hypothetical predictions are predictions made in spite of knowledge to the contrary. The existence of such counter-evidence has to be signaled to the hearer, who may not share the speaker's knowledge.

Sentences (2) and (3) differ in actual time reference, but they also differ in the strength of hypotheticality. The choice between weak and strong hypothetical forms in these examples seems to be dictated by the strength of the counter-evidence the speaker chooses to ignore in making her prediction. Thus in the case of (2) the speaker is aware that a rainfall is an unlikely thing to happen – she heard a very optimistic weather forecast, she lives in a country where rainfalls are very rare, etc. In the case of (3), however, she knows that it did not in fact rain and that the match took place without impediments. The main difference, then, is that in (2) the possibility of rain is not excluded completely, while in (3) it is.

Interestingly enough, strong and weak forms can sometimes mix in one sentence (see examples [16] and [17]), but they cannot mix with non-hypothetical forms. For example, (26) and (27) are unacceptable sentences:

(26)   *If your mother had been here, she will be in tears.
(27)   *If John wins in the election, it would be a shock.

These sentences indicate that we ought to be concerned not with individual hypothetical assumptions to be expressed differently in different clauses of the construction, but rather with **hypothetical conditional constructions** (as opposed to non-hypothetical ones), which reflect hypothetical thinking. The *if*-clause of a hypothetical sentence creates a mental space which differs in some way from the reality space, but the apodosis holds within the same hypothetical space, and therefore has to receive the same hypothetical marking.

Such an approach is very much in agreement with the predictive analysis offered above. Adding an unpredicted assumption (like *If John wins in the election*) to one's stock of knowledge simply creates more grounds for prediction, but the old asumptions as well as the new one are now legitimate grounds for prediction. In other words, the new predictive mental space has the assumption *p* in it, but it also inherits all other assumptions of the base space, where there is no incompatibility involved. It does not matter that John is in fact not expected to win (by the speaker of *If John wins, it will be a shock*), since the very form of the protasis suggests that *p* is put forward to be taken into consideration along with all other available assumptions. If the speaker had chosen a hypothetical form (like *If John won in the election*) she would have also signaled to the hearer that this assumption is to be treated differently from others, and that, consequently, the status of the prediction made on its basis is different. This is because the assumption in *p* is incompatible with some assumption in the base space. That is, the speaker may have compelling evidence against *p*, as in the case of *If your mother had been here*, and then a straightforward prediction would not be likely. It is difficult to imagine somebody knowing that the hearer's mother is dead and still saying *If your mother sees you in your cap and gown, she'll be in tears*. But when *p* and its counter-assumption can be reconciled, there is a choice between a non-hypothetical or a hypothetical prediction. However, the choice once made is made for the whole construction, not for one clause.

That hypothetical sentences are hypothetical as wholes also finds some support in the observation made by Fillmore (1990b) that in colloquial use the protases of strong hypothetical sentences may appear with the form *had've*, rather than just *had* + Past Participle. Fillmore has noted sentences like *If we hadn't've met Harry, where would we be now?* to be present in the speech of a significantly large group of American English speakers. I tend to interpret this form as an attempt to signal hypotheticality in both clauses of the construction, because, in a sense, they "feel" hypothetical in the same way. In fact, languages which use conditional mood in hypothetical constructions, like e.g. Polish and Breton, may mark it obligatorily in both clauses.

In the discussion above I argued that all three types of backshift (*if*-backshift and weak and strong hypothetical backshift) appear to be features of constructions rather than clauses alone. This is due to the fact that predictive conditional constructions are representative of a type of reasoning in which the protasis and the apodosis are linked together and are both interpreted as valid in the same mental space. In different terms and to somewhat different ends, the idea that such sentences represent a specific kind of reasoning that involves both clauses was also advanced by Dudman in his discussion of "projectively parsed sentences." Interestingly enough, his interpretation provided inspiration for an account of conditionals which focuses on the use of verb forms with respect to the well-formedness alone, regardless of interpretation (Hornstein 1990). Since in the discussion above I have claimed that the choice of verb forms in conditionals is primarily governed by the kind of reasoning a construction represents and by the assumptions constituting the background to the reasoning, it will be interesting to consider an approach which offers to describe the choice of verb forms in terms of syntax of tense alone.

Hornstein's (1990) analysis develops its formalism from Reichenbach's logical theory (Reichenbach 1947) relating the location of the event time E to the moment of speech S and the reference point R. Thus a Simple Past form represents a configuration in which the points E and R are contemporaneous and both precede S, in a Simple Present form all three points converge, while in an expression of the Future S precedes E and R, which are contemporaneous again. The Perfect forms are different in that the reference point never coincides with the event point: in Present Perfect E precedes contemporaneous S and R, in Past Perfect E precedes R, which precedes S, while in Future Perfect S precedes E, which precedes R. In his theory, Hornstein attempts to show how these basic tense structures interact with temporal adverbs and how tense configurations in complex sentences come about. Conditionals will be our case in point here.

In Hornstein's analysis, combining clauses to form complex temporal sentences (conditionals are taken to be a subcase of this broader category) occurs according to two general principles. One principle states that, first, in derived tense structures the configuration of basic tense structures of participant clauses has to be preserved, that is, the sequence of points S, E, and R cannot be changed, and that, second, the derived configuration cannot present the points as contemporaneous unless they are contemporaneous in the basic structure, but points contemporaneous in basic structures may be separated in derived structure. The second principle, specific to temporal connectives, governs the way in which two basic structures of the participant clauses yield the derived structure of the complex sentence. It requires that the S points and the R points of the two structures be aligned without the violation of the first principle. If violation occurs, then the resulting derived structure is ill-formed and the purported tense configuration is ruled out as representative of a grammatical sentence of English. The operation of the two principles correctly predicts the acceptability of sentences like *John came after Harry arrived/had arrived*, and also rules out sentences like **John came as Harry arrives* or **John had come when Harry arrives*.

As Hornstein says, though, the mechanism proposed is strictly formal; that is, the principles do not account for how structures as wholes will be interpreted and no claims are made about temporal interpretation of tense forms. The reservation is particularly relevant in the case of conditionals, says Hornstein, because they display a variety of interpretations, but nevertheless adhere to the principles proposed.

Hornstein's account of conditionals uses the ideas of Dudman discussed earlier in this chapter. Following Dudman's proposals, Hornstein claims that the sentences which I called non-predictive (the non-backshifted ones) are not proper conditionals and their clauses make their choice of tense forms independently of each other; this means that the principles summarized above do not apply. He also gives a separate treatment to generic conditionals, where his principles apply in a rather straightforward manner. The interesting part of the analysis is that pertaining to conditionals Dudman describes as "projectively parsed," which I have termed predictive (backshifted). Hornstein's formalism is thus claimed to correctly predict that sentences like *Grannie will walk/would walk/would have walked home if she misses the last bus tonight/were to miss the last bus/had missed the last bus on Friday* are well-formed. This is indeed the case, if one assumes, as Hornstein does, that the forms *would* and *were to* represent the Present tense, and only the modal + *have* structures are Past tense forms. Actually, Hornstein's treatment of verb forms makes no statements at all about the nature of modality and attempts to present all aspects of verb use through the basic present/past contrast. This does not seem to be sufficient in the case of conditionals, even if the question of actual interpretations is carefully avoided.

First of all, the assumptions Hornstein makes lead to a somewhat misleading representation of what counts as a tense configuration characteristic of a conditional. The weak hypotheticals, for instance, are presented as if the standard form in the protasis were *were to*, as in *were to miss* in the example above. The use of the past forms like *missed*, which undoubtedly dominate in actual usage, is marginally mentioned in a footnote. Also, Hornstein explicitly rejects treating such forms as past, because the adverbs used with the conditionals that have this form are ones like *tomorrow*, rather than ones like *yesterday*. So *missed* and *were to miss* are presented as variants of each other, both of them being some sort of a subjunctive or conditional. The solution proposed is not in fact supported by the major descriptions of English, where *missed* would not be a subjunctive, and in fact the form *were to* is not often called subjunctive either. But this is not the crucial question. What really seems to be the problem is where the line between form and interpretation is drawn. If a form is identical to the past but is not used with *yesterday*, is it because it is not past at all, as Hornstein would have it, or because pastness involves a concept of distance which can be re-interpreted from temporal to epistemic or social distance? This is somewhat similar to a chicken and egg problem, but it seems that in the case of conditionals dealing with form without the interpretation causes more problems than it solves.

A good example of the confusion is Hornstein's claim that his principles correctly reject clausal couplings which mix weak and strong hypothetical forms. His examples are indeed difficult to process: **Grannie would walk if she had missed the bus* and **Grannie would have walked if she were to miss the bus*. It is not clear, then, how we should qualify sentences (16) and (17) discussed earlier in the chapter: *Tom wouldn't be so hungry if he had eaten a proper breakfast* and *If Ann had a better memory for faces, she would have recognized you*. These sentences are fully acceptable, and structures similar to them are quite common (even pedagogical grammars mention them). In terms of the verb forms used (16) and (17) are identical to Hornstein's examples, and if one followed his assumptions about which forms are past and which are present, they would yield the same tense structures as Hornstein's examples do, and thus should be ill-formed. But they are not. The difference, then, is not in the morphology or syntax. As it seems to me, the problem is in the interpretation. Even Hornstein's bad examples can become acceptable with the changes that reveal the kind of reasoning involved. For example, if we are waiting for Grannie, who is late, and then we see a person looking like Grannie coming up the street, we could say *This can't be Grannie. She would never walk if she had missed the bus*. The problem is that such examples are hard to process if all we have is two non-contemporaneous events which cannot be interpreted sequentially. If we provide a background in which there is a plausible reasoning link between such events, the sentence is acceptable. And the acceptability depends on aspects of interpretation, rather than on syntax of tense alone.

Interpretations of hypothetical predictions are indeed quite context-specific, as we have seen. Another question one may ask is why they are ever made. In general, as Fauconnier (1985) argues, they choose a specific mapping to make a particular point, rather than hypothesize for the sake of hypothesizing or creating a possible world. This approach contrasts with that advocated by Dudman, who sees all hypotheticals as cases of fantasy. We could note, however, that a typical fantasy, which is of a "day-dreaming," or "fairy-tale" type, is just one of the possible uses of hypotheticals, and, in its own way, it also makes a point. Fantasies are usually timeless and are thus best expressed through weak hypothetical verb forms, as in *If I had a million dollars, I would never have to go to that office again*, or *If I were President, I would refuse to eat broccoli too*. The existence of evidence contradicting the content of such protases does not seem to be the most salient aspect of the interpretation here, it is rather a kind of "willing suspension of belief," if I may paraphrase the classic. After all, as Fauconnier 1996 would suggest, the speaker's empathy with the broccoli-hating president is more important in interpreting such a hypothetical conditional than the question of what situation would arise under the speaker's hypothetical presidency – so there is no reason for an interlocutor to worry about wrong predictions of fact, here. Other weak hypothetical sentences have other "points to make," though. Many sentences use weak hypothetical forms to perform speech acts, as in (28) and (29), where putting oneself for a moment into somebody else's shoes helps express advice and warning:

(28)   If I were you, I would accept the offer.
(29)   If I were you, I would never say that again.

More frequently, though, hypothetical forms are useful in performing speech acts which involve looking at possible consequences of situations which did not in fact occur and thus evaluating one's decisions and behavior. These speech acts require that strong hypothetical forms are used. Thus (30) is an expression of regret, (31) of accusation, (32) of relief, and (33) of self-criticism.

(30)   If I had been more careful, I wouldn't have broken the vase.
(31)   If you had been more careful, you wouldn't have broken the vase.
(32)   If I had invited John, there would have been a scandal.
(33)   If I hadn't been such a fool, I would have accepted the offer.

The types of situations in which it is more useful to present a hypothetical prediction through weak or strong forms are linked with the way in which the existence of counterevidence is signaled in these two types of constructions. What seems to be the case is that the difference between weak and strong hypothetical forms is in the strength and scope of the assumptions which are counterevidence to the particular prediction. In the case of the weak forms the contradicting assumptions block straightforward prediction, but the hypothetical prediction made is not excluded as a possibility. In choosing the strong forms, on the other hand, the speaker presents the situation as *irreversible*. It seems that special emphasis should be put on the choice the speaker has here, especially since the same situation can sometimes be presented in more than one way, for the future and the present can be talked about through the weak and strong forms alike (compare [2] and [15], also [8] and [13]).

It seems that the choice of one or the other set of hypothetical forms is not dictated by any straightforward evaluation of what is possible or impossible in reality. Why would one say that the appointment with the doctor in (15) makes having lunch together impossible, while everyone knows that a phone call could change the situation? On the other hand, why would offering someone a ride still be a possibility in (9) if the car is clearly not there for the speaker to use? In trying to account for the choice between weak and strong hypothetical forms by reference to what is possible or impossible in reality, we are just giving a different wording to the problems raised by many existing accounts: counterfactuality as part of the meaning of the construction, the realis/irrealis distinction, etc. The only explanation that seems to account for how these forms are used is the one which focuses on how the speaker chooses to present the situation, not on what the actual situation is. For example, suppose that we engage in a jocular exchange in which someone sarcastically offers to make us wings to fly with (so we can get to an appointment on time for once) and we respond in the same spirit by saying *OK, if I have wings by tomorrow, I'll fly (but as it is, you'll have to accept my coming late when the traffic is heavy)*. In a more "fantasizing" mood, though, we would probably prefer to use distanced forms, as in *If I had wings, I would fly (and wouldn't have to worry about traffic any more)*. But it is *how* the speaker presents the situation, not *how "real"* it is, that dictates the choice of forms.

Hypothetical forms are indicative of the distance that the speaker wants to mark towards the prediction in question. Strong hypothetical forms are more distanced than weak ones. The choice may be influenced by the actual time reference, because temporal distance is one of main reasons for using distanced forms – however, it is not the only reason. Thus it is, not surprisingly, almost obligatory to present past hypothetical situations as more distanced, because knowledge of past events and their consequences constitutes the strongest possible counterevidence to the prediction communicated. With future situations or present situations used in predicting future ones it is more likely that the speaker will use weak, less distanced forms, because the evidence one can have about the future is less compelling. But if the speaker is invoking an assumption which constitutes compelling evidence against a certain future development, strong forms can legitimately be used. Thus an important aspect of the speaker's choice is the degree to which the assumption considered in the protasis is in conflict with other assumptions the speaker holds – the counterevidence, as I called it above. But it is a matter of the speaker's choice just how much of the actually available counterevidence she wants to take into account in portraying the situation to the hearer. In other words, the amount of base space structure transferred to the conditional space depends on the particular mental space set up in context by the particular utterance.

An argument for the claim that the choice of hypothetical forms is dictated by the speaker's evaluation of the knowledge she has (and specifically her evaluation of it as contradicting the prediction she is making) and by her choice of how to present the situation can be found in the examples where the speaker's attitude towards a future event changes as the discourse progresses. A very compact example of that is (34):

(34)   We have provisionally programmed your seminar for Thursday 14th February. If you *give* it on the first Thursday you are here, you'll get more worthwhile feedback than if you *gave* it at the end of your visit.

The text in (34) is a fragment from a letter I received. In the first conditional, which is only marked with *if*-backshift, the provisional arrangement mentioned (giving the seminar on the 14th) is used as a ground for a prediction (getting better feedback). In the second conditional, however, this provisional arrangement is used as a piece of knowledge contradicting the prediction being made. The addressee may prefer to choose a later date, but the results of such a choice can only be predicted in the context of that choice. Such a prediction will thus inevitably be based on assumptions different from the ones provisionally taken as binding. But also, it is the choice of *gave*, rather than *give*, that signals to the reader that the first option is in fact preferred.

We have thus seen how the choice of verb forms used in predictive conditional constructions indicates the type of mental space set-up introduced by *if*, and, consequently, the particular source of the unassertiveness in the presentation of p and q. In any predictive statement, it seems, the assumption in the scope of *if* is interpreted as not being itself predictive, but its provisionally assumed future truth is necessary for the prediction made in q to be valid. Additionally, it may be the case that the whole predictive statement is presented hypothetically: this signals to the hearer that the prediction is made in spite of a piece of knowledge the speaker possesses which makes the assumption in the scope of *if* not only not predictable at the moment of speech, but also possibly unassertable or necessarily unassertable. Sentences (1)–(3), although examples of two distinct backshifting relationships, can thus be interpreted as related cases of using temporal distance to mark lower degrees of assertability: the further the verb forms used go back in time, the lower the predictions are on the scale of assertability.

2.4.3   Hypothetical conditionals and the narrator

In this section I would like to illustrate different aspects of distancing in conditionals through attested examples. The sentences examined all come from Kurt Vonnegut's novel *Hocus Pocus* (1990). Among 151 conditional sentences which I was able to find in the text, 66 are hypothetical. Of these 66, 44 have strong hypothetical forms, 17 have weak ones, and 5 mix strong and weak forms in one sentence.

The majority of strong hypothetical examples have past reference, and are interpreted as counterfactual. This should not be surprising in view of the fact that the narrator tells his life story as an elderly man, often trying to show the reader how a different turn of events could have made a different memoir. Strong hypothetical forms are specifically useful in showing how one apparently insignificant fact can start a chain of causes and results which eventually give the most unexpected course to one's life. Thus, early in the story, the narrator talks about Time and Luck as two prime movers in the Universe. Then the reader is told how the major events in the narrator's life crucially depended on the fact that a certain Henry Moellenkamp was dyslexic. Several paragraphs that create the setting for the ensuing narration each begin with a strong hypothetical sentence which, like (35) and (36), start with the following clause: *If Henry Moellenkamp had not come out of his mother's womb dyslexic . . .*:

(35)   If Henry Moellenkamp had not come out of his mother's womb dyslexic, Tarkington College wouldn't even have been called Tarkington College.

(36)   If Henry Moellenkamp had not come out of his mother's womb dyslexic, these heights above Scipio might have been all darkness on the cold winter night 2 years ago . . . when 10,000 prisoners at Athena were suddenly set free. Instead, there was a little galaxy of beckoning lights up here.

It will be later in the story that the reader will see the chain of causes and effects linking these events, but the ground has been created.

Both (35) and (36) are clearly interpreted as past and counterfactual and the use of strong hypothetical forms is thus fully justified. But there are other examples, like (37) below, where the pastness and "counterfactuality" are not sufficient to require the use of strong forms.

(37)   If my Socialist grandfather . . . could read the letter from Mrs. de Wet . . . he would be grimly gratified. There was a clear-as-crystal demonstration of . . .

The sentence is used to introduce a short section structured around the (mistaken) Socialist perceptions of "the poor and powerless." Mrs. de Wet and her views are described in the preceding section; the grandfather is mentioned here for the first time. The ensuing paragraphs revolve around the following strong hypothetical clauses about the late grandfather: "He would have seen the exploitation of the poor and powerless in the growth of the prison across the lake . . .," "The prison to him would have been a scheme for . . .," "By the time I got to Tarkington College, though, he would have been wrong about the meaning of the prison across the lake . . ." Why, then, is (37) not formulated with strong forms, though it is clear that the grandfather could not and did not read Mrs. de Wet's letter and was consequently deprived of the opportunity to be grimly gratified? It seems that the reason is rooted in the discourse function of (37), which is to state the topic of the section which follows. The sentence is apparently not about "how the world would be different if the grandfather had read the letter," but rather about "how Mrs. de Wet's views could be interpreted by someone like the grandfather." This is an introduction to an argument about why such an interpretation would be mistaken. In other words, the distancing that is necessary is only on the level that proposes a certain point of view, but there is no need to deal with actually different courses of events.

The choice of weak or strong forms also helps identify the point in narration where sentences are nested. (35) and (36) look back at history from the temporal vantage point of the narrator as he is now. In other instances, as in (38), weak forms are used because the sentence represents the evaluation made at the past point in the story, not at the present point when it is told.

(38)   I understood that this stupid girl was as dangerous as a cobra. It would be catastrophic if she spread the word that I was an anti-Semite, especially with so many Jews . . . now sending their children to Tarkington.

The reader already knows that the girl did indeed spread the word and that the narrator was consequently expelled from the college. But the sentence is a comment on one of the exchanges in the dialogue between the narrator and the girl and is made from the perspective of that dialogue. It is again not sufficient for the knowledge of past events to trigger the use of strong hypothetical forms.

Not surprisingly, weak forms are chosen where there is no adequate knowledge of the course of past, present, or future events. The narrator had a "reputation as the campus John F. Kennedy as far as sex outside of marriage was concerned" (1990: 93). His comment is:

(39)   If President Kennedy up in Heaven ever made a list of all the women he had made love to, I am sure it would be 2 or 3 times as long as the one I am making down here in jail.

Taken more or less seriously, the protasis of (39) may refer to any period of time between Kennedy's death and the infinite future. The point is not really whether he ever had the intention of making up such a list. Again, the sentence is an introduction to a paragraph about how different the women in the narrator's and Kennedy's lives were, not about the actual course of events, as is the case in (35) and (36).

Sentence (39) is also interesting in its use of *I am sure* and *I am making*, whose form is not affected by the surrounding hypothetical assumptions. An even better example of this is (40):

(40)   If he hadn't hired both of us for Tarkington, where we both became very
         good teachers of the learning-disabled, I don't know what would have
         become of either of us.

The non-hypothetical forms of *we both became* and *I don't know* clearly separate these clauses from the hypothetical prediction. And rightly so, because these assumptions are not used in the predictive argument. The fact that the narrator and his friend became good teachers of the learning-disabled is a consequence of the fact that they were both hired. The latter assumption, in turn, is not communicated in the sentence, but implicated as counterevidence to the hypothetical protasis. As for *I don't know*, it is even more interesting. It is involved in the prediction being made, but is not presented as the prediction proper. The interpretation seems to be roughly as follows: I am invoking an assumption (a counterfactual one) such that "we were not hired for Tarkington College" and trying to see what prediction it yields against the background of what I otherwise know about "us." But there is no such clear prediction. Still, the fact that *I don't know* is not itself predicted from p, it is a "meta-predictive" clause (if such a category can be postulated) which qualifies the highly underspecified content of the actual q (that something would have become of us). It has been pointed out to me that another way to interpret (40), which could be revealed in a different clause order, is to see the whole conditional, not just the apodosis, as embedded in the scope of *I don't know*. Under this interpretation the "meta-predictive" function of the phrase is even clearer and the choice of verb forms uncontroversial. The main point is that in both (39) and (40), clauses with non-hypothetical forms are marked this way in opposition to those which truly participate in the predictive reasoning – either as initial assumptions, or as the predicted consequences.[5]

Let us consider one more example of a sentence in which the choice of strong hypothetical forms seems to be guided by factors other than time reference. (41)

---

[5] For an analysis of similar sentences in terms of mental spaces, see Sweetser 1996b.

is what the narrator says to a UPS man who has just delivered to him a box with the contents of his old footlocker from Vietnam, years after the war ended.

(41)   "If the Vietnam war was still going on," I said, "it might have been you in
        there." I meant he might have wound up in a casket.

The protasis uses weak forms, while the apodosis uses strong forms, even though the known present state of affairs is implicitly referred to in both as evidence that the assumptions presented cannot be true. Apparently, the protasis is just the "let's imagine" kind of use, where counterevidence does not need to be explicitly refuted, while the apodosis does something to the contrary. It seems to be saying: "look, you are alive, and many young men like you were not that lucky." The strength of the hypotheticality highlights the contrast between the two scenarios.

As we have seen, hypothetical forms in conditionals can be used in narration to perform functions which cannot be reduced to past reference and counterfactuality. They help in organizing the narration, indicate the theme of larger pieces of prose, or help identify the narrator's point of view. The different kinds of unassertability, or distance, that they bring into the text have a crucial role in structuring the narration.

2.5   Non-predictive constructions

Predictive conditionals were defined above: they represent predictive reasonings, and they are therefore marked with *if*-backshift in the protases and have a predictive modal in their apodoses. This kind of pattern can then be further backshifted to mark hypothetical distance.

Other conditionals do not show any regular patterns of verb forms, and in particular they do not require any form of backshift. Most generally, we can say that the verb forms in non-predictive conditionals refer to the time they indicate. In other words, they are not backshifted and are used according to the general rules governing non-conditional constructions. They are also not constrained in terms of the sequence of tenses. The two clauses of a non-predictive conditional look as though they have been formed independently of each other and entered the construction as individual assumptions. That is, the conditional format of the construction *if p, q* and the fact that there is presumably some relation between the clauses do not affect the choice of verb forms in any part of the construction. Also, as I will show in chapter 3, the non-predictive format is much more open to different types of protasis/apodosis relations, which is an additional indication of the fact that non-predictive constructions are generally

much less conventionalized than the predictive ones. Consequently, their interpretations rely to a greater degree on contextual factors, and they are overall
less central examples of conditional constructions.

One of the consequences of the relative independence of p and q is that it is
possible for the time expressed in p to be later than the time expressed in q. This
is the case in both (18) and (20) above, which I will repeat here for convenience
as (42) and (43):

(42)   If he won't arrive before nine, there is no point in ordering for him.
(43)   If she is in the lobby, the plane arrived early.

The clauses of (42) and (43) are formed according to general rules and are
interpreted in basically the same way as independent sentences; among other
things, this makes it possible for *will* to be used in an *if*-clause, as in (42). In
both cases the clauses of the construction mention the events they describe non-
sequentially, in reversed order – in (42) the protasis is future and the apodosis
present, while in (43) they are present and past respectively.

Not all of the sentences having non-predictive forms are temporally
reversed: the events represented may be (roughly) simultaneous, as in (44)
below, or the sequence of clauses may follow the natural course of events, as
in (45). However, in all non-predictive sentences, whether temporally
reversed or not, the sequence of clauses does not necessarily correlate with the
sequence of events in the situation described by the construction (see chapter
3 for a broader discussion of sequentiality in predictive and non-predictive
conditionals).

(44)   If Mary said she liked the movie, she was just showing off.
(45)   If she is giving the baby a bath, I'll call back later.

The next question is what type of unassertability is signaled in the protases of
such sentences. They are clearly different in this respect from the backshifted
protases of predictive conditionals which present tentative, non-predicted
assumptions, where no knowledge of any kind is presupposed. In sentences
(42)–(45) the protases sound as if they have already been grounded in the
context. In the simplest case, some other participant in the conversation may
have said or suggested something that now allows the speaker to access the previously communicated assumption and use it in the protasis. The role of such
protases is clearly to provide the background against which the apodoses can be
felicitously communicated. For instance, (45) might plausibly be said in a telephone conversation wherein the speaker has learned that the person she wanted
to talk to is giving the baby a bath. The speaker can now use this assumption as
a background against which her decision to call back later is communicated.

Thus the protasis of (45) represents an assumption which the hearer acquired indirectly. The fact that X is giving the baby a bath is not really known to the speaker of (45), she has only been told that this is the case. It can, however, be known to be true, and thus unquestionably assertable, to the person at the other end of the telephone line. Similarly (42), (43), and (44) can readily be contextualized in situations where somebody, but not the speaker, has communicated their protases as facts. The speaker can use such assumptions in communicating other assumptions, but the evidential distance involved is marked by *if*. There are in fact many possibilities for interpretation of such examples – both in terms of types of contextual grounding of non-predictive protases, and in terms of the ways in which they themselves provide background to their apodoses. Both of these issues will be taken up in chapters 3 and 4.

Non-predictive conditionals can thus be introductorily characterized with reference to three parameters: the relation between tense and time (the former is indicative of the latter), a different level of iconicity (the sequence of clauses does not have to be iconic of the sequence of events), and the interpretation of conditionality as evidential distance.

2.6   Generic constructions

Outside the predictive/non-predictive contrast that we explored above, there are conditional constructions which seem to share some features of both of the classes. These are sentences like (46):

(46)   If I drink too much milk, I get a rash.

What such sentences seem to share with non-predictive constructions is that their verb forms are used in the same way as outside the conditional format. The use of the Present tense found in (46) can also be found in independent statements such as *You drink too much milk* or *I often get a rash*. The use is characteristic of many types of general statements, and is often called generic or iterative. That is why I refer to constructions like (46) as "generic." On the other hand, what the constructions seem to share with predictive sentences is the type of connection between *p* and *q*, such that *q* is construed to be the result or consequence of *p*. They can, however, be treated as generalized predictions, such that every occurrence of *p* can be predicted to bring about *q*.

Another similarity between generic conditionals and predictions is that in both cases there is some degree of similarity between a sentence with *if* and an analogous one with *when*. Both *if* and *when*, as we have seen, introduce assumptions which help arrive at predictions. In the case of generic constructions, they can both introduce similar clauses as well, with *whenever* as a third possible conjunction in some cases. Let us consider the sentences below:[6]

(47)   If/When/Whenever you heat ice, it melts.
(48)   If/When/Whenever you press its tummy, it squeaks.
(49)   If/When/Whenever you pressed its tummy, it squeaked.
(50)   If/When John comes on Saturdays, they play tennis.
(51)   If/When/#Whenever you live in a suburb, you pay taxes there.
(52)   If/When/#Whenever you lived in a suburb, you paid taxes there.

Whenever, which can modify sentences denoting a repeated occurrence of an event, is not readily acceptable in (51) and (52), since these examples refer to states (*whenever* seems more acceptable if we interpret them as referring to someone who moves between suburbia and the city all the time). *If* and *when* are equally applicable everywhere, whether the sentence has present or past reference. However, one should note that in all sentences except (50) there are no restrictions on the time of the application of the rule formulated there, except the basic division into rules which were binding in the past (expressed with Past verb forms) and those which are binding now or at all times (expressed in Present form). In (50), however, the mention of a regular interval at which the action may be repeated (every Saturday) provides the clue about the difference between *if* and *when*. As Keith Mitchell pointed out to me, the reading of (50) with *when* suggests that John comes every Saturday, while the one with *if* – that there are Saturdays when he does not. This seems to result from the role *if* plays. On its own, the assumption about John's coming on Saturdays suggests that he does come every week. When the assumption is preceded by *when*, some generalization is made about all of the possible occasions which the assumption can represent. In the presence of *if*, on the other hand, the iterative statement about John coming on Saturdays is weakened, presented non-assertively. The most likely relevant interpretation is thus the one under which there are Saturdays when John does not come.

The distinction outlined above holds true for all of sentences (47)–(52), but it is obliterated in all the temporally open-ended cases, that is all except (50). But it is still the case that *when*-sentences talk only about the situations where the assumption in the subordinate clause is the case, while *if* sentences imply the existence of situations to the contrary. This can also be seen in (53):

(53)   If I lived in a suburb, I paid taxes there/When I lived in a suburb I paid taxes there.

---

[6] I owe examples (48), (49), and (50) to Keith Mitchell (personal communication); the first two can be used in talking about a teddy bear.

The first person pronoun used in (53) deprives the sentence of its impersonal, universal character. It is still a habitual statement about a certain state of affairs, with respect to, again, the choice of the verb and the verb form. But the variant with *if* makes sense only in the situation where the speaker moved from one place to another several times, and happened to live in a suburb more than once, so that the implication of the situations to the contrary has some support in the past reality known to the speaker. The *when*-sentence, on the other hand, is most relevantly understood as referring to a period of time when the speaker lived in a suburb. It does not imply that there were several periods like that, but it does not imply the opposite either. It just talks only about the time which the speaker can describe by saying *I lived in a suburb*.

The remarks above should clarify how in the case of generic constructions, as in the other types, the interpretation of the sentence relies on the use of the verb form and on the variety of unassertability introduced by *if*.

2.7 Time in conditionals: a summary

In the present section I will sum up the observations made above concerning temporal reference of *if*-clauses, assuming, however, that it is established on the basis of a number of parameters, among which the verb form plays an important, but not a unique role. Other factors contributing to temporal interpretation are as follows: other explicit temporal indicators; the semantic class of the verb (state or event); the context; and the overall interpretation of the sentence as being hypothetical or not, and predictive or not.

It is clear from the data discussed earlier that the verb forms in conditional protases are not unambiguously indicative of time. Let us first look at the protases which have a Present tense form. Such a protasis has a possible interpretation as an *if*-backshifted background clause of a future-reference predictive conditional, but it is also open to a generic reading, or to a non-predictive one; the ambiguity can be resolved only by coming up with an interpretation of the whole sentence. If the apodosis uses predictive *will*, the overall interpretation is predictive, if it uses another form, the overall interpretation is non-predictive. *If*-clauses with Past tense verbs are three ways ambiguous, depending on whether the whole sentence is weak hypothetical (then *would* + V appears in the main clause), Past generic (then the apodosis also has Past generic use), or non-predictive. In the non-predictive case the apodosis can have any verb form, referring to the future, the present, or the past.

The central claim of this chapter was that the choice of the verb form encodes some aspects of the interpretation independent of time. Perhaps the most direct evidence that this is so lies in the fact that future, present, and past reference each have several different possible encodings in *if*-clauses, depending on other aspects of the conditional interpretation.

The future in a protasis can be encoded in four ways. It can be expressed by *will* + *V* (example [18]), and in these cases the assumption expressed in the clause is marked with evidential distance. When the verb is in the Present tense (as in [1]), the clause expresses a non-predicted assumption which is, however, necessary for making the prediction expressed in the main clause. The remaining two forms, Past and Past Perfect ([8] and [15]), appear in weak and strong hypothetical sentences respectively, with the former suggesting that the speaker has some evidence against the plausibility of the prediction to be made in the main clause, and the latter making a stronger claim about the irreversibility of the situation that the speaker has knowledge about at the moment of speech. Among these, the only case where the future is seen as "uncontrollable" is the use of the modal-less Present tense in *if*-backshifted sentences. As we have seen, contrary to the generally held philosophical standpoint, speakers do not treat the future as impossible to know in any useful way.

The future is thus seen as "knowable" at least to a degree; but there are degrees to the certainty of the knowledge, hence the careful marking of evidence for or against the predictions made and the source of the prediction. A variety of attitudes towards the future is further manifested in English by modal and non-modal forms indicating intentions, plans, arrangements, decisions, immediate future, etc. (Leech 1971). Many of these forms can also be used in conditionals (modals appear in them very naturally, but consider also the role of the progressive in [15]). All of these make a rather complex epistemic network whose main task is to supply the speaker with tools for giving a possibly faithful and precise account of her knowledge of the future.

As regards the conditional representation of the present (with all the reservations made above as to the scope of "the present"), there are three possibilities: the Present tense, the Past tense, and Past Perfect. The Present tense is commonly a marker of non-predictive constructions, where the assumption expressed in the protasis is attributed to somebody else, not the speaker. In such a case the tense is often combined with Progressive and/or Perfective aspect (as in *If she is giving the baby a bath . . ., If I have met him . . .*), or may be a state verb describing the state of affairs holding at the moment of speech (*If she is in the lobby . . .*). The Past and Past Perfect are respectively markers of weak and strong hypotheticality, again reflecting the strength of the evidence the speaker has while formulating a hypothetical statement about an imagined situation.

The Present in protases often refers to the ongoing speech setting. This seems to stand in contrast with the fact that conditional protases present situations as in some way unassertable. However, the fact that the discourse setting is manifest to the speaker does not mean that all of its aspects and their implications are known to the speaker directly. Some aspects of it may be brought to her attention by other participants in the conversation, and in these cases she may use non-backshifted forms in the scope of *if* to mark evidential distance. This seems to be the case in sentences like (8) – *If she is in the lobby, the plane arrived early* (see chapter 4 for more discussion). On the other hand, even having strong assumptions about the present leaves room for imagining a different state of affairs (in hypothetical constructions), and the broader the span of the interval understood as "the present," the more plausible it is to postulate weak hypotheses, whose realization is not presented as impossible. Still, the speaker may also present hypotheses about the present in a way which suggests that she has strong grounds for considering the hypothesis implausible. These two types of hypotheticality are exploited for different communicative purposes, and different speech acts are performed by making use of the two sets of forms.

The range of verb forms is most restricted in *if*-clauses referring to the past, as the choice is only between Past tense – marking either evidential distance concerning assumptions about past events or generic use, and Past Perfect marking strong hypotheticality. It should not come as a surprise that only strong (as opposed to weak) hypotheticality can mark statements about the past, for the past is certainly seen as irreversible, not subject to possible change. More interesting is the simple fact of the difference between hypothetical Past Perfect and non-hypothetical Past tense, in view of the fact that the past is always irreversible. The explanation for this contrast lies at least partly in the fact that the past, being undoubtedly understood as irreversible, is not necessarily known to the person who wants to talk about it. The evidential distance marked with the use of Past tense may indicate that the speaker has acquired the assumption from somebody else, or may show the speaker's genuine lack of knowledge of the past events. The sentences in (54):

(54)   If she had been wearing her safety belt, she would be still alive/If she was wearing her safety belt, she may be still alive.

are different in that the hypothetical version seems felicitous in a situation where the speaker knows about the accident and about the death it caused, while in the non-backshifted version she might well be indicating that she knows about the accident, but does not know whether the driver survived. Again, we can summarize the difference by distinguishing between facts that are "knowable" and those that are known to someone. The latter category further subdivides into facts known directly to the speaker and those communicated to her by someone else. However, the distinction that is linguistically marked by the contrast between hypothetical and non-backshift constructions is the distinction between facts known to the speaker directly, and facts that are "knowable" or known to somebody else. Imagining developments is done against a background of direct knowledge, and is different from speculating about the course of past events, which is known to somebody, or exploring consequences of assumptions communicated by others. Both these kinds of reasoning involve non-assertability, and thus find their expression in *if*-clauses.

In examples like (54), it is interesting to note that the speaker's knowledge is crucial to the interpretation regardless of whether the language in question distinguishes between hypothetical and non-hypothetical forms. As Akatsuka observes (1985), East Asian languages like Japanese, Chinese, Korean, Mongolian, Semai, and Thai do not make a formal distinction here and thus interpreting sentences similar to (54) as "subjunctive" or not relies primarily on the context and on the knowledge of facts available to the participants. On the other hand, languages like Polish mark hypotheticality even more pervasively than English does: hypothetical sentences use a different conjunction than non-hypothetical ones, conditional mood is then marked in both clauses, and strong hypotheticality can optionally be marked by a (somewhat formal and obsolete) past conditional verb form. But the distinctions in question still mark what is or is not known and brought to bear in interpreting the conditional.

As should be clear from the discussion throughout the chapter, in predictive, backshifted constructions the verb forms are indicative of the predictive interpretation of the whole construction and of hypotheticality, but not unambiguously of time. In fact, the examples analyzed earlier in the chapter as temporally indeterminate are all examples of hypothetical constructions. We can claim with confidence that hypothetical constructions do not encode temporal interpretation through verb forms in any regular manner.

As for the non-backshifted constructions, their verb forms are admittedly indicative of time; but simply by virtue of not being backshifted (and not obligatorily sequential), they are also indicative of not being predictive. Thus their function is to signal not only time, but also non-predictive interpretation, lack of predictive modality. The non-predictive meaning of the verb forms has many further consequences: a different understanding of the non-assertiveness of *if*, relative independence of the two clauses, a different relation between the clauses, changes in intonation, etc.

The choice of verb forms in conditional constructions, then, has a primary function of signaling the predictive or non-predictive character of the construction.

Another important question concerning time in conditional constructions is whether at any level they receive a temporal interpretation as wholes. Apparently, different answers to this question can be given for different constructions.

In the case of non-predictive constructions, clauses seem to be temporally independent. Such sentences are frequently mixed in tense reference as well as in tense forms, they are often not interpreted as sequential, and the role of the *if*-clause is that of an independent assumption providing motivation for the statement in the main clause. Thus the overall interpretation of the conditional relation can only be found in the kind of reasoning of which it is an icon, or in the type of (non-causal) relation between the clauses. Thus, *If she is in the lobby, the plane arrived early* invokes an assumption about the present and draws a present conclusion about the past course of events from it. Similarly, *If she is giving the baby a bath, I'll call back later* announces a decision made at present which, however, concerns the future.

As regards generic constructions, their overall interpretation seems to be directly related to their participant clauses. They make generalizations about the relationship between the classes of events described in *p* and *q*. These relations are presented as valid over extended periods of time: generic present or generic past.

In *if*-backshifted non-hypothetical constructions like (1), (24), and (25) the overall interpretation is future regardless of the verb form used in the main clause. This results from two aspects of their interpretation: the predictive character of the whole construction and the temporal reference of the *if*-clause. A predictive construction encodes the kind of reasoning in which states of affairs can be predicted via assumptions which are not themselves predicted, yet have to be true prior to the state of affairs being predicted. This is a sequential reasoning, which Dudman refers to as "thinking steadily futurewards." The assumption in the *if*-clause represents a state of affairs that cannot be predicted now, and it is thus subject to no evaluation at the present moment. Consequently, whatever is predicted to follow the non-predicted state of affairs can only be imagined in the future. As we saw in examples (24) and (25), however, the prediction is not necessarily concerned with a state of affairs, but also with a conclusion, and it may refer to the non-predicted assumption via an implicature.

Hypothetical sentences are most varied in their time reference, but as wholes they are still predictive in meaning and basically sequential, hence one could claim that the overall time reference is established with respect to the time in the hypothetical prediction – that is, in the main clause. However, as we saw throughout the discussion above, time reference of hypothetical constructions is established on the basis of a variety of factors, the context being often the decisive one, and establishing the time in the main clause alone poses essentially the same problems.

I noted above that imagined situations, which hypothetical sentences describe, often do not seem to have any specific time reference. Imagined situations can be timeless, and they often are (recall [11] and [12] above). Or the speaker may mark the intended time by adding time adverbials or other explicit time indicators. What is temporally determinate, however, is the interpretation of the assumptions that underlie the imagined situation. For instance, example (33) (*If I hadn't been such a fool, I would have accepted the offer*) goes back to an assumption about the past, such that "I did not accept the offer," while the *if*-clause of (15) (*If I hadn't been seeing my doctor tomorrow . . .*) refers to an assumption "I'm seeing my doctor tomorrow." For a sentence like (8) (*If you drove to the city on Monday, you would avoid the weekend traffic*), the future reference of which is established on the basis of the time adverbial and the type of the verb, the underlying assumption is "you are planning to go to the city Sunday night." These assumptions are not encoded into the hypothetical construction in a straightforward manner, they are "the background knowledge." It is an oversimplification to claim, as many analysts do, that the underlying assumption is negatively represented in the construction (by mechanical transformation of the form of the presented assumption), and to suggest on the basis of this claim that the time of the underlying assumption and the time of the fantasy are automatically the same.

What I am suggesting, then, is that temporal reference is a largely contextually controlled aspect of the interpretation of a hypothetical construction. It can be signaled by explicit temporal indicators, it is sometimes restricted by the background assumptions which the speaker considers, and it is also restricted by the choice of the verb form – in that weak hypothetical forms exclude past reference, while the strong ones favor it. But it is not obligatorily encoded in a unique and systematic manner.

There remains the question of mixed hypothetical sentences. It has usually been assumed that sentences such as (16) (*Tom wouldn't be so hungry if he had eaten a proper breakfast*) and (17) (*If Ann had a better memory for faces, she would have recognized you*) have different time reference in each of the clauses, in other words, that they are mixed temporally. They appear in basically two patterns. The first one (represented by [16] and apparently much more common) has strong forms in the *if*-clause and weak forms in the main clause. It represents a sequential, causal chain, such that a past event, which is thus presented through strong hypothetical forms, results in a present situation. The second pattern has weak forms in the protasis and strong forms in the apodosis. The verb used in the *if*-clause is a state verb, and thus the situation described is presented as permanent. In the underlying assumptions of (17), for instance, Ann is characterized as a person with a poor memory for faces, which is a timeless, permanent characterization, used to account for an irreversible instance of her behavior – not having recognized the hearer. It would be possible to use strong hypothetical forms in both clauses of (17) without changing its temporal interpretation – but in that case Ann would be portrayed as irreversibly unable to remember people's faces. The whole sentence in both cases explains a past event underlying the apodosis. Temporal interpretation of mixed sentences is arrived at in the same way as in other cases of hypotheticality, and the overall temporal reference of the sentence will, as in other predictive sentences, be established with respect to the time established for the main clause.

3 Relations between the clauses in conditional constructions

In chapter 2 I distinguished two major classes of conditionals on the basis of their usage of verb forms. I argued that the verb forms are indicative of the overall interpretation of a conditional construction as predictive or non-predictive. I further suggested that the choice of verb forms also helps to specify (or at least constrain) the nature of the relation between the protasis and the apodosis. In the present chapter I will discuss the types of such relations and their relationship to other parameters of conditionality.

The protasis/apodosis relation seems to be a particularly important aspect of conditional interpretations. As I argued above, neither of the clauses of a conditional construction is asserted in the construction, even though the content of a clause may be brought into the construction after being asserted in the context (e.g. in *If she is giving the baby a bath, I'll call back later* the protasis is not asserted by the speaker, but it quotes a statement of the other participant in the conversation). The *if*-clauses of predictive sentences thus cannot be interpreted as asserting their protases (or, consequently, their apodoses). As I have argued, the presence of *if* in the construction marks the assumption in its scope as unassertable. As a result, the assumption in the apodosis, which belongs to the same mental space as the protasis, is not treated as asserted either. It seems that the only assertion that is made in a conditional construction is about the **relation** between the protasis and the apodosis (cf. Sweetser 1984, 1990). That this is indeed the case is best seen in distanced predictive constructions, where the *if*-clause and the main clause may be interpreted as contrary to fact, or expectation, while the predictive link between *p* and *q* is what is actually being communicated.

Is there a level at which all protasis/apodosis relations can be given a common characterization? In the majority of analyses offered, the protasis of the construction is described as expressing the condition on whose fulfillment the occurrence of the situation described by the main clause is contingent. This view is sometimes narrowed to what is called the Sufficient Conditionality Thesis, which treats what is said in the *if*-clause as a sufficient condition for what is said in the main clause.

The proponents of Sufficient Conditionality Thesis (Van der Auwera 1986, Sweetser 1990) go on to say that sufficient conditionality may hold on various levels of linguistic interpretation. Prototypically, an event or a state of affairs in the protasis is a sufficient condition for the occurrence of an event or state of affairs in the apodosis. The relations may hold also on the level of speech acts, so that the content of the *if*-clause conditions a performance of a speech act, Sweetser (1990) also introduces the level of epistemic relations, such that the knowledge of p is a sufficient condition for concluding q. These, as well as other relations, will be considered in the sections to follow.

3.1   Sequentiality

In chapter 2 above I referred to the temporal order of events described by the clauses of a construction as a criterion which helps distinguish between predictive and non-predictive constructions. In the former, which reflect thinking "steadily futurewards," the time of p precedes that of q; in the latter no restrictions are imposed and it is in fact common for non-predictive sentences to present events in a non-iconic order. The question is how important sequentiality is in the interpretation of a conditional sentence.

The motivation for sequential interpretation of strings of clauses has been discussed from a variety of perspectives. From the point of view of the analysis of conditionals, which is my primary concern here, there are three major questions to explore. First of all, I will look at some general mechanisms responsible for sequential interpretation of various strings of clauses. Then, I will review the application of these principles to conditionals, and, finally, I will consider the question of how strictly sequentiality can be defined for the purposes of my analysis.

The dominant view of how multi-clausal structures are interpreted is that (when not otherwise marked) they tend to be treated as iconic of the sequence of events or steps in the reasoning they represent. Haiman (1980), for example, quotes Greenberg's influential observation that "the order of elements in language parallels that in physical experience or the order of knowledge" (Greenberg 1966: 103) and applies the principle to a number of linguistic phenomena, including coordination. Interest in the general iconicity of human language has stimulated a number of interesting studies of various syntactic and morphological forms (e.g. the papers in Haiman 1985, Givon 1990, Bybee, Perkins, and Pagliuca 1994). It has also been observed (see Lightbown and Spada 1993) that the pervasiveness of iconic thinking is also reflected in language acquisition. Children tend to produce sentences like *You took all the towels away because I can't dry my hands* (example from Lightbown and Spada 1993) not because they fail to grasp cause–effect relations, but because they consistently want to state events in the order of occurrence.

The connective which has been discussed most often in terms of iconicity and sequentiality is *and*, even though not all of its interpretations are sequential. Haiman (1980), for example, suggests that all the varied meanings of *and* may refer iconically to some concept of addition or connection, "setting two items side-by-side," as Sweetser puts it (1990: 87). Thus in examples like *He knows French and Italian* (often referred to as "symmetric") the order of conjuncts can be freely reversed, while in sentences like *He had a headache and drank a glass of brandy* ("asymmetric" use) reversing the order also changes the interpretation: either he first had a headache and then drank his brandy, or he drank first and got a headache later (possibly as a result of it). As Sweetser (1990) argues, the order of *and*-conjuncts may be conventionally interpreted to be iconic of a narrative sequence. If the word/clause order parallels the sequence of events in the real world, temporal succession will be read into the interpretation. Sequentiality is thus related to the more general concept of "putting things side by side" in that it arises as an inference from how they are set side by side.

It has also been noted that sequentiality arises not only in *and*-conjoined but also in full-stop sentences. In fact, as regards sequentiality itself, there seems to be no difference between sentences such as (1) and (2):

(1)   I bought some flour and made pancakes.
(2)   I bought some flour. I made pancakes.

In both of these cases, the usual interpretation is that the speaker bought flour before she made pancakes. It also seems that both instances can be sufficiently explained with the idea of discourse segments being iconic of narrative sequence. In both cases, one may add, our knowledge of the fact that flour is needed for making pancakes motivates the further interpretation whereby flour was bought precisely so that pancakes could be made.

A somewhat different account of such examples is generally offered by truth-conditional theories of meaning. Since it is assumed in truth-conditional accounts that sequentiality arises independently of truth conditions (which are the same regardless of the order of the conjuncts), the source of sequentiality is sought in the pragmatic interpretation, mainly in implicature. As was noted by Cohen (1971), however, the truth conditions may change when the order of the conjuncts is changed (e.g. for the asymmetric uses of *and* mentioned above) and thus the interpreted sequentiality must be part of propositional content. For pairs of sentences such as *A republic has been declared and the old king has died of a heart attack* versus *The old king has died of a heart attack and a republic has been declared* the truth conditions (of the most accessible interpretations) are clearly not the same. On the basis of these and many similar sentences, Wilson (1990) claims that the sequential interpretation of events described in the conjuncts is not an implicature, but a pragmatically determined aspect of propositional content. Depending on how broad a concept of pragmatics one assumes, this proposal may seem similar in spirit to the iconicity-based accounts mentioned above.

One of the ways in which Wilson's and Sweetser's proposals address the data in a similar way is to note that *and-* and full-stop utterances are not interpreted in the way suggested by implicature-based or similar accounts in any regular way – that is, it is not always the case that the conjunct which appears earlier in the discourse describes an event that occurred earlier in time. As Wilson (1990) observes, it is also possible that it comes later in time (as in *She is a blonde now. She dyed her hair*), that the two states of affairs are simultaneous, or that their temporal ordering is not relevant to the overall interpretation. Sweetser (1990) offers a convincing explanation of many of such cases (though her discussion focuses on the uses of *and*) by claiming that these are also instances of "putting things side-by-side," but not in the real-world domain (which she calls "content" domain).

(3)   Question: Why don't you want me to take basketweaving again this quarter?
        Answer: Well, Mary got an MA in basketweaving, and she joined a religious cult. (. . . so you might go the same way if you take basketweaving).
(4)   Thank you, Mr Lloyd, and please just close the door as you go out.
        (both examples from Sweetser 1990)

Clearly, the uses of *and* in (3) and (4) do not relate events in the real world. Rather, *and* in (3) conjoins logical premises which should lead the hearer to the intended conclusion, while the one in (4) conjoins speech acts. In Sweetser's framework, presented briefly in chapter 1, (3) represents the use of *and* in the epistemic domain, and (4) in the speech act domain. Consequently, Haiman's concept of iconicity and Sweetser's concept of cognitive domains seem jointly to account for a variety of uses of conjunctions like *and*.

We can expect that full-stop utterances, though similar in many respects, will not behave identically to *and*-utterances. On the scale of clause integration proposed by Givon (1993), *and*-utterances with continuing intonation occupy the highest (most integrated) position, while utterances with segments separated by a period are at the other extreme of the scale. Carston (1993) also discusses important differences in the way in which full-stop and coordinate utterances are processed. Givon claims further that the degree of grammatical integration of clauses is proportionate to the degree with which two events or states are semantically or pragmatically connected in the discourse. Thus we can expect the connection to be closer in (1) above, and looser as well as more context-dependent in (2), because of their different degrees of syntactic integration. That loose syntactic ties invite less integrated interpretations is clearly seen in *She is a blonde now. She dyed her hair*, which reverses the temporal sequence and offers an explanation of a state of affairs described in the first clause. The temporal continuity of events which is readily constructed in the interpretation of (1) and (2) provides a greater degree of thematic coherence than we find in the most likely interpretation of the "hair-dying" utterance (which only pro- vides continuity of perspective). Givon's concepts of grammatical integration and thematic coherence will also explain why in the content-domain sequential uses of *and* usually have a continuing intonation pattern, while epistemic and speech act uses represented in (3) and (4), which call for more abstract and global continuity, separate their discourse segments with a comma.

We have thus identified iconicity, cognitive domains, the degree of grammat- ical integration, and thematic coherence as important factors *generally* in inter- preting multi-clausal discourse structures as sequential. What remains to be examined is whether the same factors play a role *specifically* in the interpreta- tion of conditionals. Sequentiality indeed seems to be present in the interpreta- tion of many conditionals, and this even seems to be obligatory in the case of predictive sentences. Thus a sentence like *If you take an aspirin, your tempera- ture will go down* is normally interpreted to mean that one has to swallow the pill before the temperature goes down. The source of this part of the interpreta- tion seems to rely to a large degree on the same factors which were seen to be relevant in coordinate structures (taking the sequence to be iconic of the sequence of events, encyclopedic knowledge, etc.), but there are also surface signals of greater grammatical integration in conditionals. It could be argued, for instance, that in the case of a conditional construction a sequential inter- pretation arises on formal grounds, since the clauses are quite distinct in their marking with conjunctions (*if* marks the protases, while *then* or zero marks the apodoses) and there is a standard clause order in which *p* precedes *q*. Also, as we have seen in the preceding chapter, predictive conditionals show a high degree of integration thanks to the patterns of verb forms which are character- istic for predictives and which normally do not mix freely with other, non- predictive forms. Furthermore, hypothetical forms will not mix with non-hypothetical ones. As the discussion in chapter 5 will show, the intonation patterns of predictive conditionals also point to a high degree of integration and continuity. In other words, the constructional features of predictive conditionals, combined with the overall interpretation whereby *q* is contingent upon *p*, create an environment in which sequentiality arises most naturally. Conditionals in general can perhaps be characterized as "putting things one after another," rather than "side by side," since what is contingent on the validity of the condition has to come after what constitutes the condition. In the case of predictive conditionals, which function in the real-world, content domain, this translates as temporal sequentiality.

However, as we saw in the preceding chapter, non-predictive conditional constructions are different in that their verb forms do not form patterns which would suggest thematic continuity. Also, as I will show later, they often display much less regularity as regards clause order and intonation. Will sequentiality turn out to be relevant in interpreting these constructions as well?

The answer depends on how we understand sequentiality. If sequentiality is to be understood in a strictly temporal sense (in other words, in the real-world, content domain), then only predictive conditionals regularly have it as part of their interpretation. Among non-predictive constructions, content-domain sequentiality is not a rule, and temporally reversed sentences are common and acceptable, as in *If she is a blonde now, she dyed her hair.* Such examples are certainly not iconic of (content) temporal sequence, but they can still be claimed to be iconic of the pattern in which things to be communicated are ordered with respect to a certain principle, and thus adhere to the general idea of "putting things one after another." In this case, however, the "things" are premises and conclusions, and it is indeed a feature of logical inference to put premises first. In other words, such conditional constructions are sequential on a different level, or, in Sweetser's terms, in the epistemic domain. As I will argue in the sections to follow, conditionals can display various relations between their protases and apodoses, but a particular type of connection (or domain) will preserve an order of *p* and *q* which is appropriate to the sequential structure of that domain.

Let us now return to temporal sequentiality. As Wilson (1990) observed with respect to *and-* and full-stop utterances, temporal relations between the clauses do not have to be sequential, as there are also cases of simultaneity or even non-temporal interpretations. Apparently, similar cases can be found among conditionals. For example, simultaneity is present in the interpretations of many types of constructions – predictive, non-predictive and generic:

(5)   If the baby is asleep, Mary is typing.
(6)   If you live in a dorm, you don't have enough privacy.
(7)   If public transport is on strike tomorrow, getting to work will be a nightmare.
(8)   If people drove more carefully, roads would be safer.

Simultaneity is clearly not unusual in non-predictive constructions (as in
[5]), because there is no restriction on the temporal configuration of the clauses.
Generic sentences, like (6), can also express simultaneity of some kind, because
they scan over unrestricted periods of time. And predictive sentences like (7)
and (8) also seem to cover parallel periods of time in the protases and apodoses.

   The fact that all the types of conditional constructions which I have distinguished can involve *p* and *q* referring to simultaneous states or continued
activities poses an interesting question about other aspects of their interpretation. In many discussions of conditionals and coordinate structures (e.g.
Dancygier and Mioduszewska 1983, Comrie 1986, Wilson 1990), sequentiality
is related to causality, since these two aspects of interpretation of an utterance
are often inseparable. Sequentiality is not viewed as inferred from causality:
most accounts follow the classical *post hoc ergo propter hoc* approach that we
inherit from Hume. With respect to this we need an explanation of the fact that
sentences (6)–(8) are understood causally, even though they are not prototypically sequential – event *p* does not strictly precede event *q*.

   The same has been noted by Wilson (1990) in relation to *and-* and full-stop
utterances – she concludes that causality and sequentiality should perhaps be
admitted to arise independently in the interpretation. I believe that the difficulty
that has emerged can more convincingly be solved by looking again at simultaneity. It can be noted, for instance, that all of the clauses in sentences (6)–(8)
describe continuing states of affairs, rather than events, and that the inception of
the state of affairs interpreted as a cause precedes the inception of the state interpreted as a result. In other words, one has to start living in a dorm to experience
lack of privacy, the strike has to begin to cause inconvenience to commuters,
etc. Thus some interval, however minute it is, seems to separate the events of *p*
and *q*, with *p* starting earlier than *q*. Wilson herself mentions the problem of the
interval as essentially pragmatic, in the same sense as the problem of
sequentiality and causality. One could thus argue that in situations such as ones
described in (6)–(8) the interval is pragmatically determined to be "nearly
null."

   There are, however, examples of full simultaneity, though, as regards conditionals, they are found among non-predictive constructions only. These are the
cases where the two clauses contributing to the utterance (whether an *if . . .
[then]*, *and-*, or full-stop structure) describe two inseparable aspects of a phe-
nomenon – as two faces of the same coin. The clauses are then not just two
descriptions of two states of affairs, but two assumptions which logically entail
each other. For instance, any combinatorial order is possible in the case of pairs
of sentences like *The king is bald* and *The king has no hair*, or *It is a bird* and *It*

has wings. These sentences are not interpreted sequentially or causally, regardless of the form of the utterance – conditional, conjoined, or full-stop. They are not common in everyday speech, but this is due to the fact that they repeat the same message twice, in different words. Whether a sentence like *If the king is bald, he has no hair* is of interest as a part of a logical argument, or as a source of particular implicatures, it is licensed by the relationship between the meanings of the expressions used (*bald* and *no hair*). But similar sentences can in fact also be licensed pragmatically, as seems to be the case with (5). If the speaker knows that Mary can only sit at the typewriter when her baby is asleep, she can say either *If the baby is asleep, Mary is typing* or *If Mary is typing, the baby is asleep*, both of which will present inferences of *q* from *p*, rather than causal or sequential statements about the relation between *p* and *q*. Needless to say, *and*- and full-stop variants licensed by the same rule (e.g. *It is a bird and it has wings* or *Mary is typing. The baby is asleep*) are also more plausibly interpreted inferentially, and not causally or sequentially. What seems to be important here is that the states in question are, contrary to those described in (6)–(8), temporally not restricted, so that the moment of their inception does not have to become an aspect of the interpretation.

The fourth possibility considered by Wilson is that the temporal relation between the conjuncts does not arise in the interpretation at all. This may be claimed to be the case for some *if*-sentences, such as *Her table manners make me sick, if I may put it that way* (to be discussed in section 3.5.2). The two clauses do not describe two events or states of affairs which could be related in time, for one of them is a comment on a particular expression used in the other. It should be noted that such sentences also have a markedly lower degree of grammatical integration (different clause order and intonation, free verb forms), and that the relation between the clauses cannot be interpreted on the content domain level.

To sum up, the case of conditionals seems to support Wilson's conclusion drawn for *and*- and full-stop utterances: the "sequentiality" implicature does not arise for all conditionals. At the same time, temporal sequentiality is regularly involved in the interpretation of a major class of conditional constructions – the predictive ones. This is related to the fact that predictive conditionals are invariably interpreted in the content domain, as expressing relations between events or state of affairs. In other types of constructions, where the relation between the clauses is not that of the real world level, the temporal ordering of the events referred to in *p* and *q* becomes largely irrelevant. Instead, the sequence of the clauses may impose a sequence of a different type, for example that of premise and conclusion.

Conditionals are thus uniform in that their canonical *if p, q* order is iconic of a sequence ("putting things one after another"). But some sentences (the predictive ones) are interpreted as sequentially ordered with respect to the events described, while others reflect sequences such as premise–conclusion, statement–explanation, statement–comment, etc. It seems that such a solution is also plausible for types of utterances other than *if*-sentences; for example, temporally reversed full-stop utterances such as *She is a blonde now. She dyed her hair* also preserve the required sequence of a statement and an explanation. I will return to this problem in the sections to follow.

3.2   Causality

There is practically no account of conditionals which would fail to note that *if*-clauses tend to express causes, while the apodoses are interpreted as effects, even though causality does not offer a sufficient account of a conditional construction. Thus, a sentence like

(9)   If you add whipped cream, the fruit salad will taste better.

has as part of its interpretation the proposition that adding whipped cream will result in the salad tasting better, but the overall interpretation will also contain assumptions about temporal reference, non-factuality, sufficient conditionality, etc. In what follows, I want to discuss the relationship between the causal aspects of conditional interpretation and these other aspects of interpretation which appear to be linked to causality.

Sweetser (1990) views the causal interpretation of conditionals as related to the cognitive domains in which sentences are understood. She notes that standardly observed causal interpretation arises when *p* and *q* refer to real world events, which are interpreted as causally related in the real world. She refers to this as interpretation in the content domain. Interestingly, causality of the same type can be found in some disjunctive sentences as well:

(10)   On Friday nights Mary goes to see her aunt, or her parents call her and scold her on Saturday morning.
         (Sweetser 1990)

The affinity of such causally interpreted disjunctive utterances with some conditionals can be seen if we paraphrase (10) as *On Friday nights Mary goes to see her aunt. If she doesn't, her parents call her and scold her on Saturday morning.* The paraphrase also reveals the sequential interpretation of (10) more clearly. This seems to suggest that sequentially ordered sentences in the content domain (about real world events) are likely to invite causal interpretations (because the way they are presented by the speaker suggests both sequentiality and "relatedness"), regardless of the type of conjunction and syntactic frame of the construction. It is thus not surprising that causality was found to emerge also in *and-* and full-stop utterances.[1]

(11)   You say one word and I'll kill you.
(12)   The road was icy and she slipped.
(13)   The road was icy. She slipped.

The temporally sequential interpretation of such utterances has commonly been seen as arising on pragmatic and/or iconic grounds (see the review in 3.1). Nonetheless, it is agreed that this normal interpretation involves causal relations between the clauses; and this causality is associated with sequentiality and often seen as deriving from it. Causality has been claimed to arise as an implicature from sequentiality, on the assumption that the speaker observes the Maxim of Manner.

Wilson (1990), however, sees causality in the same terms as sequentiality: it is a pragmatically determined aspect of propositional content, not an implicature. It arises on the basis of the hearer's encyclopedic knowledge (e.g. about typical cause–effect chains) and the principle of relevance. The relevance-theoretic approach is also advocated by Blakemore (1987), whose analysis of examples like (12) and (13) presents causality as a feature of coherent discourse, where information made available by a discourse segment (whether a sentence or a clause) is used in establishing the interpretation of the segment that follows. Thus in Blakemore's view, causality may be inferred in the process of arriving at the optimally relevant interpretation, and is then added to the propositional content.

Wilson's (1990) and Blakemore's (1987) view of causal interpretations as pragmatically grounded offers an interesting answer to the question of why causality sometimes becomes a part of the interpretation, but sometimes it does not. In the case of *and-* and full-stop utterances causality seems to derive primarily from sequentiality and the interlocutors' background knowledge of possible cause–effect chains. Though both of these factors play an important role in conditionals as well, there are other independent motivations for causal reading of conditional constructions – and that reading is more pervasive than it is for coordinate clauses or sequential sentences.

First of all, in conditionals the clauses are not just "put side-by-side," as they are in *and-* and full-stop utterances. The *p* clause is not simply juxtaposed with the *q* clause, it is subordinate to it; and the ordering of the clauses, such that *p*

---

[1] Examples (12) and (13) are quoted from Blakemore (1987).

precedes *q*, is so pervasive that it was at some point postulated to be universal. Second, the majority of analysts now assume that conditionals express assumptions that are necessarily somehow related – and by a tighter link than the general relevance-motivated one which relates any sequential utterances of a speaker. In other words, in natural language use (rather than in purely logical terms) there is a connection between the clauses of a conditional. The nature of the connection has most broadly been defined as "sufficient conditionality" (Van der Auwera 1986), which means that the realization of *p* is a sufficient condition for the realization of *q*. That is, the event or state of affairs described by *p*, if realized, will be sufficient for the realization of the event or state of affairs described in *q*. No such connection is necessarily communicated in *and-* or full-stop utterances, therefore their causal interpretations arise much less regularly than in conditionals, which actively invite causal readings, especially in content utterances.

Thus the connection between *p* and *q* is what all conditionals share, although, as we have seen, the relation does not always hold between real-world events and states of affairs, since conditional constructions can also relate clauses in other cognitive domains. However, when real-world events are put in a sufficient conditionality relation, causality is the most natural interpretation to arise. That is, if an event *p* (e.g. dropping a glass) is a sufficient condition for an event *q* (e.g. the glass breaking), then saying *If you drop this glass, it will break* can naturally be interpreted to mean that the act of dropping will cause the glass to break. The causal interpretation seems to be resulting from a number of factors here: the fact that a conditional implies a connection, that the connection is in the content domain (as the verb forms also suggest), that the events in question can be interpreted sequentially, and, finally, that our background knowledge supports the interpretation whereby dropping glass objects causes them to break.[2] Thus the interpretation stems to some degree from our general understanding of causal relations and pragmatics certainly plays a role here, but there are features specific to conditionals which give special status to the causal interpretations that arise.

Furthermore, causality in predictive/content conditionals has a special role in yet another way. The assumption throughout my argument is that the presence of the conjunction *if* gives a special status to the protasis and, consequently, to the apodosis. Namely, neither of the clauses of a conditional construction can be interpreted as a statement of a fact, that is, none of them is asserted. What is

---

[2] As I will show in the chapters to follow, causality may play other roles in the interpretation of conditionals. Causality in the content domain, however, is the only case where the cause–effect link between the clauses of a conditional is what the construction is used to assert.

asserted, however, in predictive sentences like *If you add whipped cream, the fruit salad will taste better* or *If you drop this glass, it will break* is the predictive relation itself, and prediction is automatically understood as based on a causal relation. Thus, the fact that there is a causal relation between the two events mentioned is what is (among other things) being communicated by a predictive conditional. Causal readings plays a crucial role in the interpretation of predictive conditionals, while they are not so central to the interpretation of coordinated and full-stop utterances. One may also note that conditionals, contrary to *and-* and full-stop utterances, are always asymmetric.

Not all conditionals represent content-level relations, however (for a discussion of other types of relations see sections 3.3, 3.4, 3.5): indeed, as I have argued so far, only predictive/content conditionals are typically interpreted causally. In a non-predictive sentence like (14), then,

(14)   If you are interested, he is my husband.

a causal interpretation will not arise. The clauses are related in the speech act domain, the verb forms do not suggest a predictive interpretation, and, last but not least, there is no immediately accessible knowledge which would support a causal relation between the hearer's interest and someone's being the speaker's husband.

There is, finally, the question of precisely what kind of relationships should fall under the label of "causality." The predominant view seems to be that causality should be viewed in the common, every day understanding of the word. Apparently, this reflects the way causality is understood by speakers and hearers in actual acts of communication. Sweetser (1990), for instance, notes that enablement is often linguistically treated on a par with causality, as in her example given here as (15):

(15)   If I were president, I'd sell the White House's Limoges china to fund bilingual education.

In (15), being president would enable the speaker to sell the china rather than cause her to do so. There are more examples of this type, such as

(16)   If you feel better, we'll go for a walk.
(17)   If I were an actress, I would live in Beverly Hills.

A regularity that marks all of these *if*-constructions is that their protases express states rather than events and are thus typically non-agentive. The paradigmatic causal reading is thus excluded, as prototypical causality (Lakoff and Johnson 1980: 69–76) involves agenthood and direct manipulation. However, as Lakoff and Johnson observe, this core understanding of causation "is elaborated by metaphor to yield a broad concept of causation, which has many special cases" (1980: 75). One of the special cases they mention is the emergence of an event from the state. This seems to be the case for our "enablement" sentences above. Since expressions of causality, whether sentential or lexical, have prototypical as well as non-prototypical uses, one seems to be justified in treating the "enablement" conditional constructions as basically causal.

From the discussion above it should be clear how causality in constructions with *if* is different from that in sentences with causal conjunctions. In the former, the predictive use of verb forms sets up a predictive relationship which demands a motivation in causal relations (however we can set up such relations from background knowledge), while in the latter it is introduced overtly through linguistic expressions. There are further differences, however, which are most striking in the case of the conjunction *because*. As Ford (1993) observes, *because*-clauses typically follow their matrix clauses, while *if* clauses precede them, thus having a different function in terms of topicality and discourse coherence. Other causal conjunctions (*since, as*) are used sentence-initially in the same way as *if* is. The essential difference, however, between *if* on the one hand and all causal conjunctions on the other is that causal conjunctions introduce factual, asserted information, while *if* does not.

To sum up, then, in the case of conditionals it is not sufficient to say that causal interpretations are pragmatically grounded. It is certainly important to consider the fact that sentences like (9) (*If you add whipped cream, the fruit salad will taste better*) are pragmatically "open" to a causal interpretation, while for sentences like (14) such an interpretation will not be plausible. But there are other factors to be considered as well. Example (9), as the verb forms indicate, is a predictive conditional, while (14) is not. The connection between the clauses of (9) is in the content domain, which means that the event of adding whipped cream is related to the state of the salad tasting better. The clauses of (14), on the other hand, are linked on the level of discourse, rather than content, as the protasis offers a felicity condition for informing the hearer about the content of the apodosis. As I suggested above, the presence or absence of causality depends primarily on the type of conditional construction involved. Predictive conditionals, which mark a content connection between their clauses, will be most likely to receive causal or enablement interpretations, while non-predictive constructions, to be analyzed in detail in the sections to follow, are open to different types of relations between the protasis and the apodosis.

Content domain causality (which I have elsewhere [Dancygier 1990] referred to as a second order relation, following Lyons's [1977] classification in which facts and states of affairs are entities of the second order) is thus typically found in the interpretation of predictive, backshifted conditional constructions. An explanation of this tendency emerges from the nature of prediction, which allows the speaker to make relatively certain judgments about the future with respect to her knowledge of the situation at present and of typical consequences of states of affairs, or, simply, of typical cause–effect chains. Prediction is thus inseparable from content causality, and this is why backshifted forms character- istic of predictive constructions are indicative of a content, or second order rela- tion between the clauses, and, consequently, of a causal interpretation. It seems that the indication provided by the verb forms is strong enough for the hearer to supply a causal interpretation even in the cases when the content of the clauses does not provide sufficient grounds for reading it in. For instance, a hypothet- ical paraphrase of a sentence like (14), such as *If you were (had been) inter- ested, he would be (have been) my husband* can only be interpreted as an expression of reproach, whereby the hearer's lack of interest in the problem pre- vented the marriage the speaker desired. This interpretation is causal and pre- dictive, and even though such a causal link seems implausible or unusual, the forms used motivate both predictiveness and causality. Thus the features of the construction (such as verb forms) can motivate an interpretation typical for a given construction even if the pragmatic background does not support it. This seems to give us sufficient grounds to claim that causality is an element of constructional meaning, rather than a contextually motivated addition to the content.

Predictive *if*-sentences retain their causal reading even if in the structure of the sentence the prediction (the main clause) comes first, and the cause (the *if*-clause) is added later, as a kind of afterthought:

(18)   I'll be late to dinner, if the buses are still on strike, that is.

The examples above suggest that causality remains a part of the content of a predictive conditional sentence as long as the cause is expressed in the *if*-clause and the effect in the main clause. This is not at all surprising in view of the role of the *if*-clause advocated in chapter 2 – it describes a state of affairs which is not itself predicted, but the occurrence of which has to precede the situation pre- dicted in the main clause for the prediction to be valid. Thus the order of the clauses does not matter as long as other formal parameters (the place of the conjunction and the use of verb forms) guarantee appropriate recognition of the construction as predictive.

However, it seems possible in many cases to coin *if*-constructions which present effects in the *if*-clauses and causes in the main clauses. They can be seen as "reversed" variants of causal, predictive sentences:

(19)   If Mary is late, she went to the dentist.
(20)   If Ann is wearing a wedding ring, she and Bob finally got married.

These sentences are examples of reasoning from effects to causes. They are not predictive, and they are in fact licensed by the same causal understanding of events which licenses predictive statements with a different order of p and q, such as *If Mary goes to the dentist, she'll be late* and *If Ann and Bob finally get married, she will be wearing a wedding ring*. They do not have causality as an aspect of their content, as they cannot be paraphrased as: **If Mary is late, she went to the dentist as a result*, or: **If Ann is wearing a wedding ring, she and Bob got married as a result*. The causal relation between seeing the dentist and being late, or getting married and wearing a wedding ring, is an assumption that is used in arriving at the interpretation of (19) and (20), but is not part of their content. The sentences in question express inferences, not predictions, and thus the relation predicated operates on assumptions (third order entities), not facts or states of affairs in the world (second order entities). The inferences are licensed by assumptions independent of those appearing in the actual premise and conclusion, but necessary in the context in which the conclusion is to be drawn. Thus, the conclusions drawn in (19) and (20) are licensed by assumptions about the consequences of going to the dentist or getting married. Presumably, then, (19) and (20) are not causal themselves, but are interpreted against background assumptions which are causal.

Sentences (19) and (20) are non-predictive constructions. Their interpretations are also not sequential. Contrary to predictive conditionals, whose clause order is iconic of the sequence of events, they are iconic of reasoning patterns in which a premise precedes a conclusion. It seems that many such constructions with inferential meaning are related to causal assumptions in a similar way. More attention will be given to this problem in the following section.

3.3   Epistemic/inferential relations

Sentences like (19) and (20) above have been noted to express non-causal, non-sequential relations. Thus, in sentences like these there seems to be no causal relation between the content of the *if*-clause and that of the main clause. Indeed, the most plausible readings of such sentences involve a causal relation in the reverse direction, where the event or state of affairs described in q may well be causally prior to that described in p.

In earlier work (Dancygier 1990, 1993) I referred to the relation in question as *inferential*, as the sentences are instances of reasoning in which *q* is inferred from *p*. The protasis thus presents a premise, and the apodosis the conclusion inferred from the premise. In other words, the relation holds between third order entities (assumptions), not between states of affairs, and can also be referred to as a third order relation.

Sweetser (1990) describes such sentences as *epistemic* conditionals, functioning in the epistemic, not content, domain, and connecting epistemic states, not propositions. More specifically, the knowledge of *p* is a sufficient condition for concluding *q*.

While treating epistemic *if*-sentences as distinct from content-level conditionals and admitting the possibility of their being non-sequential (on the content level), Sweetser nevertheless interprets them as causal. The causal link in question is claimed to hold between epistemic states, that is, the knowledge of *p* is interpreted as causing or enabling the conclusion in *q*.

Indeed, the premise/conclusion relation seems central to epistemic conditionals. Their protases are often extracted from the context and put on the conversational table to be considered in terms of how they fit with the beliefs the speaker already holds, that is, what conclusions will arise as a result. In a sense, drawing conclusions from newly acquired assumptions is part of the process of discovering their communicative value. This can remain a purely mental process, but the speaker may want to communicate the implications she arrived at, if she is not sure that the information in question is meaningful to the hearer in the same way that it is to her. Let us consider the context and communicative function of (21):

(21)   If they left at nine, they have arrived home by now.

The speaker has just been told that "they" left at nine. The exchange of information may stop here, or the speaker may look at her watch and say *Oh, so they've arrived home by now*, or say (21). The latter choice is different from just communicating the conclusion in that it takes the hearer by the hand through the reasoning process. But, as Sweetser (1990) argues as well, inference as a mental process is not the same as communication of utterances showing how inferences are arrived at. One can say that the former concerns the speaker and her knowledge, while the latter has the hearer's informative profit as a goal. Thus, in communicating (21) the speaker is demonstrating how she arrived at the assumption communicated by the apodosis.

Epistemic conditionals seem (at least most commonly) to be non-predictive in function. Consequently, they are also not normally used with hypothetical forms. For example, using hypothetical forms in (19) and (20) results in sentences which are difficult to contextualize and, if acceptable, certainly lose their epistemic interpretation, such as #*If Mary were late, she would have gone to the dentist* and #*If Ann were wearing a wedding ring, she and Bob would have finally got married.*[3] The limited acceptability is related to the fact that in (19) and (20) the state of affairs referred to in *p* does not precede, and is not causally prior to, the state of affairs described in *q*; the use of predictive hypothetical forms invites an interpretation wherein the order of *p* and *q* iconically represents the causal and temporal sequence of events. Thus the hypothetical forms require that (19) and (20) be re-interpreted as representative of a different order of events, and the resulting sentence is difficult to interpret because such an order seems implausible. Coming up with a hypothetical version of the sentence is easier if the original sentence is sequential, as in (21). It is possible to say *If they had left at nine, they would have arrived home by now*, but then the relation between the clauses is interpreted as causal and on the content level. The status of the protasis is different from that in (21) and the apodosis does not represent a conclusion. In fact, such an example is not a distanced version of (21), but of a prediction like *If they leave at nine, they will arrive home by X*. In order to preserve the epistemic interpretation of the sentence we would have to explicitly mention the conclusion in the sentence, as in *If they had left at nine, I would have concluded that . . .*, but this is a different sentence altogether.

The epistemic status of assumptions expressed in the main clauses of epistemic constructions may be revealed in the fact that they are often closely equivalent to rephrasings with the epistemic modal *must*, as in *If Mary is late, she must have gone to the dentist, If Ann is wearing a wedding ring, she and Bob must have finally got married, If they left at nine, they must have arrived home by now*. The epistemic character of the link between the *if*-clause and the main clause is also revealed in the possibility of replacing simple *then* with the phrase *then it means that*, as in *If Mary is late, (then) it means she went to the dentist, If Ann is wearing a wedding ring (then) it means she and Bob finally got married*, and *If they left at nine, (then) it means they have arrived home by now*.

The general characterization of epistemic conditionals will thus involve several criteria: non-predictive verb forms, the nature of the link between *p* and *q*, and tests with *must* and *it means that*. There is also the question of the epistemic status of the protasis, which will be addressed in chapter 4.

---

[3] The sentences are interpretable, but then being late or wearing a ring is seen as preceding and causing going to the dentist or getting married. It was also pointed out to me that such sentences can be instances of "style indirect libre."

3.4 Speech act relations

The fact that *if*-clauses can bear a relationship to the speech act performed in the main clause rather than to its propositional content was noted in some earlier analyses (Heringer 1971, Davison 1973, Tedeschi 1977) and has been given a more formal interpretation by Van der Auwera (1986) and Sweetser (1990). Most generally, the protases of such sentences are said to guarantee a successful performance of the speech act in the apodosis:

(22)   I'll help you with the dishes, if it's all right with you.
(23)   Take out the garbage, if I may ask you to.
(24)   If I may ask, where were you last night?

Van der Auwera (1986) calls (22)–(24) conditional speech acts and defines them as sentences in which "the protasis is asserted to be a sufficient condition for a speech act about the apodosis." They are opposed to other conditionals, referred to as speech acts about conditionals, with respect to the way in which the utterance receives its speech act interpretation: "a speech act about a conditional is a speech act whose propositional content is a conditional" (Van der Auwera 1986: 202–3). Thus (25):

(25)   If you buy a house, will you redecorate it yourself?

asks a question which concerns the content relation expressed by *If you buy a house, you will redecorate it yourself*, or, more specifically, there being a conditional relation between buying a house and redecorating it oneself.

Sweetser refers to sentences like (22)–(24) as conditionals in the speech act domain, or ***speech act conditionals***, and paraphrases them by a gloss: "If (protasis), then let us consider that I perform this speech act (i.e. the one represented as the apodosis)" (1990: 121).

In either interpretation the protases of such sentences are largely independent of the content of their apodoses, and the propositional content of the sentence as a whole does not contain assumptions of sequentiality and causality between the states of affairs described. Sweetser gives them an analysis parallel to her treatment of epistemic conditionals; that is, she treats them as being causal on a different level: the state described in the protasis may be seen as causing or enabling the speech act in the apodosis. However, as Sweetser notes too, the intended speech acts are in fact performed, not just performed conditionally. Even if the hearers of utterances like (22)–(24) appear to be highly uncooperative, in both a linguistic and a social sense, and say something like *No, it's not all right*, or *No, you may not ask*, this would rather be interpreted as a rejection of the offer, a refusal to act or give an answer, not as invalidating the condition on which the speech act was supposedly contingent. We would not expect the speakers of (22)–(24) to look for other conditions which would eventually enable them to perform the speech acts they want, but to take "No" for an answer. Also, it seems that the hearer can reject the condition and still react positively to the speech act. In the case of (24), for instance, the answer may be *In fact I don't think you have a right to ask, but I can tell you anyway – I had a date with Tom.* The causal relation here thus does not appear to be necessary as part of the overall interpretation.

The status of *if*-clauses in speech act conditionals is therefore nebulous. They do not in fact suspend the performance of the speech act intended in the apodosis (as Sweetser notes too), but function to give the hearer some option in reacting to the speech act performed, to make the utterance more polite or appropriate. A sentence like *If I haven't already told you, I'm getting married* can thus be interpreted as invoking Grice's (1975) conversational maxim of informativeness (I am informing you that X, provided it is informative for me to say X). Other sentences (e.g. [22]–[24] above) are better interpreted in terms of R. Lakoff's (1973) politeness maxims such as "Leave options" (sentence [24], for example, gives the hearer an option of refusing to answer the question in *q* if the speaker's right to ask it is not recognized). Still others, e.g. Austin's *If you are hungry, there are biscuits on the sideboard*, seem to rely on the felicity conditions of a given speech act: for example, an offer carries with it the assumption that the thing offered is wanted by the hearer.

Conditional speech acts can also be talked about within a more restricted view of speech acts in terms of formal sentence types – such as, for instance, the approach represented by Sperber and Wilson (1986), who consider only acts of saying, asking, and telling. We could note, then, that these major groups of acts are performed conditionally with the use of specialized expressions: *if I may ask* can accompany a question, *if I may ask you to* – an imperative, *if I may say so* – a declarative statement. It is not the case, however, that they can be applied indiscriminately to any speech acts performed by these sentence types. If, for instance, an imperative is meant as an order, not a request, a condition like *if I may ask you to* is inappropriate (unless used ironically), for orders are specifically meant not to leave the hearer any options. On the one hand, this seems to suggest that conditions on speech acts are better viewed in terms of types of speech acts commented upon that formal sentence types. On the other hand, the observation seems to support the claim that many conditional speech acts, at least among those most commonly considered, are primarily concerned with politeness. One could also note that many of such "polite conditions" on speech acts are ready-made formulae, rather than spontaneously coined expressions –

and polite expressions are often fossilized. What is more, their formulaic character is often exploited in irony, as in *I'll give you a bath now, if you don't mind*, said to a child who always screams when confronted with a bathtub.

Yet another observation confirming the formulaic character of conditions on speech acts is that not all speech acts and not all of their felicity conditions are presented conditionally with the same ease. It would not, I assume, be common to make a sincere apology by saying *I apologize for being late, if that calls for an apology*, unless the speaker intends the utterance to be taken ironically or jocularly. The same can be said about all institutional acts, or, roughly speaking, all declaratives (consider *I declare you President of Ruritania, if I am authorized to do so*).

The above scattered remarks can be concluded by saying that the usual examples of the so-called speech act conditionals (or conditional speech acts), unlike other conditional constructions considered so far, constitute a rather restricted class and one which is frequently instantiated by formulaic or idiomatic forms. Their *if*-clauses are stylistic devices meant to ensure appropriateness of what is communicated in their main clauses, often, though not exclusively, by making them more polite. The fact that they are presented in the scope of *if* (and hence not asserted) is interpreted as indicating that the speaker, who believes them to be true and believes them to provide sufficient justification for what she communicates in *q*, is not sure whether the hearer shares these beliefs. However, the assumptions presented conditionally are not assumptions about facts and states of affairs, they are assumptions about optimal communication and successful social interaction – either specifically between the speaker and the hearer or in the society as a whole. Rules of cooperative conversation and social interaction are not coined spontaneously, so it is not surprising there should be a ready-made idiomatic repertory of protases expressing standard background assumptions about the interactional structure. Invoking these assumptions in an unasserted form cannot be interpreted as marking lack of knowledge on the part of the speaker, but rather as indicating lack of confidence that the hearer shares her view that a given rule applies to the particular exchange between the particular interlocutors. In other words, the speaker is making it clear why she believes what she communicates to be appropriate, but admitting the possibility for the hearer to see the situation differently. In some cases the justification concerns previous exchanges between the same interlocutors, as in *If I haven't already told you*, in others – the hearer's wishes, as in *If you are interested, If you want to know*, in still others – the relationship between the speaker and the hearer, as in *If I may ask, If you don't mind my asking*, or general politeness rules: *If it's not rude to ask*, etc. In other words, conditional speech acts can perhaps be glossed as "I believe *p* and I communicate *q* on this ground. I admit that I am not certain if you believe *p*."

Conditional speech acts are non-predictive constructions, and there are no restrictions on the verb forms used in both clauses. This is not to say that none of the forms used in hypothetical constructions can appear in a speech act conditional. On the contrary, past forms of modals, such as *might*, *could*, or *would*, are often encountered, but they are used as expressions of politeness, and thus are frequently found in *if*-clauses: *I'll get it for you, if you'd like to wait, Give me a ring, if I might/could ask you to*, etc. Such forms certainly invoke distance to indicate politeness, but it is not the hypothetical distance postulated for predictive conditionals.

Among non-predictive constructions, speech act conditionals can be distinguished with respect to several features. The specific status of the assumption expressed in the *if*-clause was discussed above. We can also note that the form of the construction forbids the marking of closer relation between the content of *p* and *q*: it is not possible to use *then* in front of *q*. The conjunction *then* (see section 6.3) suggests that there is a way in which the discourse segment it introduces can be seen to follow the preceding one, or to follow from the preceding one. The impossibility of using *then* signals the implausibility of any such interpretation. This observation is further confirmed by the fact that the clauses of speech act constructions are very often both pronounced with sentence final intonation.

The clause order in speech act conditionals also marks the relative independence of the assumptions in *p* and *q*. It is equally acceptable for the *if*-clause to occur before the main clause or after it, as in *I can type it for you, if you'd like me to/If you'd like me to, I can type it for you*. There is a certain preference for the *q* clause to appear earlier in discourse, which perhaps confirms the suggestion that *if*-clauses in such constructions do not in fact condition the speech acts in *q*'s, but rather give expression to the speaker's uncertainty about assumptions she and the hearer have to share for the utterance to be appropriate.

In the discussion above, it was noted that some epistemic conditionals are based on inference of cause from effect, and therefore the causal and conditional structure of these epistemic conditionals inverts the causal structure of the states of affairs referred to. Often, an appropriate content interpretation is readily available for a conditional which presents the same *p* and *q* in the opposite order from the epistemic conditional (*If they arrived at 11.00, they had left at 9.00* can be glossed as "I infer *q* from *p*," while *If they leave at 9.00, they'll arrive at 11.00* is interpreted as "*P* will cause *q*"). In the case of speech act conditionals such corresponding content conditionals do not typically exist, since speech acts and content are not causally connected in the same way as premise and conclusion: *If you really want to know, Mary is a Marxist/*If Mary is a Marxist, you really want to know*. However, as Keith Mitchell pointed out to me (personal communication), some form of reversibility is possible for typical "politeness" cases, for instance in requests for permission:

(26)   I'll help with the dishes, if it's all right with you/Is it all right if I help with the dishes?

(27)   I'll open the window, if you don't mind/Do you mind if I open the window?

The plausibility of such paraphrases of the protases of (26) and (27) seems to rest on the fact that both a conditional clause and a question contain unasserted assumptions. Also, as in the speech act conditionals discussed above, in both cases it is the *hearer* who can resolve the indeterminacy, either by answering the question, or by confirming or disconfirming the assumption presented by the speaker. In fact, the apodoses of (26) and (27) also have similar features – they contain assumptions which are neither asserted (as a result of being future) nor predicted (which is as near to assertion as the future can get); and they are "in the hands" of the hearer, who can accept or reject the offer. Thus all the clauses used in (26) and (27) are at least partly interchangeable with respect to certain salient features. Last, but not least, they all possess features characteristic of polite expressions – tentativeness, leaving options to the hearer, or declaring willingness on the part of the speaker.

3.5   Metatextual relations

In his recent work on negation Horn (1985, 1989) argues that logical operators can be seen as pragmatically (not semantically) ambiguous between a descriptive and a metalinguistic use. In the unmarked descriptive use, which is found in all standard cases of sentential negation, *not* operates on propositions and focuses on their truth or falsity. In the metalinguistic use, which is a marked extension of the descriptive one, the focus is on the assertability of the utterance.

Two terms in Horn's analysis require some discussion. First of all, Horn sets his account of negation against a broad background of two major approaches, one of which (incorporating the Aristotelian–Russellian tradition, as well as more recent work by Karttunen and Peters [1979]) considers negation to be ambiguous, while the other (including, among others, Atlas 1974, Kempson 1975, and Gazdar 1979) sees no need for distinguishing more than one negation operator. Horn himself argues that negation is indeed ambiguous, but pragmatically, not semantically. He uses the term "pragmatic ambiguity" following the work of Donnellan 1966, Wertheimer 1972, and many others, claiming that negation displays a duality of use: it is either a descriptive truth-functional operator, or a metalinguistic operator which is essentially non-truth-functional and in fact non-semantic. The latter use, represented by sentences such as *I'm not a Trotskyite, I'm a Trotskyist*, does not negate a proposition, but objects to some aspect of the utterance.

The second term which distinguishes Horn's analysis is "assertability." In Horn's definition, metalinguistic negation expresses the speaker's "unwillingness to assert, or accept another's assertion of, a given proposition in a given way"; it is "a device for objecting to a previous utterance on any grounds whatever, including conventional or conversational implicata it potentially induces, its morphology, its style or register, or its phonetic realization" (Horn 1989: 363). This definition stems from a crucial distinction in which Horn builds on the earlier work of Grice (1967) and Dummett (1973), that between the truth of a proposition and the assertability of a sentence. As he claims, the term "assertable" should be understood as elliptical for "felicitously assertable" or "appropriately assertable." As I have already pointed out, this understanding of the term is similar to the notion of (un)assertability used throughout this work to discuss the interpretation of conditionals.

In what follows I will argue that Horn's pragmatic interpretations are better described as generally metatextual (commenting on a selected fragment of an utterance for any reason, including its contribution to interpretation), rather than specifically metalinguistic (commenting on the choice of linguistic expression). To support this viewpoint I will first show that interpreting the use of negation in Polish requires that Horn's proposals be broadened in such a way. The revised concept of metatextual use will then be used in showing that some conditional sentences can be interpreted along the same lines. In such sentences, *if*-clauses are used as metatextual comments on some aspect of the apodosis.[4]

3.5.1   Metatextual negation

The most interesting cases among Horn's examples are those where *not* is used in its sentential negation position, and yet is interpreted metalinguistically. Many, though not all such examples have parallel Polish translations. An equivalent translation can, for instance, be provided for the sentences in which pronunciation, morphology, or appropriateness of a given constituent are com-

---

[4] Many of the ideas discussed below were first proposed in Dancygier (1986, 1992).

mented upon (all English examples are taken from Horn 1989, all Polish examples are as close as possible to word-for-word translations of the English sentences they follow):

(28)   He didn't call the [*pó*lis], he called the [po*lís*].

(29)   Nie wezwał pol[*i*]cji, tylko pol[*i*:]cję.
       (Not called [3rd PERSON SING PAST] pol[i]ce [GEN], but pol[i:]ce [ACC].)

(30)   I didn't manage to trap two **mongeese** – I managed to trap two **mongooses**.

(31)   Nie złapałem **dwu głuszeców**, tylko **dwa głuszce**.
       (Not caught [1st PERSON SING PAST] two capercaillies [GEN], but two capercaillies [ACC].)

(32)   Grandma isn't *feeling lousy*, Johnny, she's *just a tad indisposed*.

(33)   Babcia nie **korkuje**, Jasiu, tylko **troszkę źle się czuje**.
       (Grandma not feel-lousy [3rd PERSON SING PRES], Johnny, but a bit feel-indisposed [3rd PERSON SING PRES].)

Example (29) contrasts the substandard pronunciation of *policja* with the standard one, while (31) rejects morphologically deviant forms *głuszece* (ACC), *głuszeców* (GEN), in favor of *głuszce* (ACC), *głuszców* (GEN) (the noun refers to a subspecies of grouse, and was chosen to mark the kind of contrast Horn exemplifies with the forms *mongeese* and *mongooses*). In (33), the item objected to is the slang verb *korkować* ("feel very bad").

Like the English versions ([28], [30], [32]), all of the Polish examples ([29], [31], [33]) have the form of full negative sentences. This is marked in three ways:

- the negative particle *nie* precedes the verb,
- pronominal subjects could occur in (29) and (31) only in the position before *nie* (*On nie wezwał* . . . [He did not call . . .], *Ja nie złapałem* . . . [I did not catch . . .]),
- the direct objects of (29) and (31) are marked with the genitive case, which is obligatory for negative sentences in Polish. In affirmative sentences direct objects are in the accusative case. Thus, the noun phrases *policja* and *dwa głuszce* appear in the genitive form in the first clauses of sentences (29) and (31), and in the accusative form in their second clauses.

We should also note that all of the examples in Polish obligatorily introduce the second ("repair") clause with a "contrast" conjunction. In (29), (31), and (33) the conjunction used is *tylko*, in some of the examples below we will also see *a*, another conjunction similar to *but*. Also, the second clause is (also obligatorily) elliptical in all the cases where the verb is identical to that in the first clause. As regards Horn's examples, their metalinguistic reading arises in spite of the fact that the sentences retain their "plain" negation format. In other words, Horn's examples are interpreted metalinguistically, although they are structured identically to the case of standard sentential negation. It seems, then, that metalinguistic negation in Polish, which makes more specific demands on the form of the construction, appears in a much more marked and conventionalized pattern than Horn's English examples.

Furthermore, only some of the possible translations of Horn's examples into Polish do in fact follow the unmarked, sentential-negation format found in English. Such a translation is indeed plausible in the case of (32), as we can see in the "sententially-negated" form of (33), but the cases of (28) and (30) are different. Their translations offered in (29) and (31) are more conventionalized than the English sentences (due to the use of a special conjunction and ellipsis) and they are in fact less likely to be used than alternatives such as (34)/(36) and (35)/(37), whose form is still more conventionalized:

(34)   Wezwał nie pol[*i*]cję, a pol[*i:*]cję.
       (He called not *pol[i]cję*, but *pol[i:]cję*.)
(35)   Nie "wezwał pol[*i*]cję," tylko "wezwał pol[*i:*]cję."
       (Not "called the *pol[i]cję*," but "called the *pol[i:]cję*.")
(36)   Złapałem nie **dwa głuszece**, a **dwa głuszce**.
       (I caught not two *głuszece*, but two *głuszce*.)
(37)   Nie "złapałeś **dwa głuszece**," tylko "złapałeś **dwa głuszce**."
       (Not "you caught two *głuszece*," but "you caught two *głuszce*.")

Unlike sentences (29) and (31) above, (34) and (36) do not contain sentential negation. In (34) and (36) any pronominal subject would have to occur directly before the verb (*On wezwał . . .* [He called . . .], *Ja złapałem . . .* [I caught . . .]). Further, they differ from sentential negation in that *nie* does not precede the verb and the case of direct objects is accusative. In these examples, then, the metalinguistic negation takes the form of constituent or focus negation, with the negative particle *nie* preceding the phrase being objected to. Such constructions in English (e.g. *He called not the [pólis], but the [polís]*) are apparently less common, though they are fully acceptable.

Examples (35) and (37) contain direct quotations from the utterances just heard, which are marked in pronunciation by a pause between *nie* and the material quoted. The particle *nie* directly precedes the quote, and the expression under scrutiny is marked by a fall–rise intonation within the quotation. Furthermore, the deleted subjects can be recovered only within the quotes: *Nie "on wezwał . . ."* (Not "he called . . ."), *Nie "ty złapałeś . . ."* (Not "you caught . . ."). Most crucially of all, the objects in these examples are accusative, not genitive.

It seems, however, that in spite of the fact that in Polish constituent negation prevails as an expression of metalinguistic objection, sentential-level metalinguistic negation is possible both in English and in Polish. The possibility of interpreting Polish *nie* metalinguistically in its sentential negation position is largely due to the overall echo–repair format of the construction in which it appears.

We should note here that the format of many sentential and constituent negation clauses involves an "echo" of somebody else's utterance which repeats the form without subscribing to the content of the quote at the same time. This kind of use was discussed by Sperber and Wilson (1981, 1986) under the rubric of "mention" (in the use/mention distinction), "echoic use," or "interpretive use." Sperber and Wilson's primary example of such use is irony, but it seems that the cases of metalinguistic negation quoted above are interpreted in a similar way: they echo somebody else's utterance and interpret it in a way which is not necessarily identical to what was originally intended.

I argued above that Polish requires specific constructional formats to accomplish metalinguistic negation. However, in some sentences in Polish the format of the construction alone does not ensure acceptability. For instance, a metalinguistic reading will not be possible for a sentence in which negation focuses on the content verb in an SVO structure:

(38)   Chris didn't *manage* to solve the problem – he solved it easily.
(39)   *Krzysztof nie *zdołał* rozwiązać problemu (GEN) – rozwiązał go (ACC) z łatwością.
        (exact translation of [38])

Sentence (39) is a contradiction – it first asserts that Chris didn't solve the problem, and then that he did. Similarly in a scalar example:

(40)   Around here, we don't *like* coffee, we *love* it.
        (Horn 1989).
(41)   *My tu nie *lubimy* kawy (GEN), my ją (ACC) *kochamy*.
        (exact translation of [40])

Examples (39) and (41) are unacceptable as wholes, because the echo-repair format and the fall–rise focus on the verb do not suffice to prevent the reading of negation in the first conjuncts as descriptive. The standard preverbal position of the negative particle and the genitive case marking on the object override the intonational contour. Let us recall that in the Polish equivalents of (28) and (30) above, which are very similar syntactically to (39) and (41), the rejected expressions could be identified as inappropriate without any reference to their meaning: the objection was directed exclusively at the form of the utterance –

pronunciation, morphological form, or style. In (38) and (40), on the other hand, which, according to Horn, object to conventional and conversational implicatures respectively, the expressions in question are rejected with respect to their contribution to interpretation, not form.

Interestingly enough, at least (41), though not (39), can be saved if we formally mark the echoic character of the first clause by changing the case of the object from the genitive, characteristic of negation, to the accusative, which must have been used in the previous utterance referred to. With such a change, (42) is still unacceptable, while (43) now is. The change to an accusative object makes it clear that (43) is a negative comment on positive content, rather than an expression of a negative proposition:

(42)   *Krzysztof nie *zdołał* rozwiązać problem (ACC) – rozwiązał go (ACC) z łatwością.
        (Chris didn't manage to solve the problem [ACC] – he solved it [ACC] easily.)
(43)   My tu nie *lubimy* kawę (ACC), my ją (ACC) *kochamy*.
        (Around here, we don't like coffee (ACC), we love it [ACC].)

The only plausible explanation of the difference in acceptability of (42) and (43) is that the former has fewer surface signals of the metalinguistic reading intended, because it does not offer repair of the phrase objected to – instead, it explains the reason for the rejection. The repair – the information that Chris solved the problem – is implicit in (38) and its translation (42), but it is not given explicitly, as in (40) and (43). In fact, if an explicit repair is offered instead of an explanation, (42) becomes acceptable:

(44)   Krzysztof nie *zdołał* rozwiązać problem (ACC) – po prostu go (ACC) rozwiązał
        (Chris didn't *manage* to solve the problem – he simply *solved* it.)
        (The speaker feels using the word *manage* is inappropriate; what happened can be sufficiently described by the verb *solve*, perhaps because there was no difficulty involved.)

Further, with an explicit repair a constituent negation variant is also acceptable, such as *Nie "zdołał rozwiązać," a "rozwiązał"* ("Not 'managed to solve,' but 'solved'"). With an explanation instead of a repair, however, the only acceptable translation of (38) is with the phrase *To nieprawda, że . . . (It's not true that . . .)*, as in (45):

(45)   To nieprawda, że Krzysztof *zdołał* rozwiązać problem (ACC) – rozwiązał go (ACC) z łatwością.
        (It's not true that Chris managed to solve the problem (ACC) – he solved it (ACC) easily.)

This might be taken to suggest that in the case of an objection to conventional implicature the difference between the descriptive and metalinguistic reading is blurred. Horn rejects the phrase *It's not true that* as a proof of descriptive use, for, as he claims, it can also be ambiguous between a descriptive and metalinguistic reading. Nevertheless, clearly *It's not true that* is not an acceptable paraphrase of all examples of metalinguistic negation. For instance, it is rather unlikely that the phrase would be used to reject the pronunciation or morphological form of an expression, as in *?? It's not true that I caught two mongeese – I caught two mongooses. It's not true that*, even if not unambiguously descriptive, is thus much more likely to be used as a comment on meaning-related phenomena than on pure form.

Comments on form are also different from comments on the content in that the specific reason why the utterance is considered inappropriate is clearly marked only in the cases pertaining to form (pronunciation, morphology, style), while in other instances the aspect of the message being rejected can only be understood in contrast with the alternate message offered in the repair.

The examples above suggest that there is a difference between metalinguistic comments on form and those objecting to aspects of meaning. Interestingly enough, these differences disappear in the constituent negation format. A possible explanation is that a metalinguistic comment has to first of all make it clear which part of the previous utterance is being objected to. If the expression echoed is inappropriate in form (pronunciation, morphology, style) or rhematic (as in the case of copula sentences), it is easily identifiable. In the case of comments on aspects of meaning, such as implicature, sentential negation fails to be understood metalinguistically because nothing singles out a particular implicature as the subject of the comment. Constituent negation format, which puts the expression in question directly in the scope of *nie*, helps to single out the part of the sentence responsible for the implicature in question.

Thus, the asterisked examples above are found unacceptable for just one reason – that it is not clear whether *nie* negates the whole sentence or only part of it. This seems to suggest that metalinguistic negation is first of all an objection to a localizable ***part of the text*** of the previous utterance; what the speaker of a metalinguistically negative sentence has to achieve first is to make clear which fragment of the utterance she objects to. And, as we have seen, all of the formal devices used in the examples above (echo-repair format, intonation, change of case, constituent negation, ellipsis) primarily function to highlight the part of the utterance which is called into question. Inasmuch as the overall interpretation relies heavily on such formal features, rather than solely on negation and context, metalinguistic negation is perhaps better handled as an instance of a *construction*, rather than being described as a specific use of a logical operator independent of other aspects of form.

The above observations have raised certain questions about the use of the term "metalinguistic negation." Horn's use of it seems to imply that this type of negation objects to a preceding utterance because of the language used in it. In fact, Horn explicitly claims that it is the *way* in which the proposition is asserted, not the propositional content itself, that is being objected to. The distinction between metalinguistic and descriptive negation is thus based on the distinction between semantic/truth-conditional meaning (where descriptive negation is appropriate) and pragmatic meaning (where metalinguistic negation is possible). However, in the data considered above metalinguistic negation seemed to take different forms with respect to whether an *aspect of form* or an *aspect of meaning* were being objected to, rather than along any other dividing line. Also, the variety of forms used seemed to have a common major function: proper identification of the fragment objected to. That is, the objection raised by the speaker is not so much against the proposition to be asserted in a given way, but against a specific part of the text of the utterance to be used in that utterance to contribute to an interpretation which adequately describes a given state of affairs. In other words, the speaker using metalinguistic negation identifies the state of affairs whose description was attempted by her interlocutor, but believes that a certain fragment of the utterance is responsible for the description not being fully adequate, because of either imperfect use of forms or inadequate choice of words. In what follows I will thus argue that the uses of negation exemplified above can more appropriately be described as *metatextual*. First of all, the term seems to appropriately reflect the "text selecting" function of formal devices the construction employs. Also, it will allow me to look afresh at the data not fully accounted for by Horn's model. Finally, it will appear useful in the analysis of conditionals in section 3.5.2 below.

The revision of Horn's terminology suggested above admits various understandings of what the "text" is. In the majority of cases, exemplified above, the fragment in question is a word or a phrase. But it is also possible to make a metatextual comment on the whole utterance, if the aspect of the utterance which is questioned can only be derived on the basis of its text as a whole. A good example is quoted by Horn (1989) after Wilson (1975: 152):

(46)   I'm not his daughter – he's my father.

The echo and the repair seem to communicate the same message in this case and there are no formal signals of focus on any of the expressions. The only aspect that can be calculated as being objected to is an overall framing of the clause's content. In other words, what is really being questioned is (obviously) not what the word *daughter* standardly means, but what is conventionally associated with one of the possible construals of a parent/child relationship. In the terms suggested by Langacker (1987), the two phrasings represent reversed trajector–landmark relations and thereby differ centrally in their framing of otherwise common conceptual structures. Clearly this is an aspect of the utterance content which is not readily qualifiable in terms of the categories considered by Horn.

Throughout the discussion, I have looked at examples of metatextual negation which comment on the form of the expressions in question or on the implicated aspects of interpretation. Horn explicitly rejects the idea that such negation can qualify the propositional content of the utterance. However, there seem to be examples of metalinguistic/metatextual comments objecting to aspects of meaning traditionally seen as propositional content. Horn mentions some of them, but classifies them as metalinguistic on the grounds of their form:

(47)   John was born, not in Boston, but in Philadelphia.
(48)   John wasn't born in Boston, but in Philadelphia.
(49)   John wasn't born in Boston, he was born in Philadelphia.

All of these have exact equivalents in Polish. In all versions of these examples, English and Polish, it is clear from the sentences that it is not true that John was born in Boston. The repair, on the other hand, states that he was born in Philadelphia. These are, surely, statements concerning the core of content, and not implicature, form, or style. What makes them metatextual, then?

First, they are objections to the previous utterance directed at one of its aspects, against an implicit background of acceptance of the rest of that utterance. Also, they have the form of a metatextual construction, that is, they contain the echo part and the repair part, whether in sentential or constituent format. But they do not comment on the language used in one of its pragmatic or formal aspects, they reject a part of the text of the previous utterance on the basis of its contribution to the content. However, like our previous examples, they focus on a part of the text of the previous utterance.

What all the examples considered above share is the attempt to reject only a part or aspect of the previous utterance which the speaker finds unassertable. In the examples concerned with form only, the speaker agrees with the whole of the content, but rejects part of the wording. In those directed at implicatures, the essential part of the message remains untouched (e.g. he did solve the problem, we are indeed fond of coffee, etc.). In the cases like (47)–(49), there is a part of the message which is rejected, and which is profiled against a backdrop of general acceptance of the rest of the mesage. (The speaker might be saying something like: "John was indeed born in an East Coast city with historic tradition, but the city was not Boston – it was Philadelphia"). The cases described by Horn, which comment on the choice of expression, can be referred to as metalinguistic, but they seem to be a part of a larger class of utterances, which I proposed above to call metatextual, which comment on the contribution made by a given part of the utterance to the overall message – whether the objection raised refers to form or to any aspect of content.

The view that emerges from the above considerations is that we are dealing with something more than an ambiguity of negation, even if it is a pragmatic ambiguity. The ambiguity arises in a specialized construction, whose pragmatic function is to find the most effective expression of the thought one of the interlocutors – let us continue envisaging him as the hearer – purports to communicate. The context for using such a construction is the situation where the hearer has communicated an assumption in a certain way, in the belief that the utterance will be appropriately understood by the speaker. The utterance produced was thus meant to communicate a thought and the form is believed to give the thought the best expression.

The other interlocutor – the speaker – has received this utterance and assumes she understood the message – the thought. But she believes that the utterance does not give an optimal expression to the thought. She thus offers an improvement on the formulation of what she assumes to be the intended message. The speaker does not reject the whole of the utterance, but one of its aspects, and the comment offered has to make it clear which aspect it is. It does so by echoing and revising the fragment of the text the speaker rejects. With the objections to formal aspects of the utterance, such as pronunciation, morphological form or style, the corrective effect is ensured by the very juxtaposition of the form rejected and the form meant to substitute for it. Hence, as we saw above, such cases require only minimal marking of the echo and the repair parts of the construction.

In the cases in which some part of the meaning is under scrutiny, more surface signals may be required for the hearer to understand the objection (as we saw in the examples from Polish, the range of available means of focusing on the right part of the text may be quite broad). In some cases, as in (47)–(49) above, the rejected part of the text may be objected to with respect to its content. However, this does not mean that the utterance is rejected as false, but that it is not a fully adequate expression of what the hearer wanted to communicate. In the examples like (47)–(49) the speaker does not concentrate on the falsity of the statement about John being born in Boston, but on getting right the purported message about John's place of birth. The sentence is still concerned with unassertability, not falsehood, as in Horn's definition, but one can say that the speaker considers the previous utterance unassertable with respect to an aspect of (propositional) content. The fact that in semantic terms the unassertability renders the sentence false does not concern the speaker of a metatextual utterance, because her point is to get the message right, whether with respect to form or intended interpretation. She does not even have to assume that the hearer holds a false belief in such a case; she may treat the inaccuracy as a lapse of memory or even a slip of the tongue.

In the examples related to interpretation, not form, we are thus dealing with a cline of comments on meaning, ranging from conversational implicature, through conventional implicature, to propositional content. None of these can really be qualified as a comment on the choice of language, that is, as a metalinguistic comment, because what the repair concerns first of all is **what** the hearer has said (or implicated), and not **how** he has said it. Regardless of whether the aspect of meaning in question is described as pragmatic or semantic, it remains an aspect of the overall interpretation, and may thus be evaluated as being more or less adequate as a description of the state of affairs in question.

3.5.2 Metatextual conditionals

Horn (1985, 1989) notes that pragmatic ambiguity between descriptive and metalinguistic uses is characteristic not only of negation, but also of other operators, such as disjunction and conditionality, and of some constructions, such as questions.

Horn's chief examples of metalinguistic conditionals, such as (50) and (51), are constructions he calls "Austin conditionals," after Austin's (1961) famous sentence *If you are hungry, there are biscuits on the sideboard.* Such conditionals, as Horn claims, are metalinguistic in that they are concerned with specifying conditions for the appropriateness of asserting the antecedent, and not for its truth.

(50)   If you haven't already heard, Punxsutawny Phil saw his shadow this morning.
(51)   If I may say so, you're looking particularly lovely tonight.
        (both examples from Horn 1985, 1989)

In some works on conditionals, however, (Van der Auwera 1986, Sweetser 1984, 1990), such examples are described as speech act conditionals, and their antecedents are thus seen as conditions on the appropriateness of a speech act purportedly performed in the consequents. In the Austin example above, then, the *if*-clause does not qualify the appropriateness of ***asserting*** that there are biscuits on the sideboard, but gives a justification for ***offering*** biscuits to the hearer. Similarly, the antecedents of (50) and (51) justify acts of informing and complimenting, respectively.

It can further be noted that Horn's sentences in fact show little similarity to his examples of metalinguistic negation. They are not contextualized in the same way, as they do not refer to the previous utterance, and they do not contain parts identifiable as "echo" and "repair," or as "echo" and "explanation." Even more importantly, they do not seem to distinguish among individual aspects of the utterance, such as pronunciation, morphological form, style, implicature, etc.

On the other hand, examples displaying exactly these features can be found:

(52)   He trapped two mongeese, if that's how you make a plural of "mongoose."
(53)   He trapped two mongeese, if "mongeese" is the right form.
(54)   Grandma is feeling lousy, if I may put it that way.
(55)   Grandma is feeling lousy, if that's an appropriate expression.
(56)   Chris managed to solve the problem, if solving it was at all difficult for him.
(57)   Chris managed to solve the problem, if "manage" is the right word.
(58)   The Queen of England is happy, if not ecstatic.
(59)   John was born in Philadelphia, if that's where they keep the Liberty Bell.

Sentences (52)–(59) have much in common with examples of metatextual negation considered in the previous section. The utterance in the "antecedent" presents a given thought in a given way. The speaker, however, is not sure if she chose the right expression to render an aspect of the utterance – whether pertaining to form or interpretation. To mark the lack of certainty, she appends to the utterance an *if*-clause expressing her doubt about a part of the text. The *if*-clause may highlight the fragment in question by echoing it (as in [53] and [57]), or refering to it anaphorically (note the use of *that* in [55]). It may also offer a potentially more appropriate expression, as in (58), or explain the reasons why the speaker is not sure about the expression being an appropriate one – this is the case in (52)–(56) and in (59). The comments offered may concern any aspect of the utterance – its form (see [52] and [53]), its style (as in [54] and [55]), its implicata ([56]–[58]), or an aspect of its propositional content (as in [59]).

The similarities between metatextual conditionals like (52)–(59) and metatextual negative constructions are striking: the comments in both cases are comments on assertability, they object to a part of the previous utterance, and they pertain to the same range of phenomena. The difference lies mainly in the fact that in metatextual conditionals the speaker comments on her own utterance, and the comment follows the utterance in the same construction. In cases of metatextual negation the speaker usually objects to an interlocutor's utterance (although, as Horn shows, it is possible for the speaker to create a special rhetorical effect by rejecting what she has just communicated), and the metatextual utterance is therefore formally independent of the one it comments upon. Also, the objection expressed in a metatextual conditional is understood as doubt, or uncertainty, not as outright rejection of the previous utterance as unassertable. This seems to follow from two factors: first, the use of *if* dictates a weaker interpretation of the objection than in the case of *not*, and, second, if the speaker were sure that the utterance is not assertable in a given way, she would (or, at least, should) initially choose a different means of expression.

To account for these data, we need to postulate a class of **metatextual conditionals**, which is independent of speech act conditionals (such as Austin's famous example) and bears a striking resemblance to Horn's cases of metatextual negation.

Speech act conditionals and metatextual conditionals are still similar in many respects. First of all, both types express conditions on appropriateness, and thus do not involve any real-world dependence between the contents of their antecedents and consequents. Neither of the classes admits the use of predictive verb forms, and consequently speech act or metatextual conditionals typically do not use hypothetical forms. If such forms are used in metatextual conditionals, the invited interpretation is, as in the case of epistemic and speech act conditionals, predictive and causal. Thus *?Grandma would be feeling lousy if that were an appropriate expression* (though perhaps acceptable as "style indirect libre"), cannot be interpreted parallelly to its non-hypothetical counterpart *Grandma is feeling lousy, if that's an appropriate expression*. It loses its metatextual, comment-like meaning and suggests a genuine, real-world condition on Grandma's health.

The similarities are not incidental. Both speech act and metatextual clauses are comments on utterances presented in their "consequents," and are thus markedly different from both predictive and epistemic conditionals. Their parenthetical role can be seen also in the fact that they can be used as comments on other conditionals, as in (60) and (61), presenting a metatextual and speech act conditional respectively:

(60)   I'd love to go if I didn't feel so lousy, if that's an appropriate expression.
(61)   If I know my daughter, she'll go mad if you tell her.

It seems possible, then, to refer to speech act and metatextual examples jointly as **conversational conditionals**.

But there are significant differences between the classes, too. As I have noted, for instance, speech act conditionals are often specific to a given speech act force or sentence type, and may explicitly refer to its preconditions. Thus, *if*-clauses such as *if I haven't already asked . . ., if it's not rude to ask . . .* can only function with questions as "consequents," while *if I may say so* typically accompanies a declarative. There are no such restrictions in the case of metatextual comments, since they focus on a fragment of the text regardless of the utterance's force or sentence type. Another argument for treating the two classes independently is that an utterance can be qualified by both types of comments simultaneously. In (62), for instance, the initial *if*-clause justifies the appropriateness of asking a question, while the final one focuses on the phrase *my husband*.

(62)   If I haven't already asked, when did you last see my husband – if I can still call him that.

Let us also note that it is rather unlikely that the same speech act would be hedged twice, by means of two independent *if*-clauses, while two metatextual comments on two formal aspects of an utterance would be acceptable.

Speech act and metatextual conditionals also differ with respect to their preferred clause order. The former are most often used with their *if*-clause in the sentence-initial position, but a reversed clause order is equally acceptable (as in a paraphrase of [50] above: *Punxsutawny Phil saw his shadow this morning, if you haven't already heard*). The metatextual ones, on the other hand, are typically sentence-final, apparently due to the fact that a metatextual comment must echo the text in question or refer to it anaphorically, and thus has to follow it. Further, as in the case of negative metatextual constructions, it has to be clear which part of the text is being focused upon. The sentence-final position of a metatextual "antecedent" ensures the text–metatext proximity only if the focused-on "text" appears in the predicate phrase, or otherwise in the rheme of the preceding "consequent." If it is a sentence-initial part, the link may be lost, as in (63):

(63)   *My husband hates onion soup, if I can still call him that.

In such cases, due to the required transparency of the text–metatext relation, the speaker has the unique possibility of putting an *if*-clause inside the "consequent," as in *My husband, if I can still call him that, hates onion soup*. The fact that such sentence-medial clause order is (as we shall see later) rather uncommon for other types of conditional constructions suggests that such *if*-clauses focus on an aspect of the text in a way similar to negation, which seems to justify the use of the term "metatextual" (rather than "metalinguistic") also in this case.

Metatextual conditional sentences have been shown here to be strikingly parallel to the negative constructions discussed by Horn. Further, the two types of metatextual uses seem to co-occur in some contexts. In a sentence like *The Queen of England is happy, if not ecstatic* (example [58] above) we are dealing with a conditional metatextual comment on the scalar implicature triggered by *happy*. The *if*-clause is obligatorily negative and can be interpreted as suggesting that *ecstatic* is perhaps a better term than *happy*. Under this interpretation the negation, interestingly enough, is also interpreted metatextually, for the speaker is not necessarily saying that the Queen is not ecstatic.

The difference between a negative metatextual utterance like *The Queen of England is not happy, she is ecstatic* and a conditional one like (58) is that in the former negation focuses on the term related to a lower position on the scale (*happy*), and in the latter on the one having a higher position (*ecstatic*). In the metatextual conditional the weaker term has actually been used, and is questioned, rather than rejected, while the stronger term (e.g. *ecstatic*) is only considered as an alternative. A possible gloss to clarify the actual scope of negation here is: "It is appropriate to use the word 'happy' to describe the Queen's emotional state, if it is not more appropriate to use the word 'ecstatic.'" The affinity between the scalar uses of metatextual and negative constructions can also be seen in the fact that the conditional examples involving scalar implicature are the only ones suggesting an alternative expression (a potential repair).

Earlier in this section I suggested that the metalinguistic uses of negation are perhaps better described as a type of construction than as an independent ambiguity of negation alone. Our observations on metatextual conditionals also point to features (such as clause order, intonation, and use of verb forms) which characterize the constructions, rather than just the use of *if*. What is more, conditionals cannot be claimed to fall into just two classes (descriptive or metalinguistic, to use Horn's terminology), for their epistemic and speech act interpretations are clearly independent of the metatextual ones. It would be difficult to argue that any of the particular classes of constructions should be described unambiguously as "descriptive" (that is, if "descriptive" is in any way related to the logical operator). Furthermore, conjunctions in general do not seem to display the dichotomy Horn argues for. For example, the conjunction *or*, which, as Horn claims, can also be seen as a (pragmatically) ambiguous operator, has been shown by Sweetser (1990) to have epistemic and speech act uses which go far beyond the suggested descriptive/metalinguistic dichotomy Horn offers for logical operators. Sweetser's analysis also covers *and, but, since, because,* and *although,* and in each case what we see is multiplicity of interpretations in different cognitive domains, rather than two-way ambiguity of the type Horn suggests for *or* or *if.*

As a final point, we should consider a group of conditional constructions which are metatextual in character, but do not involve echoic use and are not concerned with explanation or repair. Instead, a linguistic expression used in one of the clauses functions itself as a justification for a parallel or contrasting expression used in the other clause. The first examples of such use were noted by Ducrot (1972) (and quoted by Horn 1985, 1989):

(64)   If the Cité is the heart of Paris, the Latin Quarter is its soul.

Ducrot (1972) sees the *if*-clauses of such examples as offering justification for the metaphor used in the "consequent." It can perhaps be added that both clauses of (64) are metaphorical, and justify each other against a background of a broader metaphor in which Paris is envisaged as a human being.[5] The reciprocity of the justification can be seen in the possibility of reversing the order of the clauses: *If the Latin Quarter is the soul of Paris, the Cité is its heart.* Such sentences can thus be called **symmetric** metatextual conditionals.

The symmetric metatextual sentences can also express contrast, as in *If Velazquez soothes, Goya terrifies.* The clauses can again be reversed without affecting the stylistic effect. They cannot be reversed, though, if the rhetorical device used is intensification, not symmetry or contrast: *If Mary is just pleasantly pretty, her sister is a real beauty.*

A metatextual analysis in terms of intensification can also be postulated for a sentence first discussed by Jespersen (1940), then commented upon by Haiman (1978) and Sweetser (1990):

(65)   If I was a bad carpenter, I was a worse tailor.

The example has most commonly been seen as concessive, but it seems to be best interpreted as "If *bad* is the right expression to describe my carpentry, *worse* has to be used to describe my tailoring." As we can see, in such constructions the "text-selecting" is achieved by much more subtle means than echoing and commenting, but there is no doubt that symmetry is an important constructional feature here.

Furthermore, as Sweetser (1996a) has shown, symmetrical mappings like that in (64) define an independent class of conditionals which she calls

---

[5] Metaphorical mappings in conditionals have been explored by Sweetser (1996a).

meta-metaphorical. Example (64) above is a good representative of the class, as it uses a general metaphorical mapping (as defined by Lakoff and Johnson 1980) relating big cities to human bodies. The sentence can be glossed roughly as saying: "If it is acceptable to call the Cité the heart of Paris, then it is also acceptable (via the same mapping) to call the Latin Quarter its soul."

In the analysis above two main points have been made. First, it was argued that Horn's idea of metalinguistic use is better captured in terms of a comment on a part of the text of the previous utterance, objecting to it in any of its aspects, including its contribution to propositional content. In the second part, it was shown how the function of metatextual commentary is realized in conditional form. Metatextual conditionals will thus constitute another class of conditional constructions distinguished with respect to the relation between the protasis and the apodosis.

4 *Knowledge and conditional protases*

As I argued in the earlier chapters, *if* as a marker of a conditional protasis instructs the hearer to treat the assumption in its scope as not assertable in the usual way. There are various reasons for the speaker to mark an assumption as non-assertive; most of these reasons, except in the rather exceptional case of commentary on linguistic form, are related to the speaker's state of knowledge. As I have tried to show, the type of unassertability influences the choice of verb forms in the sentence. Thus in predictive conditionals the speaker may mark two different types of lack of commitment with two types of backshift. The *if*-backshift marks the content of the protasis as in a sense "not knowable" – it is not factual and thus cannot be known to be true or false, and it is also not predictable on the basis of the present situation and its potential consequences. The hypothetical backshift marks both the protasis and the apodosis as even more difficult to assert, because of some other beliefs which the speaker holds. Thus, in hypothetical conditionals, the protasis is still not knowable or predictable, and is then further distanced because of the clash between its content and the content of other assumptions the speaker holds or entertains. The apodosis is then marked with the same distance, for its assertability crucially depends on that of the protasis.

The second type of non-assertiveness was found in epistemic conditionals, in which the protasis may contain an assumption which, in most cases, was acquired by the speaker indirectly. Such an assumption is knowable, and potentially known to somebody, as it is grounded in the context of the interaction. But it is not known directly to the speaker and is thus marked with a conditional *if*, to indicate what I have tentatively called evidential distance.

Finally, the protases of conversational conditionals (speech act and meta-textual ones) are presented to the hearer as only tentative, for they express conditions on the appropriateness of the apodoses and refer to rules of politeness and linguistic usage that the hearer may not share.

In the present chapter I will consider some further questions related to the use of conditional protases as expressions of unassertability. First, I want to explore the actual role of context in the marking of evidential distance: what kind of contextually acquired knowledge would be marked as conditional, and why? The next section will look for an explanation of the use of *will* in conditional protases: what modality is expressed by *will* in such cases? Finally, I will consider in more detail the relationships between the type of unassertability, verb forms, and the nature of the connection between the protasis and the apodosis.

4.1 "Contextual givenness" and degrees of distance

It has often been observed that the protases of non-predictive conditionals such as (1), (2), or (3) bear a special relation to the context.

(1)   If she is giving the baby a bath, I'll call back later.
(2)   If she is in the lobby, the plane arrived early.
(3)   If I ever read this book, I have forgotten it altogether.

The way such sentences are interpreted usually assumes the content of *p* to have been expressed earlier in discourse, most commonly by the hearer. Thus such protases are called "contextually given" (Van der Auwera 1986, Akatsuka 1986) and often paraphrased by adding a phrase such as *as you say*. That is, the most common interpretation of the protasis of (1) is *If, as you say, she is giving the baby a bath* . . . As this suggests, such protases are seen as quotations from previous discourse.

Such an interpretation is based on a rather restricted view of the context as preceding co-text. If we follow this interpretation of the role of such protases, that is, if we treat them simply as echoed utterances of the hearer, we are also oversimplifying the reasons for which they are brought up as background to their apodoses. First of all, echoic use, as Sperber and Wilson have shown (1981, 1986), does not necessarily imply that the speaker shares the belief in the assumption echoed. Second, accepting the role of such utterances as mere "quotes" from preceding discourse presents a rather restricted view of mental space construction involved. As Fauconnier argued (1996), the building of conditional mental spaces involves the creation of mental constructs on the basis of the cognitive, cultural, contextual, and epistemic concepts available to the discourse participants, for the purposes of a given exchange. It is thus a process which involves a background much broader and more complex than a "preceding utterance" alone can offer.

We can get a better understanding of the source of such protases if we assume a different concept of the context. For example, Sperber and Wilson (1986), argue that in any discourse the context in which a given utterance is processed is dynamically constructed for the purposes of processing this particular utterance – a claim much in the same spirit as Fauconnier's proposals. In the theory of relevance, the context is characterized as a dynamic cognitive structure built up for the purpose of the interaction. Such a notion of the context can be used in explaining both how speakers construct their utterances and how hearers interpret them, and it may in fact apply to all levels of message construction.

Naturally, the context most easily accessible to conscious analysis is that of the preceding utterance, as well as the immediate history of the current speech exchange stored in the short-term memory of the interlocutors. But the context may also contain the history of the relationship between the interlocutors, and their encyclopedic knowledge related to the concepts occurring in the utterance to be interpreted. Let us imagine a woman saying *Let's go into the dining room.* When she and her husband then sit down at the table to celebrate the twentieth anniversary of their marriage and she says *We've come a long way*, her husband is unlikely to interpret her utterance as a complaint about the distance she had to walk from the kitchen to the dining room. In order to arrive at the intended interpretation he has to consider what the dinner is meant to celebrate, which does not relate to previous discourse. What is taken to be relevant context is thus a matter of choice; and the choice is governed by various factors, not necessarily of a linguistic nature.

This view of the context allows us to see many conditional protases as **contextually bound**, without defining this contextual binding narrowly in terms of "quotations" from previous discourse. Such protases contain contextually motivated assumptions which are communicated to justify the discourse segment that follows – in particular, the apodosis of the *if*-construction. For example, having heard an account of a conversation with a person who would not be convinced to change his mind, one might say:

(4)   If he's so dumb, it's no use talking to him any more.

In a sentence like (4), *p* verbalizes a conclusion or a contextual implication which arose in the course of interpreting previous discourse, but it does not necessarily echo any part of preceding discourse. It thus would probably not be tagged with a comment like *as you say.* The range of possible attributive/ evidential phrases which reveal the source of a contextually bound protasis is in fact quite broad and includes expressions such as *as you seem to believe/suggest, as one might conclude/think,* or *as far as I could understand* (cf. Lakoff 1972b, Sweetser 1987 on hedges and evidentials). The assumptions expressed in "given" protases may thus arise as tentative formulations of implications derived from previous discourse, the speaker's guesses at the message intended by the hearer, etc. In other words, for any of the protases in the non-predictive examples above to be contextually bound it is not necessary that someone said *p* in the immediately preceding context, but only that *p* can be concluded from what has been said, whether by the hearer or any other participant in the conversation, or even by some ancillary participant (e.g. the third person talking to one of the interlocutors on the phone). In fact, the assumption may be still further detached from linguistic context, as it may be a part of the speaker's and the hearer's background knowledge or even a fact observable in the discourse setting.

As Akatsuka (1985, 1986) also notes, such protases, even if actually communicated in the preceding context, do not necessarily represent the speaker's *knowledge*, because having heard an assumption communicated as true does not oblige the addressee to accept this as his own belief. Akatsuka refers to this epistemic status of an assumption as *information*. The "uncommitted" status of non-predictive protases, together with the fact that they often arise as conclusions arrived at on the basis of the context (not just co-text), suggest, as I pointed out earlier, that we should interpret them as special cases of unassertability. Clearly, the assumptions which non-predictive protases represent are not presented by the speaker as known to her and they are marked with distance (by *if* and the choice of verb forms). The distancing may be evidential in nature, and thus mark the protasis as acquired indirectly, or, in a weaker case like (4), it may mark the protasis as a contextual implication derived from previously communicated or simply manifest assumptions; in such a case the distancing is not strictly evidential, but still epistemic in nature. Since "epistemic" seems to be a broader term than "evidential," I will use the term *epistemic distance* to refer to all such cases of unassertability.[1]

The speaker marking epistemic distance is thus using the *if*-clause to represent an assumption which is possibly assertable and possibly true, but is not presented as a belief the speaker holds at the moment of speech (or as assertable at the moment of speech). As in the case of predictive sentences, the protasis presents an assumption which the hearer is not meant to interpret as the speaker's

---

[1] We should note that such a use of conditional protases probably matches the definition of "interpretive" use offered by Sperber and Wilson (1986), because they do not represent the speaker's thought, rather, they interpret a thought expressed by another participant. However, Smith and Smith (1988) have suggested that the so-called counterfactual conditionals can be claimed to be instances of the interpretive use as well. Since I have offered an interpretation of conditionals which treats hypothetical predictive constructions (the best examples of "counterfactuals") in a very different way, I am not sure to what degree the concept of interpretive use really applies in drawing the distinctions I am advocating.

assertion about a certain state of affairs. The difference is, however, that a protasis of a predictive statement presents an assumption not derivable from the speaker's knowledge (including contextually derivable knowledge), while a protasis of a non-predictive one represents an assumption derived from the context. In particular, the assumption may have been acquired indirectly, from what somebody else has communicated – thus the protasis may be a quotation of an assertion, a verbalization of its intended implicature, or a contextual implication arrived at on the basis of what the hearer said and what the speaker knew before. Being rooted in the context, the assumption, even if not believed, is equally accessible to the speaker and the hearer: it can thus be shared without being "given." In the limiting case, the assumption is manifest to the speaker in the speech setting, which again does not necessarily mean (see Sperber and Wilson 1986) that she believes it to be true or even treats it as a "fact," for not all of what one perceives and interprets is automatically incorporated into one's set of beliefs and stored in memory.

The protases of non-predictive conditionals can be seen as signaling many possible degrees of epistemic distance between speaker and content. We may in particular remark on the variety of specific ways in which the assumptions in the protases can be bound by the context. In possibly the most typical case, the speaker just abstains from presenting p as her own belief. One reason for this may be illustrated in an example like (1), where the assumption is marked as acquired indirectly.

Another possibility is that the speaker wants to use p to show the hearer how she arrives at the assumption in q, and thus wants to put aside her own beliefs for the sake of the argument. When a teacher says to the class *If two and two make four, four is an even number*, she is "putting aside" her knowledge of the fact that two and two make four not to suggest that there is any possibility that the assumption is false, but to present it as background leading to q. In other words, p is used in arriving at a statement, but is not itself asserted. The reason why it is not taken as an assertion might well be that it has been communicated before, in a class that has come to talk about even numbers, and so need not be asserted here. Here the epistemic distance arises not on the contextual basis of one interlocutor quoting the other's previous utterance, but on a basis of a speaker's reliance on knowledge common to all participants, quoting an assumption acquired earlier in the history of the exchanges among the participants.

Another interesting, though uncommon, case is when the protasis of a non-predictive sentence contains an assumption which is manifest in the speech setting, to both the speaker and the hearer, and was not communicated either in the preceding or broader context. An example is (5), said to someone eating a steak:

(5)   If you're having a steak, you're not a vegetarian.

The assumption in the protasis will not be interpreted as expressing an assertion of the belief that *p* is true, even though *p* may be true to the hearer and is at least manifest to the speaker. It is precisely with respect to the manifestness that it is highly unlikely that the speaker would want to tell the hearer that *p*, as this would have no communicative effect. But the whole sentence may be an introduction to saying something like *But you may like vegetarian food once you try it*, which refers to the conclusion drawn in *q* of (5). The example shows again that the purpose of putting an assumption in the scope of *if* is to show that, and how, it is used in arriving at assumptions which can be communicated with appropriate contextual effect. Giving such relationships explicitly saves the hearer processing effort. It is thus the act of expressing the protasis, rather than the content expressed, which gives rise to new contextual effects.

The way in which *if* marks epistemic distance in (5) is similar to what happens in the case of *If two and two make four . . .* Since *p* is manifest to both the speaker and the hearer, the speaker may refer to the assumption as contextually bound even though it has not been asserted in previous discourse – it is enough that it is present in the speech setting.

So far I have been talking about the cases of epistemic distance where the speaker does not present *p* as *her* belief, but is not inclined to object to its validity. There are also instances, however, where an assumption communicated or implied by the hearer as true is not immediately accessible to the speaker of an ensuing conditional as being possibly true. A sentence like (6):

(6)   If she called last night, it was while I was out.

refers to the assumption the hearer holds that X called the speaker the night before. The speaker did not receive the call, however, and needs to reconcile two contradicting assumptions: that of the hearer (X called) and her own (X did not call). She does not want to show distrust in the hearer's words and comes up with an explanation which reconciles what the hearer says with what the speaker knows.

The speaker may also be left genuinely puzzled by the assumption in question. In (3) above (*If I ever read this book, I have forgotten it altogether*), there seems to be a suggestion that the book should be known to her even though she has no recollection of reading it. The issue is left unresolved, for the speaker cannot call up additional evidence in favor of or against the suggested assumption.

As Akatsuka shows, a non-predictive protasis may also be meant by the speaker as an outright rejection of the truth of the hearer's words. This is the case of the so-called indicative counterfactuals like (7), which I quote after Akatsuka (1986):

(7)   If you're the Pope, I'm the Empress of China.

Sentence (7) (which was briefly mentioned in chapter 1) is a purportedly authentic reply of a telephone operator to a caller identifying himself as the Pope. Offering a blatantly false, and also blatantly irrelevant conclusion as necessarily derivable from *p*, it thus presents *p* as false. The difference between Akatsuka's account of such conditionals and a truth-conditional one is that in terms of material implication *p* can only be treated as false, while an account based on the effect of the speech exchange allows us to motivate the conditional marking of these protases via an understanding of the fact that *p* is treated as "true" to the hearer but "false" to the speaker. In this case, however, in contrast with (6), the speaker is not trying to find a reconciliation between the hearer's belief and her own. Her purpose in putting *p* in the scope of *if* is to mark epistemic distance – to indicate unwillingness to assert *p* as the speaker's belief. The interpretation of (7) as a complete rejection of *p*'s truth arises from the speaker's further distancing herself from *p* by drawing an implausible conclusion from it.

The non-predictive protases analyzed above differ with respect to the source of the assumptions they contain, as well as with respect to the degree of epistemic distance marked. What they share is that the speaker does not take the responsibility for asserting *p*. This is, then, the kind of non-assertiveness signaled in *if*-clauses whose verb forms are not backshifted, following general rules for tense use. This should not be surprising, as the protases discussed above are in fact independent assumptions – either literally communicated or potentially communicable.

4.2   Future protases of non-predictive conditionals

An added advantage of the interpretation of non-predictive protases which is offered above is that it provides us with an explanation of the use of verb forms in a group of conditional constructions which have so far escaped a convincing and uniform explanation. This is the class of constructions with *will* in their protases.

There are essentially two types of such constructions. The first type has been described (e.g. by Quirk, Greenbaum, Leech, and Svartvik 1985) as the use involving volition. Thus, in sentences such as *If you will look after our luggage,*

I'll go and get a taxi the speaker is in fact making an indirect request, asking the hearer to look after the luggage. The same content could have been expressed through a question, as in *Will you look after the luggage? I could go and get a taxi then*. Other similar uses associated with the types of modalities expressed by *will* might be described in terms of "insistence," as in *If you will watch TV in the dark, what can you expect?*, which can be glossed as "If you watch TV in the dark, you should not be surprised if it affects you (e.g. your eyes hurt). But you will do it!"

Recently Fillmore (1990b) has offered a re-interpretation of *will*-protases (and other related uses of *will* outside conditionals) as the expressions of the positive interests of the participants. This explains why (8) and (9) are easily interpretable, while (10) and (11) seem odd:

(8)   If you would speak to my father about that, I might get permission to go.
(9)   If the sun'll shine, we'll be able to have our picnic.
(10)   ?If you would speak to my father about that, we'd get into serious trouble.
(11)   ?If it'll rain, we'll have to cancel the picnic.

In (8) and (9) the protasis and the apodosis present desirable developments, while (10) and (11) are odd in that they present undesirable situations as if they were in the participant's positive interests.

It seems that Fillmore's interpretation covers the so-called volitional uses, as well as many others, and describes the intended meanings more adequately than the previous accounts. But it is restricted to sentences which I would call predictive, that is those which have predictions (distanced or not) in their apodoses. Under the interpretation advocated here, (8) and (9) seem to be saying that the situations described in *p* are not predictable, but desired, precisely because they result in (and allow the conditional prediction of) other desirable situations. (NB, (10) and (11) will be acceptable if for some unusual reason the speaker desires to be in trouble or to have the picnic canceled).

Non-volitional uses of *will* in *if*-clauses have also been addressed in several papers. Close (1980) sees the contrast between the present tense and *will* in the protasis as that between "prediction" and "likelihood" respectively. Haegeman and Wekker (1984) view the problem in syntactic terms, assigning the *if*-clauses with *will* to the class of "peripheral" clauses, which either are comments on speech acts or "provide a motivation why the proposition is expressed in the way and at the time it is expressed" (1984: 487). Comrie (1982, 1986) notes that *will* appears in the *if*-clauses which are "contextually given," and that such sentences are often not sequential. This seems to refer to examples like (12):

(12)   If he won't arrive before nine, there's no point in ordering for him.

Sentences like (12), as I argued in chapters 2 and 3 are non-predictive. This would suggest that we in fact have two distinct uses of *will* in protases, one expressing positive interest and found in predictive sentences, the other contextually bound and found in non-predictive sentences. However, there are also sentences like (13) and (14), the protases of which do not seem to be contextually bound, and which are also not predictive in the sense postulated in chapter 2.

(13)   If you will be alone on Christmas Day, let us know now.
(14)   If it will amuse you, I'll tell you a joke.

Sentence (13), quoted from Close (1980), is an attested example. It appeared in a poster on the door of a social welfare institution, two weeks before Christmas. The use of *will* in its protasis is difficult to explain; and backshifting the verb along the lines of predictive constructions (*If you are alone on Christmas Day . . .*) creates an uninterpretable result, for the sentence then instructs the hearer to wait two weeks, see if he is alone, and then go back in time to tell the social welfare people about it.

The second example is quoted from Comrie (1986). Comrie argues, and the argument can be extended to (13), that the sentence differs from the most common constructions with *will* in the *if*-clause in that the *if*-clause is not contextually given in the way it is, for instance, in (12) above. I would like to add that (14) is also not predictive, because backshifting the protasis into *If it amuses you . . .* changes the interpretation again. The backshifted version might elicit a generic interpretation of the protasis, or, as in the case of (13), possibly calls for a sequential, predictive interpretation, such that the joke will be told after it has caused amusement. It would seem, then, that the "positive interest" interpretation does not apply to either (13) or (14), because neither of them is predictive. Also, while being amused may be desired, being alone on Christmas Day normally is not: indeed, the poster is based on an assumption that it is undesirable.

Comrie's explanation of (14) is that *will* signals a "bicausal" interpretation (prospective amusement causes telling a joke, the joke causes amusement). This, however, seems to be an isolated explanation of an isolated example. As I argued in Dancygier 1993, the protasis of (14) contains a condition relevant to the present making of the offer: the speaker offers to tell a joke, but leaves it to the hearer to decide whether he wants to hear one. Sweetser (1990) has also argued convincingly that (14) should be interpreted along the lines she suggests for other speech act conditionals, with the protasis spelling out the reasons for making the offer to tell a joke. The example is thus no longer isolated with respect to its causal structure, but the use of *will* still remains to be explained.

As I argued in earlier work (Dancygier 1988a, 1993) the use of *will* in (13) and (14) can be explained along the same lines as (12) above, namely, as a predictive use. The reason why (12) has been seen as different from (13) and (14) is that its protasis (under its most natural interpretation) is a very clear example of contextual boundness, for apparently someone has said that *p*. Under the analysis advocated above, someone made the prediction that "X won't arrive before nine," which the speaker quotes, not making the prediction herself, but basing the following clause on it. It is thus a use of a predictive assumption in a non-predictive construction: *p* predicts, or cites a prediction (and is thus marked with *will*), but the conditional construction itself does not make use of *p* to **predict q**, and it is thus not a predictive conditional. The same can be said about (13) and (14), which are not contextually bound.

Pieter Nieuwint (1986) also claims that *will* in conditional protases is essentially predictive, and contrasts such *if*-clauses with those having Present tense and future (or, as he argues, non-past) reference, which, in his view, are concerned with events, not predictions. However, he also claims that these two interpretations of the protases arise independently of the relation between *p* and *q*. I agree with Nieuwint in my analysis of *will* protases of (12), (13), and (14) as expressing a prediction, but I see this aspect of the interpretation as a part of the overall characterization of the construction. Thus, we need to say that while the *will* in (12), (13), and (14) is predictive, the whole constructions are not. In fact, the use of predictive *will* in a protasis is restricted to non-predictive conditional constructions. This follows necessarily from our understanding of predictive conditionals. Both *if* and *when* present a clause *p* as background to a prediction made in *q* – the predictive relationship between *p* and *q* is asserted, but the *p* clause itself is neither asserted nor predicted. Only in a non-predictive conditional, therefore, can a predictive *will* occur in *p*.

The "prediction interpretation" gives us a common denominator for all *will* protases except "positive interest" ones, which involve a different modality, probably based not on predictive modality but on volitionality. But it does not provide us with a full explanation of the way in which essentially the same kind of epistemic distance is marked in (12), which is contextually bound, as in (13) and (14), which are not. What is shared between these examples is that the predictions in the *will*-protases are clearly not to be attributed to the speaker, but to the hearer (or the context as seen from the hearer's viewpoint). Thus, in (13) and (14), as in other non-predictive constructions, the protases express assumptions which the speaker does not want to be responsible for. In (13) the hearer is requested to make a prediction about being (or not being) alone on Christmas Day. If his prediction is that he will be alone, he is asked to inform the agency about it. His prediction, according to the interpretation offered above, will be taken as well grounded, and thus he can expect the social welfare people to offer an alternative way of spending the holiday. In (14), very similarly, the hearer is asked to decide whether he will be amused by a joke (some people usually are not). If he can predict that he will be amused, it makes sense for the speaker to make her offer, but otherwise it does not. Thus in (12), the speaker is using *will* in the same predictive sense as in (13) and (14); and as in (13) and (14), the prediction is not hers.

The difference is that in (12) we might assume that the prediction has already been overtly made by the hearer, and can thus be quoted, while in (13) and (14) the hearer is invited to make it, and the consequences of his making it are presented in *q*. The essential difference, then, between *If it rains, the match will be canceled* on the one hand and (12), (13), and (14) on the other, is that in the former case the protasis assumes *the speaker's perspective*, while in the latter ones *p* expresses what is more likely to be *the hearer's perspective*. In the "rain" example the speaker is making a prediction (the apodosis), while at the same time signaling that there is an additional necessary assumption (the protasis) which she cannot predict. In the sentences with *will* protases, the speaker is not making any prediction herself, but communicates *q* as a speech act justified against the background of a prediction which only the hearer can make.

To sum up, there seem to be two types of uses of *will* in conditional protases: one is the "positive interest" use connected with predictive constructions, the other represents the hearer's, rather than the speaker's perspective. The latter use is characteristic of non-predictive conditionals.

4.3   Epistemic distance, hearer's perspective, and the type of *p/q* relation

As we have seen above, the epistemic distance marked in the protases of non-predictive conditionals is perhaps better explained in terms of the hearer's perspective than through contextual boundness alone, especially since contextual boundness, as I have described it, is a much broader category than previous understandings of contextual givenness. The concept of the hearer's perspective is also perhaps more useful in explaining why non-predictive inferential sentences are often mere "displays" of possible inferences – that is, why the speaker uses the whole conditional where the conclusion in the apodosis would apparently have been sufficient. Suppose the speaker has been informed that "they left at nine," has accepted this information as an assumption, and has concluded from it that "they have arrived home by now." If the speaker wishes to communicate her conclusion, she has two options. She may simply announce her conclusion (*they have arrived home by now*), or she can use the hearer's point of view to show him what contextual implications his assertion licenses (*If they left at nine, they have arrived home by now*). In so doing, she exposes her reasoning processes and invites the hearer to share them. This communicative goal explains why the speaker would explicitly communicate an assumption that the hearer shares with her at some contextual level.

It seems, then, that an earlier mention in the context alone does not offer a sufficient explanation of epistemic distance, and consequently, of non-predictive conditionality. Indeed, predictive sentences do not lend themselves to inferential interpretations even if their protases are recoverable from context: as we have seen, they are invariably sequential and causal. Thus in a sentence like (15) an inferential interpretation will not be possible, even though it may be preceded by a discussion about the subject's prospective marriage to John:

(15)   If she marries John, she'll quit her job.

The contextual source of the protasis of (15) can be made explicit by adding an appropriate comment to the protasis, as in *If she marries John, and we both know/you say/everybody says she will, she'll quit her job*. Still, it seems to me, an inferential interpretation is not a plausible one. Apparently, a protasis of a predictive sentence, even if recovered from the context, is used differently from the protasis of a non-predictive one and is not contextually bound in the sense discussed here. It marks the speaker's rather than the hearer's perspective.

Predictive conditionals, then, formulate their protases independently of their context, while non-predictive inferential ones present the content of their *p*'s from the hearer's perspective, using the contextual resources shared by the participants.

Another interesting issue is how the contextual grounding and the type of unassertability relate to the type of the relation between *p* and *q*. We have seen in chapter 3 that predictive sentences are invariably sequential and causal. On the basis of what has been said so far, it is tempting to claim that non-predictive ones, which are contextually grounded and mark epistemic distance, are never causal at the same time. Examples such as *If he had lasagne for lunch, he won't want spaghetti for dinner* seem at first glance to be candidates for a causal analysis – the eating of lasagne for lunch might be a possible cause of refusing Italian food for dinner. However, as Sweetser (1990) has argued, in epistemic conditionals the causal relations between the states of affairs described in *p* and *q* are completely independent of the epistemic conditional relationship itself.

Admittedly, causality may have some role in the processing of a non-predictive construction, especially an inferential one. Inferences are drawn from premises, but the conclusions they lead to may also be licensed by other assumptions which never appear explicitly in the inferential chain proper. In (2) above the unspoken assumptions are that a passenger can only appear in the airport lobby after the plane has landed and that the expected time of arrival of the plane transporting her is still ahead. In (5) the conclusion is justified by the knowledge that vegetarians do not eat meat, and in (6) by the fact of the speaker not having received the call. In some instances, the conclusion is licensed by the knowledge of a causal assumption. This seems to be the case in (16):

(16)   If you drank some milk straight from the bottle, it will turn sour by tomorrow.

Sentence (16) presents an inference the speaker can draw out of the contextually grounded assumption that the hearer drank some milk straight from the bottle. The inference is licensed by the assumption that drinking non-pasteurized milk straight from the bottle results in the contents turning sour in one day. The apodosis is a prediction, but the conditional construction presents the *if*-clause as an explanation of how the speaker arrived at this prediction, rather than as a cause of the predicted state of affairs (as would have been the case if (16) were a predictive conditional construction). As it is, the prediction in *q* is a non-conditional, independent prediction, justified by a contextually bound assumption about the hearer having drunk some milk straight from the bottle, and licensed by the knowledge of what makes milk turn sour. Causality thus constitutes a part of the interpretation, but only as a background assumption, not an aspect of the content. Its status is similar to that found in full-stop utterances with non-iconic clause order, like *She slipped. The road was icy*, which use the second sentence to explain the cause of the event in the first one, but do not assert causality at any level.

Interestingly enough, inferential conditional constructions can be ambiguous with respect to the underlying assumptions which license them:

(17)   If Greg read chapter 4, he understands Verner's Law.

With the assumption that one has to understand Verner's Law to be able to successfully read chapter 4, (17) can be interpreted as a temporally reversed construction in which *p* is used to draw a conclusion about Greg's understanding of Verner's Law prior to reading. It is thus a case of inferring a cause (or an enabling factor) from knowledge of its effect. However, if the speaker believes the reading of chapter 4 to be a step towards a proper understanding of Verner's Law, the sentence's presentation of the sequence of described states of affairs is not temporally reversed, and is an instance of reasoning from knowledge about the cause (or enabling factors) to a conclusion about its expected effect. Under this reading (17) can be paraphrased as "If (as I have grounds to assume) Greg read chapter 4, I can conclude that he now understands Verner's Law as a result." The sentence is thus essentially epistemic, but based on the knowledge of a causal chain of which the sequence "*p, q*" is an instance.

Humans readily engage in reasoning from known causal factors to likely effects, and also from known effects to likely causes of those effects. They may also base inferences on non-causal factors, in particular on regular correlations of any kind. As Sweetser (1990) has observed, this means that inferential sequences will simply be orthogonal to the causal sequence of the state of affairs reasoned about. We may well need to construct causal relations between the contents of *p* and *q* to understand inferences presented in epistemic conditionals; but the conditional construction marks the relation between a premise and an inference, not the relation between the contents of those belief-structures.

We can conclude now that, in accordance with the earlier suggestion, predictive conditionals involve causality and their protases are marked for "not-knowableness" and "non-predictableness," while protases expressing epistemic distance (contextual grounding, hearer's perspective) are not causal in the same way. And indeed, the protasis of (16) cannot be construed as "not knowable," because it refers to the past – and the past is "knowable," though it does not have to be known to the speaker directly.

Let me note that sentences like (16) make a prediction in the apodosis but are not termed predictive conditionals. This is because the term was coined to refer to sentences reflecting predictive (rather than, for example, inferential) reasoning, and using backshifted (rather than non-predictive, unmarked) verb forms. Just as the presence of the prediction in the protasis did not make a predictive construction, now the presence of the prediction in the apodosis also does not on its own make the conditional predictive. Predictions can be used as premises, and apparently they can also be arrived at as conclusions. But both of these situations are different from a predictive conditional, which involves a special type of protasis leading to a predictive apodosis via an assertion of a causal relation between them.

We have seen, then, how the choice of verb forms in different conditional constructions is indicative of various aspects of the construction's meaning, among others, of the type of reasoning, the type of relation between *p* and *q*, and of the type of unassertability indicated by the presence of *if*.

4.4   Contextually bound questions

In the discussion above, I have dealt mainly with the examples of non-predictive conditionals which had apodoses in declarative form. However, interesting questions seem to arise in the analysis of non-predictives whose apodoses are questions. The discussion was opened by Van der Auwera (1986), who distinguishes between "questions about a conditional" and "conditional questions." The former class is represented by sentences like *If you buy a house, will you redecorate it yourself?*, and can be described within the framework advocated here as questions about predictive conditionals, where the inquiry is about there being (or not being) a causal or enablement relation between the proposition of *p* and that of *q*. The latter have been described in earlier chapters as non-predictive speech act conditionals, such as *If it's not rude to ask, when did you come home last night?*

However, there seem to be some examples of conditionals with interrogative apodoses which very much resemble conditional questions, but differ from them in some respects. An example was first noted by Holdcroft (1971) and is then extensively discussed by Van der Auwera (1986), who calls it the "Holdcroft question":

(18)   If you saw John, did you speak to him?

Example (18), as Van der Auwera notes, is not quite a question about a conditional, that is, it does not ask a question about there being a relation between seeing John and speaking to him, and yet it is not a conditional question, as it does not directly refer to conversational rules. In view of the criteria used in section 3.4, it should also be seen as different from typical speech act conditionals in that it is not an idiomatic politeness device and that its protasis is not specifically meant to accompany a question.

Sweetser considers (18) to be a conditional speech act, along with Austin's *If you are hungry, there are biscuits on the sideboard.* Her example is (19):

(19)   If you went to the party, was John there?

In these sentences, as Sweetser argues, the speech act in the apodosis is presented as conditional on some factor expressed in the protasis. They also invoke rules of appropriateness, but implicitly. Under this interpretation, a question is felicitously asked if the hearer can be assumed to know the answer, which in particular may depend on his having seen John or having participated in the party.

However, not all such examples invoke rules of appropriateness. As Sweetser notes, the sentence given here as (20) is still more "implicit" than (19), as it can be interpreted to mean that the party-going provides the background against which the question can be asked:

(20)   If you went to the party, did you see John?

And yet, (20) does not seem to be much different from (19), since they can both be understood as questions about whether the hearer managed to see John at the party. They both seem to be markedly different from other speech act conditionals, in that, among other things, they are neither politeness devices nor specifically connected with a given speech act.

It seems that the class of speech act conditionals, as it now stands, is too broad, for it includes two types of sentences with markedly different types of protases. Some speech act protases contain fossilized expressions meant to make a given speech act more appropriate, while others present spontaneously coined assumptions meant to provide some background to the speech act in the apodosis. There is no reason why these "background conditions," as we can temporarily call the protases of (18), (19), and (20), should be in any way specially identified as conditions on speech acts, for any kind of utterance can in fact be communicated along with an assumption which contextualizes the main message. In particular, many varieties of contextualizing assumptions can precede the utterance and, if such an assumption is also non-assertive, it can be given the form of a conditional protasis.

Another very important difference between examples like (18)–(20) and the kind of speech act conditionals discussed in chapter 3 is that the protases of such sentences are normally understood as given, or, in my terminology, contextually bound. (This difference in fact motivated Van der Auwera's separate treatment of [18].) And contextual boundness, as we saw in the sections above, is not in itself a useful parameter for classifying conditionals, but is connected with a specific epistemic status of the assumption in the scope of *if*. What is more, contextual boundness has so far been seen as characteristic of epistemic conditionals.

It seems that the special character of the Holdcroft question and of Sweetser's "implicit" (or "background") conditions lies not so much in the form or interpretation of the protasis, but rather in the fact that the apodosis is a question. It is because of the sentence type in the apodosis that these sentences are not classified with epistemic conditionals, because epistemic conditionals have conclusions in their apodoses and thus require a declarative sentence type and reject a question. Apparently, then, the view so far (though not explicitly stated) has been that speech act conditionals have protases that are "conversationally bound" and apodoses of various sentence types, including questions, while epistemic conditionals have protases that are contextually bound and declarative apodoses. As examples (18)–(20) seem to suggest, there are conditionals which have contextually bound protases and non-declarative apodoses. Van der Auwera and Sweetser prefer to group these with speech act conditionals. And yet, there seem to be many significant similarities between (18)–(20) ("background" conditionals) and epistemic constructions.

First, the protases of "background" conditionals are coined spontaneously, and express assumptions appropriate to a given speech event, not speech act. The same can be claimed for epistemic conditionals. Also, the protases of "background" conditionals and epistemic conditionals obligatorily precede their apodoses, while those in speech act conditionals preferably follow their *q*'s. The protases of "background" and epistemic conditionals cannot be pronounced with sentence-final intonation, while those in speech act conditionals can. Finally, let us recall, epistemic and "background" protases can be contextually bound, while the ones in speech act constructions cannot.

The above observations point to numerous similarities between the protases of epistemic and "background" conditionals. However, there is also an important difference between the two types of sentences. In epistemic conditionals the main clause is often introduced by *then*, while in speech act constructions and in "background" conditionals *then* is not acceptable. These restrictions seem to be related to the nature of the relation between the protasis and the apodosis (see section 6.3 for further comments on the use of *then*).

There remains the question of the form of the apodosis. Van der Auwera claims that the Holdcroft question has no counterparts among imperatives and assertions, for the conditionals that can be coined with a protasis like *If you saw John* are speech acts about conditionals. His examples are (21) and (22):

(21)   If you saw John, tell Mary about it.
(22)   If you saw John, then you saw that he is no longer the happy-go-lucky chap of five years ago.

In Van der Auwera's interpretation in (21) and (22) seeing John itself is a condition for seeing what kind of person he is or telling Mary about it. That is to say, Van der Auwera sees such sentences as conditionals in the content domain, or as expressions of the causal relation between *p* and *q*. Several arguments can be raised against that interpretation. First, both sentences can be paraphrased to reveal the fact that the relation holds between assumptions, not states of affairs, as in *If you saw John, as you said you were going to, then I assume you can tell Mary about it and I am asking you to do so* and *If you saw John as you said you were going to, then I conclude you saw that X/then you must have seen that X/then it means you also saw that X*. In the case of (22), the affinity to epistemic conditionals cannot be doubted, in the case of (21) the similarities are also striking, even though the apodosis is not a conclusion. Furthermore, it does not seem to be the case that the causal relation is in fact asserted in (21) and (22) as it is in predictive constructions. As in the case of (16) above, it is presented as the background against which conclusions are drawn.

As a final criterion we can consider the kinds of answers the questions above can evoke. A question about a predictive construction, such as *If you buy a house, will you redecorate it yourself?*, can be answered in essentially three ways: *Yes, I will*, or *No, I won't*, or with a full sentence, such as *Yes, if I buy a house, I will redecorate myself*. In other words, the answer concerns the validity of the prediction of *p* against the background of *q*, and will not be understood as addressing *p* alone or *q* alone. If the hearer finds the condition improbable, he may explicitly say so, but then he may well also refuse to give a straightforward answer to the question in *q*, saying instead something like *I don't think I'll buy a house, so why bother about redecorating it*.

In the answers to questions contained in conditionals typically assigned to the speech act class, such as *When did you come home last night, if I may ask?*, any direct reference to the protasis is inappropriate. That is, *Yes, you may* will not be quite felicitous because it puts unnecessary emphasis on the participant's authority to decide whether the other interlocutor may or may not ask a question. On the other hand, *No, you may not* would be considered rude because it bluntly deprives the speaker of her right to make inquiries, and we can expect that the speaker ventures to ask a question when she has reasons to believe that it is appropriate. If the hearer does not want to answer the question he would probably say something similar to *Sorry, but I'd rather not talk about it* – depending on how polite he himself chooses to be. Finally, in some contexts the hearer may deny the speaker's right to ask, but give an answer anyway, especially if it confirms the answer the speaker expected (consider *You have no right to ask, but yes, it was past midnight*).

In sentences like (18) the protasis is naturally treated as an independent assumption. The simplest case is the situation in which the hearer did indeed see John and does not need to comment on this assumption any more. He will then just answer the question posed in *q*, as in *Yes, I did. He told me . . .* He may, however, choose to confirm the plausibility of the assumption in *p* and only then give an answer – a positive or negative one – to *q*, but he will have to use a coordinate construction, not a conditional one: *Yes, I saw him and I spoke to him*, or *I did indeed see him, but I didn't speak to him*. It seems that the same independence of assumptions in *p* and *q* marks the clauses of (21) and (22), as can be seen in *I did indeed see him, but I don't feel like telling Mary about it* or *Yes, I saw him, but I don't think he has changed so much*. Thus the protases of "background" conditionals, similarly to epistemic ones, can be evaluated by the hearer separately from their apodoses with respect to how they fit with the rest of his beliefs. They thus stand in contrast to both predictive protases, which are difficult to consider separately, and speech act ones, which can be evaluated separately with respect to rules of appropriateness, not the content of the clause.

There is perhaps one more interesting aspect of some of the examples of epistemic and "background" conditionals. Apparently, their protases often extract an aspect of the full utterance of the apodosis – the one whose factuality is questioned by the speaker. Instead of saying *If you went to the party, was John there?* one could plausibly ask *Was John at the party you were planning to go to?*, and instead of *If you saw John, did you speak to him? – Did you speak to John when you were supposed to see him?* More examples of this kind can be found: *If you paid five guineas for this rug, it was a bargain*, which can be interpreted as *Paying five guineas for this rug was a bargain*. The difference in each of these cases is that the conditional construction questions the factuality of a particular aspect of the event described, and also topicalizes it, by presenting it as a ground against which the validity of the apodosis is to be evaluated.

The conclusion, then, is that the protases of both epistemic and "background" conditionals seem to contain assumptions of the same type, with contextual boundness being perhaps their most salient feature. They are assumptions about "knowable" facts – events and states of affairs – not known directly to the speaker.

This revision results in a further refinement of the proposed classification of conditionals. The class of predictives remains the same: predictive constructions are characterized by patterns of verb forms which reflect predictive reasoning, special status of the apodosis (marked with *if*-backshift), causal link between *p* and *q*, and the possibility of using hypothetical, distanced forms. Non-predictive conditionals, on the other hand, are free in their choice of verb forms and are generally not distanced and not causal on the propositional level. They fall into two subclasses. The first group of constructions, which I will call *conversational*, can be characterized with respect to several features: their apodoses perform their speech acts independently of the content of the protases, because the protases are only comments on the appropriateness of the speech acts performed or the linguistic forms used. *Then* is typically not used in such constructions, and protases rarely precede their apodoses. Thus, conversational conditionals involve speech act and metatextual relations, as defined in chapter 3.

The second subclass of non-predictive constructions is characterized mainly with respect to the type of epistemic distance attributed to the speaker's conditional presentation of the protasis (contextual grounding, hearer's perspective, or evidential distance). I have referred to this class as ***contextually grounded*** (or ***bound***). Such protases typically precede their apodoses, because they are often background conditions on the content of the main clause. They often present the apodosis as a conclusion to be drawn from the protasis, and the order of clauses is then iconic of inferential reasoning (Sweetser's epistemic conditionals). But inference is not the only type of reasoning involved, as the same type of protases are found to provide background for a variety of speech acts: decisions (*If she's giving the baby a bath, I'll call back later*), suggestions (*If he won't come before nine, there's no use ordering for him*), requests (*If you will be alone on Christmas Day, let us know now*), directives (*If you went to the lecture, tell me about it*), and questions (*If you saw John, did you speak to him?*).

The class of non-predictive conditionals can thus be characterized with respect to two parameters: the type of relation between **p** and **q**, and the type of protasis. The former parameter defines the classes of epistemic, speech act, and metatextual conditionals, while the latter divides non-predictive constructions into those which have contextually bound protases, and those which have conversational ones. In the discussion above, I argued that epistemic conditionals typically have contextually bound protases, while speech act conditionals occur freely with protases of both types. As regards metatextual conditionals, they are commonly concerned with appropriateness of linguistic expressions used (as in *My husband, if I can still call him that, hates onion soup*) and thus their protases are typically conversational. However, the occurrence of contextually bound protases is not ruled out in principle. It is possible for a self-critical speaker to respond to the hearer's remark about his hair being grey by incorporating the remark into the protasis, as in *If **your** hair is grey, what do you call **mine**?* It is clearly a comment on the use of the word *grey* (as possibly more descriptive of the speaker's hair than of the hearer's), which gives the sentence a metatextual interpretation, but the protasis is contextually bound, for it picks up the description the hearer offered and puts it in the scope of *if* to mark the speaker's epistemic distance from the hearer's statement. To conclude, then, contextually bound protases are found among all subtypes of non-predictive conditionals.

In the next section I will go back to examples from Vonnegut's *Hocus Pocus* to see if the above characterization of non-predictive protases is confirmed by the use of conditionals in the novel.

4.5   Non-predictive protases in the context of a narrative

In the text of *Hocus Pocus* there are twenty-seven examples of non-predictive conditionals – relatively few, if compared with the abundance of predictive ones. They represent all classes discussed earlier: speech act, inferential, and metatextual ones. They also represent different degrees and types of distance in their protases. Let us look at some more interesting sentences.

All the examples represent some form of contextual grounding. In the majority of cases the protases represent a tentative acceptance of some aspect of the interpretation of the preceding text, as in (23), a speech act conditional, or (24), an epistemic one:

(23)   If I was wrong, sir, I apologize.
(24)   But if he is still alive, he . . . is a grown-up now.

Sentence (24) is a response to a statement from an indignant father: *I can never forgive you for accusing my son of theft.* The protasis, *If I was wrong*, does not quote the statement in question; it also does not in any way indicate whether the narrator believes that he was wrong or that he was not. As the discussion in the previous sections indicates, this is possibly the most common example of a non-predictive conditional protasis – contextually grounded and tentative, not directly representative of the speaker's beliefs or knowledge. The conditional in (24) is quite similar. It refers to a boy whom the narrator met briefly in his youth, and who then disappeared from the narrator's life. Again, the protasis cannot be unambiguously interpreted to mean that the boy is alive or is not – this is one of those things that are "knowable," but not known. And yet the speculation about the boy is contextually grounded in the preceding story, though not in any specific sentence of that story.

There are also examples of protases brought up from the context to express doubt or to show the contrast between the speaker's beliefs and newly presented information.

(25)   So, if I did father a child out of wedlock somewhere along the line, that comes as a complete surprise to me.
(26)   If that was in the letter, I must have told his mother that.

Both sentences come from the part of the story where a young man appears claiming to be the narrator's son. The young man refers to various "facts" about the narrator's life, which he learned from a letter his mother wrote just before she died. (25) is what the narrator says to the man, precisely to show that he is shocked and puzzled by the news, as this is the first time he hears about having an illegitimate child. (26) is his comment on the revelations the letter contained, which, as it is clear to the reader, are not true; the narrator simply does not remember what he told the woman about himself. Thus in both cases the function of the conditional construction is to reconcile the incredible with the known. The content of both protases is grounded in the story, but is neither actually quoted from the addressee's discourse, nor presented as given (in the sense of "accepted by the speaker as true").

A closer look at how the narrator uses the context in conditional protases shows that the possibilities are infinitely more complex and interesting than simple quotation or even paraphrase of the previous discourse by other participants. In (27), for instance, we can see the narrator using conditional protases to spell out his thoughts, at the same time showing the reader a possible misinterpretation of the stand he takes:

(27)   If I say that the Trustees . . . were dummies . . . I hope it is understood that I
        consider myself the biggest dummy of all . . . And if I feel that my father was
        a horse's fundament and my mother was a horse's fundament, what can I be
        but another horse's fundament?

As a matter of fact, both protases are new in the discourse context. Some negative evaluation of both the Trustees and the narrator's parents was perhaps a possible interpretation of the preceding 145 pages, but it is the first time that any such pronouncement is made clearly. So what the narrator seems to be saying is something like "You thought I was trying to say that all these people are dummies (perhaps in contrast with myself), but that contrast at least was not a justified inference." And it is precisely the function of *if* here to signal that the sentences used in *p*'s and starting with *I say* and *I feel* are in fact meant to mean "You think I am saying/implying" or "You think I feel." This is what I called "a hearer's perspective" in the sections above.

In (27) "the hearer" whose perspective is taken is the reader. In (28), it is another character, who talks about the narrator's wife and mother-in-law, who are both insane:

(28)   "Funny thing-" he went on, "it never seemed to hit any of them until they
        were middle aged."
        "If I'm not laughing," I said, "that's because I got out on the wrong side of
        the bed today."

The protasis of the narrator's response hinges on the phrase *Funny thing*. The reasoning might be as follows: "You seem to think it's funny that two relatives of mine are insane, so you expect me to be laughing; you can see I'm not laughing, and it's because I don't find it funny; but you obviously haven't thought of how I might feel, so I'll explain my not being amused on the basis of something irrelevant; if I give you an absurd reason for not laughing, perhaps you'll understand it's absurd to call this funny." Regardless of what kind of gloss we provide, the conditional protasis plays a rather crucial role. It takes the hearer's phrase and shows what absurd contextual implications it licenses, thereby reprimanding the hearer for his careless choice of wording. But it is the presence of *if* that accounts for the change of perspective, because it presents the assumption *I'm not laughing* not as a true statement about the speech setting (which it obviously is), but as an assumption the speaker treats as tentative, even though it is manifestly true. This is what triggers the interpretation outlined above.

We have seen, then, that the examples considered confirm the interpretation of epistemic distance and contextual grounding outlined earlier in the chapter. Furthermore, the use of non-predictive conditionals in the text of *Hocus Pocus* seems to support the point made above that while some examples of non-predictive conditionals are unambiguously representative of the main types of protasis/apodosis relations (inferential, metatextual, and speech act), others are less clearly interpretable as just one of those, but still essentially non-predictive. Thus, (24)–(26) are inferential, for they all present conclusions one can draw from the tentative acceptance of the assumptions in their protases. Sentence (23) is a very typical speech act conditional, and so is (29); (30) and (31) are very good examples of metatextual conditionals:

(29)   If you want to know the truth, I hardly sleep at all.
(30)   I didn't have a Chinaman's chance with the Trustees, if I may be forgiven a racist cliche – not with the sex stuff Wilder had concealed in the folder.
(31)   The number of students, if you can call convicts that, is about 2,000 now.

But many other sentences have a more complex interpretation. For example, the sentences in (27) seem to invoke both an inferential and a speech act interpretation. The first one is structured around the verb phrases introducing the protasis (*I say*) and the apodosis (*I hope it is understood that I consider* . . .). At this level the meaning is perhaps more like that of a speech act conditional: "I have said *p*, so I assume it is appropriate to hope that *q*." But the overall interpretation is about the inference relation between the embedded clauses of *p* and *q*: "I have said (or at least suggested) that my parents were dummies, and you should have inferred that I consider myself a dummy as well." The second conditional in (27) has a question in its apodosis, and it looks very much like a "Holdcroft question" or a "background" condition. But it is about an inference again, and it can readily be paraphrased as "what do you conclude I am but another horse's fundament?" That is, the hearer is pushed into the conclusion suggested by the question. It would seem, then, that it is possible to mix the two types of conditional interpretation (inferential and speech act) to achieve a special effect: the sentences do not just draw conclusions, and they do not only "display" reasoning chains to the hearer. By embedding the assumptions actually used in the inference chain in the scope of "tentative belief" verbs, or by asking a rethorical question, they not only provide the intended conclusions, but at the same time reprimand the addressee (the reader) for not having drawn those obvious conclusions on his own (just in case he did not in fact draw them).

There are also interesting examples of interaction between metatextual and inferential readings. A good example of this is (32):

(32)   If there is Divine Providence, there is also a wicked one, provided you agree that making love to off-balance women you aren't married to is wickedness. My own feeling is that if adultery is wickedness then so is food.

Both conditionals in (32) are about how one belief entails another. In this sense they are like more typical inferential conditionals. At the same time, however, the whole reasoning is based on some concept of what can legitimately be called wickedness. The validity of the first instance of conditional reasoning depends on the assumption introduced with *provided* which opens the door to a metatextual interpretation. But in the second conditional the reader learns that the narrator does not in fact subscribe to such a definition of wickedness, because it leads to another conclusion which is unacceptable – that eating food is being wicked. So there is reasoning here, and there is inference, but it revolves around the question of what can legitimately be ***called*** wickedness.

One can also note that both conditionals of (32) have a symmetrical structure, similarly to some more widely discussed instances of metatextual conditionals, like the Robinson Crusoe example, given here as (33):

(33)   If I was a bad carpenter, I was a worse tailor.

Similar structure is also found in many meta-metaphorical conditionals, so labeled by Sweetser (1996a) and briefly mentioned in section 3.5.2. These are sentences like (34) and (35):

(34)   If the Cité is the heart of Paris, the Latin Quarter is its soul.
         (Ducrot 1972)
(35)   If Scarlett O'Hara is a red rose, Melanie Wilkes is a violet.
         (Sweetser 1996a)

In earlier work (Dancygier 1986) I discussed (34) as an instance of a metatextual conditional related to a metaphor portraying cities as bodies. Sweetser

(1996a) describes (35) as motivated by a metaphorical mapping "Women are flowers." She also defines meta-metaphorical conditionals as an independent class.

The second conditional in (32) is not based on metaphor, rather, it is meta-textual in the way in which (33) is. However, one cannot help noticing that the symmetrical structure of the protasis and the apodosis has its role in inviting the "meta" interpretation. It is not incidental that the verb used is *to be* – it links the pairs of objects and labels to be juxtaposed in the two clauses of the conditional. If there is no obvious explanation of the basis on which labels are assigned to objects, the very juxtaposition of two such pairings will let the hearer figure out the underlying principle. The point is that the metaphors underlying (34) and (35), as well as the conventions of label-use which underlie (32) and (33), are made available to the hearer through the sentences themselves. And the symmetrical structure seems to make a major contribution to setting up the mappings. This is, then, yet another instance of form–function relation which is characteristic of a certain type of a conditional construction. Symmetrically structured protases and apodoses will invoke a metatextual interpretation even if there is another type of protasis/apodosis relation holding between p and q.

4.6   Givenness, manifestness, and topicality

As we have seen in the sections above, conditional protases cannot be claimed to be "given" in the proper sense of the term – that is, "presupposed to be true." On the contrary, the function of protases is to present assumptions as for some reason unassertable. The contextual grounding of protases, even in the cases where the protasis does indeed quote a preceding utterance, does not ensure that the speaker necessarily accepts the quoted assumption as true; it may even be the case that she believes it to be false. Like the traditional concept of givenness, the concept of shared knowledge seems to be too strong as well, especially for those cases where the speaker brings up an assumption that was merely implicated in previous discourse, or which was not communicated at all and is only observable in the speech setting. It seems, then, that the most we can claim about such assumptions is that they are accessible to both the hearer and the speaker, though not in any direct manner. Thus "shared accessibility" is perhaps the term that we should substitute for "givenness" and "shared knowledge" in the discussion of conditional protases.

We are still in want of a better explanation of how an uncommunicated assumption can be accessed. The most adequate one that comes to mind is offered by the notion of manifestness, as proposed by Sperber and Wilson

(1986). This notion is first introduced with reference to facts and then extended to assumptions. An assumption is thus manifest if the environment provides sufficient evidence for its adoption, but it can be manifest to a greater or lesser degree. An assumption can be manifest without being known, or even assumed, because assumptions need not be believed to be true. The sources of assumptions which can be manifest to the speaker are varied – including the speech setting – and one can assume that some assumptions which have been communicated can be manifest without being known to be true. This seems to be the case with the assumptions which are sources of some contextually bound protases: whether directly communicated or implicated, they can be represented in *if*-clauses and further considered without being assumed to be true. What is more, the assumptions may be representations of facts which are manifest in the environment. In the context of a date to go to the opera together, a speaker may react to the sight of her boyfriend wearing a T-shirt and a pair of worn out jeans by saying: *If that's how you're going to go to the opera, I'm staying home.* The protasis is again an assumption which is not known by the speaker to be true, which has been acquired indirectly, which does not originate in preceding discourse, and yet which draws an implication from facts which are manifest to the speaker.

Another concept which addresses related issues and is often linked to givenness is that of topicality. In his (1978) paper Haiman made the claim that all conditionals (i.e. conditional protases) are topics, arguing on the basis of data from a variety of languages and of a definition of a topic as given or old information in the sentence, which goes back to Dressler (1974), Firbas (1964), and, importantly, Chafe (1972, 1976). Haiman's claim has usually been seen as too strong. For example, Comrie (1986) quotes Haiman's definitions and adds that conditional protases are not necessarily topical – in particular, protases which are not sentence-initial do not fit standard criteria for topicality. Work by Schiffrin (1992) also shows the relationships between clause order and topicality of conditional protases.

It has also been argued that conditional protases, even if topical, cannot be defined exclusively as being topics. First of all, the data considered by Haiman can apparently be interpreted in a less definitive manner, as was argued by Akatsuka (1986), who offers a somewhat different analysis of some of Haiman's most suggestive evidence from Hua. Jacobsen (1992) shows that Japanese conditionals, which look very much like topics, cannot in fact be described that way, and that the affinity is illusory. Akatsuka (1992) argues further that Japanese conditionals encode the speaker's affect, and not only informational or epistemic relations between clauses. What is more, as

Sweetser (1990) claims, conditional protases which are clearly topics are not the best examples of conditionals, at least in English. The most severe criticism, however, seems to be directed against the assumption made by Haiman that the topicality of the protasis is to be taken as equivalent to its "given" status – that is, its status as old information, or shared knowledge between the speaker and the hearer. The criticism of this assumption is based first of all on the existence of sentences which I have referred to as "contextually bound," which, in spite of being quotations or implications from previous discourse, may mark epistemic/evidential distance, rather than shared knowledge. The significant observation that Akatsuka makes about them is that in Japanese they constitute a separate class, as they are marked with *nara*, not *tara*, which distinguishes other conditionals. *Nara*, in turn, can replace a marker of a contrastive topic. Thus, claims Akatsuka, conditionals can be topics, but contrastive ones, which can be new information. Hence it is untenable that all conditional protases are given.

The critical remarks made by Sweetser (1990) are similarly directed centrally at the idea of topics being necessarily given. As Sweetser puts it: "A protasis is, rather, 'given' in the sense that its acceptance (even if hypothetical) must presumably precede any consideration of the contents of the apodosis: it is given only relative to the apodosis." (1990: 126).

Some of these controversial points can be elucidated by looking again at the original statements made by Haiman:

- "A conditional clause is (perhaps only hypothetically) a part of the knowledge shared by the speaker and the listener. As such, it constitutes the framework which has been selected for the *following* discourse" (1978: 583) (emphasis mine).
- Haiman distinguishes resumptive topics and contrastive ones and defines them both as given. "Resumptive topics are established by previous context. Contrastive topics, however, are selected by the speaker apropos of thoughts which he has not yet communicated to his listener. They must be established as givens by agreement . . . both [kinds of topics, B.D.] are treated as givens *after* being established in their different ways" (1978: 584) (emphasis mine).

Clearly, Haiman is not saying that all conditional protases are shared before they are uttered. He also agrees that contrastive topics present information which has not yet been communicated, that is, new information. They are contrastive, says Haiman, because they are selected from among other possible conditions, and if they are not immediately objected to by the hearer, they give the speaker the right to go on with the apodosis, because by then both the speaker and the hearer share the same frame of reference. The assumptions in conditional protases are then shared only after they are uttered. Consequently, they can then be kept in mind as a frame of reference for the following discourse (the apodoses), in other words, they are given only relative to the apodosis.

Evidently, then, there is in fact much agreement as to the way in which conditional protases are topical, and as to the very fact that they are indeed, in this restricted sense, topical. Conditionals can be seen as topics, provided that their topicality is not identified with givenness, and that the idea of "shared knowledge" is weakened to "shared accessibility." This means that the hearer and the speaker share at least an environment in which the fact represented by the assumption in *p* is manifest. It is still difficult, however, to accept the belief that prototypical conditionality can be defined in terms of topicality alone, especially against the limited understanding of topicality that conditional protases allow. First of all, we would have to be sure that such an understanding of topicality indeed applies to all *if*-clauses, regardless of their position in the sentence. This question will be addressed in the next chapter.

5 Conditional clauses: form and order

In the preceding chapters conditional constructions were characterized with respect to three major parameters: the use of verb forms, the relation between constituent clauses, and the epistemic status of the apodosis. In what follows I will discuss structural features of the construction: the form of the clauses and clause order.

5.1 Constituent clauses of the construction

A standard grammatical characterization of a conditional construction describes it as a complex sentence consisting of the main clause, or the matrix clause, and an adverbial clause of condition which is subordinate to it. Typically, both clauses are structurally complete (that is, the frame provided by the construction requires no deletions or special syntax in the clauses), and they are both declarative in form. In the sections to follow I will give an overview of some varieties of conditional constructions not conforming to this generalization.

5.1.1 Sentence types in the apodosis

Declarative apodoses are often seen as more typical for conditional constructions than interrogative or imperative ones. Linguistic descriptions concentrate on declarative conditionals, and this is carried over to pedagogical approaches, where conditionals with questions or imperatives as q's are discussed separately as exceptions. In truth-functional or logical works on conditionals, on the other hand, non-declaratives, which are uninterpretable in terms of truth value, are often entirely disregarded.

From a purely descriptive point of view, seeing declaratives as more typical apodoses is apparently a matter of statistics rather than of genuine differences in the status of declaratives and non-declaratives as parts of a conditionals structure. Declarative apodoses are certainly more frequent, but the same can be said about independent simple sentences – statements are more common than imperatives and questions, as can be seen even in a cursory review of any language corpus. In what follows I will argue that the overall interpretation of a conditional construction is basically independent of the sentence type in the apodosis.

This lack of restrictions is best seen in the case of questions. Conditionals with interrogative apodoses show the same range of verb-form options shown in declarative conditionals: note, in (1) and (2), the backshifting in the verbs of the protases, as well as the use of *will/would* forms in the apodoses. (1) shows neutral predictive verb forms, (2) standard distanced predictive forms. Both have verb-form patterns identical to parallel non-interrogative conditionals, such as *If I get a raise, I will move to a bigger house*, or *If I got/had got a raise, I would move/have moved to a bigger house*.

(1)   If you get a raise, will you move to a bigger house?
(2)   If you got/had got a raise, would you move/have moved to a bigger house?

Like their declarative counterparts, such questions are interpreted sequentially and causally. Their overall interpretation is thus a question about there being a causal link between the hearer's getting a raise and his decision to move.

As for non-predictive constructions with interrogative apodoses, they were discussed in detail in chapter 4, with the conclusion that they can be interpreted in terms of a variety of relations, not only conversational ones. Non-predictive conditionals are characterized centrally with respect to the special epistemic status of the assumption in the *if*-clause – a status which is often exploited to express doubt as to its truth or to reject it altogether. It is interesting to note how, by means of the speaker's presentation of the protasis in this manner, the interpretation of the apodosis is also significantly altered.

As Sperber and Wilson (1986, 1988) observe, an important factor in interpreting questions is the context, not only in the well-known general sense in which the context is always a factor in interpretation of utterances, but also in a narrower sense. Namely, questions are asked with answers in view (this is why Sperber and Wilson count questions among the cases of what they call "interpretive use"), but the answer (if provided at all) would, in some contexts, be more appropriately addressed to another participant, and not to the speaker (the "questioner"). For example, a speaker asking a rhetorical question does not really expect an answer.

Epistemic/evidential *if*-clauses often induce a framing of an interrogative apodosis as requiring an answer addressed to someone other than the questioner. For instance, questions like *What did you buy aspirin for?*, *Why didn't you write down the answer?*, or *Who knows the answer?*, which in isolation may be interpreted as genuine requests for information, are interpreted in a different manner if they are preceded with *if*-clauses, as in (3)–(5):

(3)   If you are allergic to aspirin, what did you buy these for?
(4)   If you knew the answer, why didn't you write it down?
(5)   If you don't know the answer, who does?

Sentence (3) seeks a reconciliation of contradictory assumptions, while (4), if considered in the context of a typical post-exam student–teacher exchange, shows the hearer that the assumption about his knowing the answer cannot be accepted as true. Thus, in (3) and (4) the potential answer will be primarily important to the hearer. As for (5), it becomes a rhetorical question, and is thus not addressed to anybody in particular. Thus (3)–(5) are interpreted quite differently from independent questions, and, at the same time, similarly to analogous conditionals with declaratives in their apodoses: *If you are allergic to aspirin, you shouldn't have bought these; If you knew the answer, you could have written it down; If you don't know the answer, nobody does.* These examples show that in the case of non-predictive conditionals, as in the case of predictive ones, the fact that the apodosis is a question and not a declarative does not influence the overall interpretation of the construction in a crucial way. The clues offered by verb forms restrict the range of available interpretations in the same manner.

Imperative apodoses have more restricted use than the interrogative ones. First of all, one can form questions using hypothetical (or, in the terminology adopted by some grammars, subjunctive/counterfactual) verb forms, but no such forms can be used in conditional constructions with imperatives. Clearly, this is because the imperative form itself cannot be marked as hypothetical, and, as was shown above, hypothetical backshift has to concern the whole sentence, not just one clause. Consequently, even though imperatives can take predictive protases, they can be marked only with *if*-backshift:

(6)   If the postman comes, let him in.

The claim that conditionals with imperative apodoses do not accept hypothetical forms means simply that one cannot use a hypothetical verb form in the protasis of (6) to convey something like "In an unlikely situation of the postman coming, let him in." If the past form were used (*? If the postman came, let him in*), the protasis would be interpreted as contextually bound, that is, as something like "If, as you say, the postman came some time ago . . ." Even though the sentence is odd and difficult to contextualize with the past form *came*, as the speaker (let us say, a parent instructing a small child over the phone) would probably use a present perfect form *has come*, the main point is not affected. Contextually bound protases, which do not restrict the tense use, can precede imperative apodoses in appropriate contexts (see the discussion of [7]–[9] below), while predictive protases with distanced forms cannot.

Under the interpretation which sees imperatives as derived from futurate sentences with *will*, a predictive interpretation of (6) is quite straightforward, for the imperatives can then be seen as variants of predictive statements. But even if we argue (with Davies 1986) against postulating an underlying unity of imperatives and predictions, there is enough semantic similarity between *let him in* and *you will let him in* to justify the acceptability of (6): both describe future developments which the speaker can expect to occur when the postman comes. As all backshifted constructions, sentences like (6) will also be interpreted sequentially and/or causally to the effect that the future potential occurrence of the situation described in the *if*-clause should prompt the hearer to carry out the action described by the imperative.

As regards non-predictive conditionals, there seem to be no restrictions on their acceptance of imperative apodoses. Imperative utterances can be accompanied by *if*-clauses in classic examples of speech act and metatextual conditionals, such as *Take out the garbage, if I may ask you to, And buy some stamps on the way home, if you can, Don't even talk to my husband, if I can still call him that* (the divorce is in progress). There are also imperative non-predictive constructions with contextually bound protases expressing epistemic distance, as in:

(7)   If you lost your car keys, take my bike today.
(8)   If Mary is coming, buy some wine on the way home.
(9)   If you called the police yourself, don't blame me for the mess they've made.

As in other examples of such non-predictive conditionals, the protases of (7)–(9) present contextually bound assumptions which are not known directly to the speaker and which provide justification for the imperative utterances in the apodoses. The imperatives in the apodoses, as in independent utterances, perform the appropriate directive speech acts. The protases, however, do not express immediate conditions of appropriateness or felicity, and do not constitute grounds for prediction, but spell out the circumstances which prompt the speaker into performing the speech acts in question. The offer to lend a bike has been brought up by the speaker's somehow becoming aware of the car keys being missing, but since the speaker cannot be sure if the hearer is still in need of some means of transportation (the keys might have been found), the offer is made in the context of an epistemically distanced assumption. Similar interpretations can be offered for (8) and (9). We can see, then, that imperative apodoses can be preceded by the majority of types of protases, in predictive (though not hypothetical), as well as non-predictive conditionals.[1]

Evidently, all three basic sentence types can appear as apodoses of conditional constructions and with all types of protases. The only restriction noted is among imperative apodoses, which can stand in causal relations to *p*'s, but cannot be hypothetical. This, however, seems to result from the formal characteristics of the imperative, and not from the implausibility of a certain kind of protasis–apodosis combination. Thus, the sentence type in the apodosis does not seem to limit the array of interpretations a conditional construction can receive. The only limits are imposed by the verb forms and the epistemic status of the protasis.

5.1.2   Elliptical *if*-clauses

If-clauses standardly have the form of declarative sentences, and are introduced into the scope of *if* without changes (except for backshift of the verb forms in the case of predictive conditionals). Sometimes, however, the clauses of a conditional construction are elliptical, that is, they appear to be missing elements which can be recovered from the context. In the most straightforward case, elliptical *if*-clauses (and sometimes also main clauses) are interpreted exactly like their full forms and seem to be reduced merely to avoid repetition, that is, for stylistic reasons. These are sentences like *I'll go, but not if John goes, If not, why not?, If not now, then when?* However, there is a class of elliptical *if*-clauses which requires a different interpretation. These sentences have often been described as concessive. In what follows, however, I will try to revise some of the claims made within this view.

In chapter 3 I delineated a class of conditionals which I called "metatextual," because their *if*-clauses comment on an aspect of the text of the apodosis. Among the examples considered there were sentences which I referred to as "scalar," because the metatextual comment concerned the scalar implicature triggered by the word (text) highlighted by the conditional. One of the examples was (10), which I will consider here along with (11) and (12):

(10)   The Queen of England is happy, if not ecstatic.
(11)   He spoke ungraciously, if not rudely.
(12)   She ate many of the cakes, if not all.

---

[1] Examples (7)–(9) are also interesting if analyzed along the lines suggested by Sperber and Wilson (1986). They are not essentially directive, but describe states of affairs which are desired by someone. In the case of (7) the imperative is meant to satisfy the wish of the hearer, in (9) – of the speaker, and in (8) – of the speaker, but possibly also the hearer, or even the third party (Mary).

Such sentences are, of course, elliptical, but they are obligatorily elliptical, for the counterparts of (10)–(12) with full protases could not be interpreted in the same way (consider *The Queen of England is happy, if she is not ecstatic* or *She ate many of the cakes, if she didn't eat all of the cakes*). They are also consistently ambiguous between two readings: a metatextual one and a concessive one. Further, in their metatextual interpretation they are different from other metatextual examples. First, they are the only metatextual conditionals which seem to require negation (without *not*, [10]–[12] are hardly interpretable); and, second, the negation involved is also metatextual (or metalinguistic, as Horn 1989 would prefer to call it). For example, under the metatextual reading, (10) is not interpreted to mean that the Queen is not ecstatic, but rather that *ecstatic* is perhaps a better word than *happy*. Finally, among metatextual conditionals, scalar sentences like (10)–(12) seem to be set apart by the fact that their protases offer a repair, rather than an explanation.

In the extant literature (Kjëllmer 1975, Haiman 1986, König 1986) only the concessive reading of such sentences is recognized. Thus, examples like (10)–(12) are treated on a par with sentences like (13), and qualified uniformly as concessive:

(13)   The salary was good, if not up to her expectations.

Sentence (13) has a straightforward concessive interpretation, and its negation is understood descriptively, as we can see in the paraphrase: *The salary was good, even if it was not up to her expectations*. As for (10)–(12), they have two interpretations. One is indeed parallel to that of (13), and can be paraphrased in the same way, as in *He spoke ungraciously, even if he didn't speak rudely*. The second, metatextual interpretation is best paraphrased quite differently, with a different expression in the scope of *even*, and no negation of the main predication: *He spoke ungraciously, perhaps even rudely*. If there is negation here, it is not in the content of any of the clauses, but rather at the level of the overall metatextual interpretation of the sentence; thus (11) can perhaps be glossed (though not paraphrased) as something like "One would call his manner of speech ungracious, even if one wouldn't quite call it rude."

The role of negation (metatextual or descriptive) is apparently the main factor distinguishing the two interpretations in question. Under the metatextual reading of (10) the speaker states that she has essentially decided on *happy* being the best description of the Queen's emotional state, but is tentatively considering an expression which indicates a higher degree of emotional temperature. Emotions are hard to measure, so it may seem to the speaker uncertain whether it is appropriate to use the word *ecstatic*. In any case, *ecstatic* is not in any sense negated, it is only used tentatively. It signals the possibility of going higher up the scale. Under the concessive interpretation, on the other hand, describing the Queen's mood as "ecstatic" is rejected. The speaker had some expectation of the Queen being more than just happy, but the expectation proved wrong. Thus, the metatextual interpretation invites the hearer to look higher up the scale than *happy* indicates, while the concessive one tells him to stop at *happy*, and not try to go higher, contrary to expectation.

Presumably, then, the scalar conditional/negative metatextual constructions should be seen as independent of the concessive elliptical constructions as exemplified in (13), even though they are formally similar. Elliptical *if*-clauses can be ambiguous between the two uses, and the choice of one interpretation or the other crucially relies on the metatextual or descriptive interpretation of negation.

We should also note that some elliptical sentences with concessive inter-pretations do not require negation at all, as can be seen in an example quoted by König (1986): *This is an interesting, if complicated, solution.* If we add nega-tion into the *if*-clause here, as in *This is an interesting, if not complicated, solu-tion,* the resulting sentence is difficult to process. There is also no possibility of metatextual interpretation. This seems to be due to the fact that such sentences are scalar in a different way. There is no scale invoked such that *complicated* and *interesting* represent two points on that scale in the same way in which *happy* and *ecstatic* do. Rather, there is a scale of conditions which cause a high evaluation of a solution, and *interesting* represents a point on that scale. *Complicated,* on the other hand, marks a negative evaluation, as solutions should not be any more complex than they need to be. But the solution in ques-tion is so interesting that one would forgive added complexity and thus, con-trary to expectation, the solution is still positively evaluated.

The concessive interpretation of *The Queen of England is happy, if not ecsta-tic* (which uses negation and also admits a metatextual interpretation) seems to be somewhat different from the one offered for the "solution" example. Most importantly, the descriptions considered (*happy* and *ecstatic*) belong to the same scale. The negation in the *if*-clause also plays a role, for saying that the Queen is not ecstatic may create an expectation that her response is not positive at all. In other words, the negation may be interpreted as the negation of the applicability of the scale of positive emotions – in such a case the expectation is created that "happy" is not an applicable description either. But, contrary to that expectation, "happy" can be used.

Finally, are there metatextual elliptical conditionals which do not use nega-tion? One candidate here is (14):

(14)   Few people, if any, enjoy paying taxes.

The *if*-clause is undoubtedly elliptical and it makes a comment on the use of a particular expression in the main clause – it focuses on the existential presupposition carried by *few*. It seems that the target of the metatextual comment is best seen if we try to develop *if any* into a full clause. Interestingly, (16), which makes a direct reference to the presupposition, seems to be a better "full version" than (15):

(15)   If any people enjoy paying taxes, few people enjoy paying taxes.
(16)   Few people enjoy paying taxes, if (in fact) there are any people like that at all.

There seem to be several other *if* expressions similar to *if any: if ever, if anything, if that*. These expressions differ from metatextual elliptical conditionals like (10)–(12) in that they indicate going down the scale, rather than up. In a sentence like *It'll take five minutes, if that* the speaker indicates that the time needed may in fact be less than five minutes. But the expression may indicate that one should go to the very bottom of the scale, as in (14), which tries to say that there may in fact be no people who enjoy paying taxes.

We have seen, then, that elliptical *if*-clauses are a varied group. The only feature they seem to share is being scalar: invoking scales either through concessiveness, or through metatextually contrasting two expressions from the same scale but occupying different positions on it. We have also seen how the type of interpretation correlates with the type of negation: descriptive negation is found in concessive uses, metatextual negation is found in metatextual ones. Also, the presence of negation in metatextual cases indicates going up the selected scale, while its absence signifies going down. A variety of factors are involved, but many of the contrasts are elucidated by setting them against the background of the crucial distinction between metatextual and descriptive uses of *if* and *not*.

5.2   Clause order, topic, and discourse

The fact that conditional constructions are usually given a general representation as *if p . . . then q* reflects a common observation that in the majority of cases *if*-clauses precede the main clauses. This is confirmed in several discourse-oriented studies of conditionals: in the data gathered by Linde (1976) the sentences with *if p, q* clause order constitute 80 per cent of conditionals used; in the study conducted by Ford and Thompson (1986) on a corpus of both written and spoken English, initial conditional clauses outnumber the final ones by a ratio of about three to one. Finally, in a study of adverbial clauses by Ford (1993), 26 conditionals have preposed *if*-clauses, while 18 have them postposed.

The same tendency seems to hold in other languages. Greenberg (1963: 84–85) postulates as a universal that the clause order with the protasis preceding the apodosis is normal in all languages. The universality of such a sequencing pattern can be attributed to a variety of factors. As suggested by Comrie (1986), the *p/q* order preference may be dictated by the need to mark non-factuality of the whole construction with a protasis-initial marker such as *if*, or by the tendency to iconically represent real-time sequence of events or of the cause–effect chain. As was noted by Lehmann (1974), *p/q* order effectively allows the interlocutors to gain common ground gradually, as the discourse progresses.

The dominance of the protasis–apodosis clause order is still clearer if we note that among the conditionals with postposed protases, there are in fact two patterns, which are distinguished by intonation. The *if*-clause of a typical conditional like (17) can be made to follow its apodosis within two different patterns: either *q if p* is pronounced without a pause, with "continuing" intonation (as in [18]), or *q* receives a sentence-final contour while a pause (marked in written form by a comma) appears before *p*. The "clause-final" apodosis intonation pattern (*q, if p*) is shown in (19).

(17)   If it stops raining, I'll take you to the park tomorrow morning.
(18)   I'll take you to the park tomorrow morning if it stops raining.
(19)   I'll take you to the park tomorrow morning, if it stops raining.

In her study, Ford (1993) attributes different discourse functions to the three patterns exemplified in (17)–(19). She confirms the dominance of the *if p, q* pattern, and sees the role of initial *if*-clauses as pivotal points in the organization of talk. They have a grounding function, they present options or explore their implications, but most importantly they organize discourse in relation to the preceding context. Final *if*-clauses with continuing intonation do not contribute to the structure of discourse; rather, they complete the meaning of a particular sentence. Sentences like (19), with ending intonation of the apodosis, are seen as "post-completion extensions" and are used for self-editing or for negotiating understanding between participants.

Another study of conditionals in discourse (Schiffrin 1992) concentrates on the role of *if*-clauses (and their position) in relation to the construction or maintenance of various types of topics (text topic, speaker topic). Schiffrin also explores the ways in which topicality and givenness are related in conditionals. A more general question she considers is whether conditionals are so readily used as topics because of some property unique to conditionals, or whether there are more general principles at work (e.g. the principle that given information precedes new information).

Schiffrin's findings on sentence-initial *if*-clauses confirm Ford's results to some degree. In expositions and narratives, conditionals are found to "serve pivotal points in the discourse by relating the message-level topics to the speaker topic" (1992: 189). *If*-clauses are here understood as given in relation to the preceding text. In question–answer and question–answer–evaluation sequences, however, the givenness derives from the contrasting options implied by a question. Thus the "pivotal" function and the "contrasting options" function of conditionals with preposed protases figure in both studies, but Schiffrin's analysis shows how these functions are motivated by their uses in topic construction and maintenance.

As regards conditionals with sentence-final protases, Schiffrin's study offers a different point of view. She does not distinguish two intonation patterns (shown in [18] and [19]), but looks at given and new information instead. Her claim is that *if*-clauses occupying the initial position in the sentence follow both of two major principles of discourse organization: they are ***topics*** and they are ***given***, so their initial position is doubly motivated. Among conditionals with postposed protases, however, some *if*-clauses are given, and thus adhere to Haiman's principle whereby conditionals are topics (even though they are postposed), while some are new, and thus follow the given–new order. The former function anaphorically, and participate in message construction at a local level; the latter function cataphorically and have a global discourse role, e.g. creating new text topics. Schiffrin's observations are thus in contrast with Ford's findings, which do not attribute major discourse roles to postposed *if*-clauses.

In what follows I will try to add another dimension to the analysis of postposed clauses. I will test the classes of conditionals distinguished in the preceding chapters with respect to their clause order flexibility. Then, I will look again at the corpus of *Hocus Pocus* to test the validity of all the proposed discourse criteria within the context of a major narrative structure such as a novel.

5.2.1   *Predictiveness, non-predictiveness, and clause order*

The studies of clause order in conditionals which I have cited focus on interpreting the data available in the corpora used by the authors. Consequently, a question which remains unaddressed is whether the choice of all of the identified patterns (*if p, q*; *q if p*; *q, if p*) is open to all possible formal *p/q* pairs. In other words, the question is whether any protasis could be used with its apodosis in any of three patterns, with the choice being dictated by discourse factors and topic construction only. In this section I will look at examples of all the classes of conditionals identified earlier and see whether any restrictions of the choice of pattern apply and what the consequences of this choice might be.

Let us look first at predictive conditionals, represented in examples (17)–(19) above. Even outside a broader context one can see that the three sentences tend to be interpreted differently, especially with respect to what is being asserted (in the speech act sense of "assert") and what is being given as background. Sentence (17), which represents the standard *if p, q* order, asserts the causal relation between *p* and *q*, since, as I argued earlier, none of the clauses can be treated as felicitously asserted. Thus, (17) focuses on the connection between the clauses, and presents *p* as backgrounded (or topical in Haiman's sense). In (18) the asserted part is again the causal relation, while the apodosis (or its part) may be topical. Thus *I'll take you to the park tomorrow morning if it stops raining* can appear in a conversation when its topic is 'the park' (not 'the rain'), or when it is a response to a question, such as *Can we go to the park tomorrow morning?* The initial position of the apodosis can thus be significant in at least two ways: either it ensures that the protasis appears sentence-finally and is thus considered as new information; or it presents the protasis in a non-salient way which nonetheless allows it to guarantee the overall coherence of the text by continuing the main theme of the conversation or being a direct response to previous discourse. But the difference between (17) and (18) is indeed mainly in organization of discourse, for the causal relation remains the focus of assertion in both cases.

Sentence (19) is different from (17) and (18) in this respect. The speaker asserts the assumption given in *q*, and adds *p* to it as an independent statement, often understood as an afterthought to *q*, or a clarification. The fact that *p* causes *q* does not appear as part of what is being said, though it may be recovered in searching for the way in which the content of *p* is relevant to the preceding assertion of *q*.

The contrast between the interpretations of (18) and (19) is clearly parallel to the one noted by Chafe (1984) and Sweetser (1990) in the case of *because*-sentences, which can also be distinguished with respect to "comma" or "commaless" intonation ("continuing" versus "ending"). As Sweetser shows, the two variants receive essentially different interpretations: in particular, only the sentences with comma intonation can function in the epistemic and speech act domain.

Apparently, some such restrictions also hold for non-predictive *if*-sentences with contextually bound protases. Consider sentences (21) and (22), which are reversed versions of an epistemic sentence like (20):

(20)   If she is in the lobby, the plane arrived early.
(21)   ??The plane arrived early if she is in the lobby.
(22)   ?The plane (must have) arrived early, if she is in the lobby.

Both (21) and (22) are preceded with question marks, because they are difficult to contextualize and interpret, and also because they do not seem to be equivalent to (20). The commaless variant in (21) cannot be understood epistemically, because the assumption in *p* is no longer interpreted in the original way. By appearing in the rheme, where new, communicatively crucial information is likely to be contained, it is no longer presented as an unconfirmed, acquired assumption, to which the speaker refers only in order to explore its consequences. The only possible (i.e. linguistically licensed), though not plausible, interpretation of (21) is causal, but our encyclopedic knowledge does not in fact license such an interpretation as acceptable. Making sense of (21) requires a special scenario which would explain a causal link such that her presence in the lobby now caused the early arrival of the plane.

As for (22), which is a "comma intonation" variant, it is still difficult to accept, but better than (21), because in this intonation pattern the epistemic modalities revealed by the expressions in parentheses are more easily read into the interpretation. What is required, apparently, is that the status of both clauses is made clear: *q* has to be interpreted epistemically (i.e. as an inferential background to reasoning, rather than as a cause of an event). *P*, on the other hand, has to be presented as an assumption which requires confirmation. Even with these changes, however, the communicative effect of (22) is different from that of (20). (20), like other epistemic/inferential conditionals, brings up a contextually bound assumption (*p*) to draw the conclusion (*q*). But the speaker of (22) draws the conclusion *q* first (with the assumption *p* somewhere in the background as its premise) and then subsequently justifies her already made conclusion by citing *p*. We cannot say, then, that the same inference process is involved in (20) and (22), even though the same premise and the same conclusion are involved.

Evidently, then, epistemic *if*-sentences with reversed clause order are like epistemic *because*-sentences in that they cannot appear with a commaless intonation, and unlike them in that they may be problematic even with a comma intonation. The explanation seems to be that for *because*-sentences the default clause order is with an initial *q*, while for *if*-sentences the default order is with an initial *p*.

Certain freedom of clause order can be expected in speech act conditionals: the act to be performed is contained within the apodosis and the protasis provides additional information or evaluation of appropriateness. This relative independence of the apodosis (as compared to the tight causal relations of p and q in predictive conditionals, for example) should allow for more flexibility in clause order. And indeed it is possible for *if*-clauses of speech act conditionals to precede or follow their main clauses, but in both cases an intonational pause between the clauses is necessary:

(23)   You're looking particularly lovely tonight, if I may say so.
(24)   If I may say so, you're looking particularly lovely tonight.

However, with the *if*-clause postposed and with continuing intonation any sentence seems to invite a causal interpretation of the relationship between p and q, rather than a speech act conditional reading. So (25):

(25)   ?You're looking particularly lovely tonight if I may say so.

changes the flirtatious compliment of (23) into a practically unusable sentence in which the speaker apparently claims that the addressee's looking lovely results from the speaker saying so ([25] thus behaves similarly to [21]).

We should also notice that the clause order flexibility (which may even involve some preference for the q, *if p* order) is observed mainly in the "classical" (conversational) speech act conditionals (like [23] and [24]). In chapter 4 I argued that the distinction between speech act and epistemic conditionals is often blurred by the fact that protases of the same kind are found with both – such protases are contextually bound, hearer-oriented, and marked with epistemic distance. The protases of (20)–(22), as well as that of (26) below, fall into this category. (26) is a speech act conditional in which a decision is presented in the context of an assumption that brings the decision about:

(26)   If she's giving the baby a bath, I'll call back later.

The speaker of (26) has just heard in a telephone conversation that the person she wanted to speak to is giving the baby a bath. Being acquired in such an indirect manner, the protasis of (26) is thus a contextually bound protasis. It is brought up by the speaker as a background to her decision to call back at a later time. With respect to the type of the protasis, variants of (26) with postposed protases behave like postposed variants of an epistemic conditional such as (20), rather than like the postposed versions of a conversational speech act conditional like (24). That is, the "comma" intonation variant (*I'll call back later, if she's giving the baby a bath*) presents the decision, and then brings up the assumption on the basis of which the decision has been made as an afterthought.

The "commaless" variant (*I'll call back later if she's giving the baby a bath*) changes the interpretation in a crucial way, because it does not present the decision as already made. Instead, it brings up one reason (out of possibly many) which may bring the decision about. The preposed version, as given in (26), is clearly preferred, and both of the postposed versions receive interpretations not compatible with the speech act reading of (26) ("I hereby make this decision, as I speak"). The conclusion, then, is that the acceptability and interpretability of different clause order versions of conditionals is related not only to the type of protasis/apodosis relation (causal, epistemic, speech act), but also to the type of protasis. As we have seen, contextually bound protases of (20) and (26) provide the kind of grounding for their apodoses which can only be achieved in the *if p, q* pattern.

The clause order considered universal for conditional constructions thus seems also to be the most open in the sense that it can freely be interpreted in terms of the widest range of relations and accommodate the greatest variety of protases. Among the reversed variants, the commaless one is highly restricted in that it requires the link betwen *p* and *q* to be causal. It appears that *q if p* sentences can only be formed as variants of the causal construction which are contextualized in a different way. Contrary to what is the "classic" relationship between topicality and conditional constructions, they have topical *q*'s, rather than *p*'s. Finally, the "comma intonation" pattern (*q, if p*) treats *p* and *q* as independent statements (and potentially independent speech acts) and leaves no room for asserting any relation between them. This is why conversational constructions are most appropriately formed according to this pattern of clause order.

Do the above observations shed any light on the question considered by Comrie (1986): why is the *if p, q* order universal? Comrie suggests that one of the main reasons is that the *if p, q* order is iconic of real-time sequences of events and of cause–effect chains. And yet in the sentences analyzed above, the only clause order pattern which is unambiguously causal is the postposed commaless one (*q if p*). The *if p, q* variant, on the other hand, has the capacity to represent a wide variety of relations between the protasis and the apodosis. Similar objections can be raised to the claim that the basic clause order is iconic of real-time sequences of events. As we saw in numerous examples in chapter 3, reversed temporal relations are common in *if p, q* sentences, but such an interpretation is not acceptable in *q if p* conditionals like (21). Finally, we can note that epistemic and speech act conditional constructions with hearer-perspective (contextually bound) protases are typically structured as *if p, q*. While not being causal or temporally sequential, they can be seen as iconic of a sequence of steps in the reasoning, which the hearer has to follow to understand. Thus, the iconicity of the universal clause order is better captured not in terms of events, but in terms of assumptions which have to be entertained prior to other assumptions.

I have not mentioned the clause order of metatextual conditionals so far. This is because the special rules governing this class of sentences seem to be directly connected with the special nature of the relation the *if*-clause bears to the main clause. The unique character of metatextual conditionals lies in the fact that their *if*-clauses focus on an expression within the apodosis, rather than on the whole apodosis clause. Metatextual *if*-clauses therefore frequently take a position as close as possible to the "text" commented on – which may mean a position *within* the main clause rather than preceding or following it. In section 3.5.2 we have seen examples such as *My husband, if I can still call him that, hates onion soup*, where metatextual protases take a position that I will call *sentence-medial*. We have also seen that there is in fact no other plausible variant in such cases, since the *if p, q* variant (*?If I can still call him that, my husband hates onion soup*) is hard to process, while the *q, if p* pattern gives an unacceptable sentence: *??My husband hates onion soup, if I can still call him that*. Finally, the *q if p* pattern invites the usual causal interpretation: *??My husband hates onion soup if I can still call him that* does not seem readily interpretable as a metatextual conditional.

We may further note that there are unusual constraints on clause order in metatextual sentences which establish a parallelism rather than commenting on it, as well as in the so-called meta-metaphorical sentences. In both cases, postposed versions are unacceptable, as in (27) and (28):

(27)   ??I was a worse tailor (,) if I was a bad carpenter.
(28)   ??The Latin Quarter is the soul of Paris (,) if the Cité is its heart.

The commaless variants once again seem to demand a causal reading (as we have come to expect with this intonation pattern). With a comma separating the clauses, on the other hand, we cannot recover the original interpretation of dependence of one metaphorical mapping on another, because the acceptance of the expressions (metaphors) in the protases has to be prior to (and is a condition for) the acceptance of those in the apodoses.

The above review of conditional classes and their clause order flexibility seems to show that the type of protasis/apodosis relation is a factor which influences the choice of a clause order pattern to a considerable degree. A particular clause order may invite some interpretations more willingly than others, and will be better suited to some discourse functions than to others. Only through a consideration of all of these factors can we explain the choice of a given pattern in each particular sentence. Still, among the existing patterns, the allegedly universal *if p, q* seems to be best suited to the functions most frequently performed by conditionals; it is also the one most open to the widest array of *p/q* relations, types of protases, and types of reasoning patterns. Nevertheless, there are conditionals (such as conversational speech act and metatextual ones) for which the standard pattern is not even preferred, and in these cases the *p/q* relations and discourse factors seem to play equally important roles in motivating the choice of clause order.

5.2.2   Postposed *if*-clauses in written narration

The analyses of clause order in conditionals referred to above (Ford and Thompson 1986, Schiffrin 1992, Ford 1993) are based on a variety of corpora, but the majority of examples are taken from spoken discourse. In this section I will present an analysis of the use of non-initial conditionals in Kurt Vonnegut's novel *Hocus Pocus*.

In this Vonnegut corpus, 47 conditional sentences out of a total of 151 have non-initial protases.[2] Among these 47 two types constitute an overwhelming majority. There are 22 metatextual sentences and 23 predictive ones, while speech act conditionals and concessive conditionals have 1 representative each. This is a significant, though not surprising result. There are no examples of epistemic, or other hearer-perspective sentences; as we observed above, they are more likely to be used in the *if p, q* order. Speech act conditionals are also more to be expected in natural spoken discourse, rather than in narrative prose, even in a narrative with dialogue passages in it.

The 22 metatextual sentences, which form an unexpectedly large group, all have commas separating the *if*-clause from the main clause. This is not surprising, since metatextual *if*-clauses comment on their apodoses with respect to the choice of expressions used rather than standing in a closer (such as content or epistemic) relation to them, and thus no causal relationship between *p* and *q* is involved. More than half of these examples (13 of them) have sentence-medial protases rather than sentence-final ones; and when the protases are final, it is because the "text" they comment upon is at the end of the main clause. Sentence (29) is a typical example of a metatextual conditional:

(29)   The number of students, if you can call convicts that, is about 2,000 now.

---

[2] I am using the term "non-initial" to deliberately avoid using the commonly applied terms "final" or "postposed." This is because a great number of examples in the corpus are not in fact sentence-final, but sentence-medial – they are situated within their apodoses.

The *if*-clause is sentence-medial, separated by commas, and its role is to comment on the peculiar use of the word *students* to refer to convicts. For the narrator they are students, because he has been hired to teach them, but the use is nevertheless not standard. Example (30) is more interesting:

(30)   It was a beautiful shot, if Darwin was really the man the College President was shooting at. He could have been shooting at me.

The comment in the *if*-clause is again on the applicability of the description "beautiful" to the shot which hit Darwin, but it is not made on the basis of a linguistic convention. Instead, it refers to the lack of knowledge of whether the College President was really aiming at Darwin. The protasis here is very much like contextually bound protases of epistemic and speech act conditionals, but its tentative acceptance provides motivation for choosing one's wording, rather than for drawing conclusions or making decisions. The problem of finding the right words to talk about events we have insufficient knowledge about seems to be the true "emploi" of metatextual sentences.

Among the 13 sentence-medial metatextual protasis clauses, 9 are elliptical.[3] Among these are 1 example with metatextual negation (*to many, if not most, of the freedom fighters*), and 3 uses of the phrase *if any*, which, as was shown in section 5.1.2, can comment on existential presuppositions carried by the main clause (e.g. *and describe their dental work, if any, and their obvious wounds, if any, and so on*). The remaining instances do not properly represent elliptical conditionals, as they were defined in 5.1.2, because the reduction of the *if*-clause seems to be primarily a necessary stylistic shortening; a longer clause would simply be too major an interruption to main-clause structure, if inserted in a sentence-medial position. We therefore find examples like *to pick up gossip, if I could, about . . .* or *they punched in their race and age and what their parents did, if they knew . . .*

Let us now look at how the intonation options are represented in the corpus. Ending intonation on the initial main clause (that is, a comma in writing) was found in 30 sentences, while 17 sentences have no comma. Twenty-two of the "comma"-intonation sentences are metatextual (all of the metatextual examples in the corpus have comma intonation). There are also, among the ending intonation examples, two speech act conditionals (one with *even if*). Thus only 6 of 23 predictive sentences are marked with an ending intonation on their preposed *q*-clauses. Four out of these 6 are hypothetical.

By contrast, *all* 17 commaless examples from the corpus are predictive. This is again not very surprising, since, as I have noted before, the postposed pattern

---

[3] There are altogether 10 elliptical clauses, 1 of which is a concessive clause of the type discussed in 5.1.2.

without a comma invites a causal interpretation, which distinguishes predictive sentences from other conditionals.

In the remainder of this section I will examine the discourse functions of the commaless sentences in the corpus, and their relation to the presentation of new and given information. I will also consider the question of the relationship between these discourse functions and other formal and functional parameters such as the position of the protasis in the sentence, the degree of givenness of protasis and apodosis, the intonation pattern, and other factors. In this part of the presentation I will concentrate on the hypothetical sentences in the corpus, since they display the most interesting ties to the structure of the narrative.

At least 9 of the sentences in question seem evidently to have important discourse-organizing functions. Most typically their apodoses complete or recount the preceding part of the story, while their *if*-clauses announce the beginning of a new story – in Schiffrin's terms, they change the text topic. Let us consider sentences (31) and (32):

(31)   Before I went to work at Athena, I had seen only 3 convicts anywhere in the valley. Most people in Scipio hadn't seen even 1. I wouldn't have seen even 1, either, if a truck with a steel box in back hadn't broken down at the head of the lake. I was picknicking there . . .

(32)   "I had to laugh like hell," he said, but he didn't crack a smile. He would have wanted to laugh like hell if he had seen me on the roof of our embassy in Saigon with my pistol drawn . . . Now I was on the rooftop, while . . .

In both sentences the apodoses are given by preceding text and provide a link with previous discourse. Both protases are new and constitute introductions to stories which continue for the next page or so. Interestingly, the apodosis of (32) maintains its chain of anaphoric references ("he") across a boundary between two separate parts of the text. In *Hocus Pocus* there are chapters which have numbers, not titles, and the text of each chapter is further divided into smaller parts by vertical lines; such chunks may be a page, a paragraph, or even a sentence long. In example (32) the first sentence belongs to one such section, the second one to the next. It is clear, then, that the essential role of q is indeed first of all to fill in the "given information" gap, so that p can start the new topic to be dealt with in the new section of text.

Such examples confirm Schiffrin's observations about the role of protases carrying new information. However, it seems that similar tasks are performed in sentences which have given protases, as in (33):

(33)   My guess is that he was a comedian, and I was not . . . I, too, might have been acceptable as a comedian if all Kimberley had taped was what I said about Yen and fellatio. That was good, topical Mohiga Valley humor . . .

This sentence looks almost like (32) above. The apodosis refers back to the "comedian" topic of the previous paragraph (and preceding section, since there is a vertical line before *I, too*). The protasis introduces the new text topic – how much truth and humor there was in what the narrator said to Kimberley about Yen and fellatio. The difference, however, between (32) and (33) is that the story of Kimberley, as well as "Yen and fellatio" remarks and other remarks that Kimberley recorded, which cost the narrator his job, are not new information in any sense. Some fifteen pages earlier a major portion of the novel (almost a chapter) is devoted to exactly what was said and recorded and what happened as a result. So the difference seems to be not in that one clause is given and the other new, but how saliently they are given at this particular point in the narration. The "comedian" theme is a natural hook on which to hang the new text topic because it is situated in the immediately preceding discourse. The "Yen and fellatio" story needs re-introduction at this point – not as new information, but as a new topic, a topic which is about to supplant the preceding one.

Examples like (33) may in fact suggest that the "given–new order" principle overrides the "*if*-clauses are topics" principle, rather than just competing with it, as Schiffrin has observed; but so far it seems that only the *q if p* clause order pattern allows this to happen. When an *if*-clause is put in a sentence-final position after an apodosis which clearly is given, it is naturally taken to be new, either on the informational level, or on the discourse level ("upcoming topic"), or both. We also have to bear in mind that both (32) and (33) are first sentences of discourse units; and since the narration in this particular novel is not always chronological, but more like a huge floor puzzle, where new pieces are added to various parts of the story all the time, it is necessary that text topics for all the scattered fragments be somehow nominated – ideally, as early in the section as possible. The *if*-clauses of (32) and (33) thus occupy special positions in the text and are readily interpreted as contributing information about discourse structure.

For comparison, if we look at sentences which are perhaps similar, but deeply embedded in the text, their interpretation will be local, as is the case in (34):

(34)   Before I could protest to the Trustees that I certainly wouldn't have said what I'd said about Yen and fellatio if I'd thought there was the slightest chance that a student could hear me, the background noises on the tape changed. I realized that I was about to hear something I had said in a different location.

This is again the beginning of a section, but its topic is no longer "what I said about Yen and fellatio," but "what I said in the basement of the Pahlavi Pavilion." The next sections are about "how I had come to say what I said in the basement of the Pahlavi Pavilion." The new topic is announced by the last clause of the first sentence: *the background noises on the tape changed*. The preceding *if*-clause, even though it presents new information and seems to appear in a position very similar to the *if*-clauses of (32) and (33), will not take any role in structuring the discourse at a higher level, because the entire conditional sentence is embedded in the background temporal clause of the topic-nominating sentence. Thus a particular position within the conditional, even combined with new information status, does not suffice to grant an *if*-clause a discourse-organizing function. Its relationship to other sentences plays a significant role.

In looking through the corpus I expected to find examples of given, sentence-final, and commaless *if*-clauses which would perform anaphoric functions of the type described by Schiffrin. Surprisingly, however, such examples proved difficult to find. First of all, only two of the commaless postposed-protasis conditionals had protases which were clearly given. One of them was (33) above, whose function is cataphoric and global, rather than anaphoric and local. The other is given as (35):

(35)   Since he already knew ice cream, it made perfect sense for him to buy the old ice cream parlor. It would have been better for all concerned if he had known a little less about ice cream and a little more about paint remover.

The conditional in (35) makes reference to the fact that the character in question died after inhaling too much paint remover. The reader has just been told that the character knew about ice cream, and he clearly did not know enough about paint remover – the message of the *if*-clause is given. It is also the final clause of the paragraph. We might expect this to be a case where the *if*-clause indeed does nothing but tie the sentence to previous discourse and complete the thought. But apparently this is not the case.

One of the recurring themes in the novel is "germs in the human body." When the paint-remover poisoning is mentioned, speculation follows immediately concerning the reaction of germs to paint-remover poisoning of their human host. Then a little more about the poisoned man is said, and at the end of the section comes (35), taking us back to the poisoning itself. The two sections which follow are again about the poisoning, and finally about poisoning (in general) and about germs. That is how the chapter ends. Thus at the local level of message construction, the *if*-clause of (35) concludes the story of Jerry Peck, but on a higher level it reminds the reader that the story of Jerry's life is only a digression, and maintains a more global topic, namely "poisons in the human body."

From the examples in this corpus, it would seem that sentence-final comma-less *if*-clauses perform important discourse organization functions more often than not, regardless of whether they are given or new.

As regards the sentences with a comma preceding their *if*-clauses, we have seen that most of them are metatextual, and thus by definition involve a very local relation between protasis and apodosis. Of the few predictive sentences in this group, most function locally as well – they complete the meaning of their protases. However, none of the protases here seems to present given information. Consider (36) and (37):

(36)   "There is much I could probably forgive, if somebody put a gun to my head, Professor Hartke," he said, "but not what you did to my son."
(37)   "You keep talking as though I could turn you loose, if I wanted. I'm as much a prisoner as you are."

Both of the *if*-clauses here are new, but they are only meant to contribute to the message on the sentence level. They complete the speaker's thought with assumptions which explain the communicative intent of the apodosis, rather than marking its relation to broader discourse structure. Characteristically, both appear in dialogues; that is, they are meant to represent spoken, rather than written discourse.

There is one example, however, which contains an apparently given protasis – and which, more importantly perhaps, belongs to the narration proper rather than to dialogue. It is given here as (38).

(38)   It is my guess that he would not have minded having the place sound like a catchment for the poor, if only he had not suffered the misfortune of having his own grandson go there.

This is the final sentence of a section of the novel. The section starts with a brief reference to the first of the Moellenkamp family who graduated from Tarkington College. Next the reader is informed that it was at the time of this graduation that what used to be The Mohiga Valley Free Institute was renamed Tarkington College. The rest of the section talks about how the change of name was introduced, and (38) concludes the story. In a way, then, the *if*-clause of (38) is at least partly given, because it recalls the graduation of Moellenkamp's grandson, which is mentioned at the beginning of the section. It is also possible for the reader to infer that the name was changed precisely because of the young man's graduation. Thus (38), as a section-concluding sentence serves to clarify the topic of the paragraph, or hammers the point in. So not only is this conditional grounded in previous discourse; it explains the significance of that discourse and brings the topic of a larger unit of discourse into focus. To conclude, an *if*-clause in a sentence with a "comma" intonation functions anaphorically, but does not have to perform a local role only. It may still contribute to more global aspects of discourse organization.

The examples in my corpus seem to point to the conclusion that, contrary to what has been suggested (e.g. by Ford 1993), postposed conditionals can perform important discourse-organizing functions. They seem to adhere to the "given–new order" principle, as most of them present new information or at least introduce new text topics. The sentences with continuing intonation seem to be better suited to performing these functions, but *if*-clauses preceded by commas can also play a more global discourse role. Schiffrin's original conclusion can thus be taken one step further: postposed *if*-clauses can play a role at higher levels of discourse construction even when they are not new information.

6 If *and other conditional conjunctions*

The purpose of this book, as stated in the introduction, is to describe complex sentences whose subordinate clauses are introduced with *if*. This is the class of sentences which I have been calling "conditionals." Different analysts, however, broaden or restrict the application of the term in a number of ways. For instance, logical accounts disregard constructions with questions and imperatives as *q*'s, some analyses (e.g. Ramsey 1931) do not consider *even if* sentences to be conditionals, Austin (1961) doubts the conditional status of speech act sentences, and even Jespersen talks about "pseudo-conditionals." Using yet another set of criteria, it is common to apply the term "conditional" to any sentence which can be paraphrased as a conditional.

In what follows I will try to show that, taking *if* to be the only explicitly conditional form in the English conjunction repertory, we can still offer a consistent explanation of *if*-compounds (such as *even if*) and of other conjunctions traditionally linked to conditionality: *unless* (as a negative marker of the protasis) and *then* (as a marker of the apodosis). In the final chapter I will also discuss the ways in which conditional meanings can arise without the presence of any overt markers.

6.1   Concessive conditional constructions

We have seen throughout this work that *if . . . then* constructions share important aspects of form and interpretation with constructions containing other types of adverbial clauses, in particular temporal and causal ones. As was noted by König (1986), concessive clauses should also be added to this list. Since the interpretation of conjunctions other than *if* is beyond the scope of the present analysis, in this section I will consider only the area of overlap between conditional and concessive clauses.

In his paper, König discusses three groups of related adverbial sentences: conditionals, concessives, and conditional concessives. The conditional class is marked with the conjunction *if*, and the most central marker of the concessive class is *although*. The conditional concessive class is claimed by König to sub-divide further into three subclasses. There are concessive conditionals which have disjunctions of conditions as their protases and have *whether . . . or* as a conjunction; there are ones whose protases are marked with a universal quantifier such as *whatever*; and there are ones which contain an expression bringing one of a set of conditions into focus – the paradigm example of the group is the expression *even if*. In what follows I will be centrally concerned with this last subclass of concessive conditionals, which are of particular interest because of the fact that the protases of some *if . . . then* constructions are sometimes inter-peted as *even if* clauses, but not as disjunctive or universal ones.

I shall assume that *if* differs in sufficiently significant ways from any of the other conjunctions mentioned above. It apparently does not introduce the same kinds of clauses which *although, whether*, and other concessive conjunctions can also introduce, but it sometimes appears in contexts which also admit the use of *even if*. The purpose of this section will be to specify the nature of such contexts. Before this task can be approached, however, I must first briefly summarize the characterizations offered for *although* and *even if*.

Sentences with *although*-clauses entail the factuality of both *p* and *q* (Haiman [1974] characterizes their verbs as "actual"). Haiman (1974) further notes that they invoke a negative assumption (a presupposition, in Haiman's ter-minology): the subordinate clause of *Although Max will come, we'll have fun* suggests that the fact of Max's coming could spoil the fun. The third feature mentioned by Haiman is that, contrary to what happens in conditionals, the assumption in the subordinate clause is not relevant to the result expressed in *q*. In other words, the clause introduced with *although* cannot be interpreted causally.

Even if, being also concessive, shares some features with *although*, but differs from it in many important respects. Since Fraser 1969 it has been gener-ally assumed that *even if* should be analyzed as a compound expression to which *even* and *if* contribute their independent meanings. In Dancygier (1988b) I argued for an interpretation based on this assumption.

Even has been invariably analyzed as free of truth-conditional meaning, so that the sentence with *even* (*Even Bill likes Mary*) has the same truth conditions as the one without it (*Bill likes Mary*). The meaning that it carries has been described in a variety of ways – as a presupposition or conventional implicature (Horn 1969, Fauconnier 1975a and 1975b, Karttunen and Peters 1979), and recently as a scalar operator pragmatically modifying the meaning of construc-tions (Kay 1990), but what all of the accounts share is the claim that *even* intro-duces a scale of unlikelihood, or negative expectation, the highest position on which is occupied by the referent of the expression in the scope of *even*. That is, a sentence like *Even Bill likes Mary* is interpreted to mean that Bill likes Mary, that there are other people who like her, but also that Bill is the least likely among them to like her. Thus what *even* seems to share with *although* is the "negative expectation" – hence its concessive use – but its most salient meaning is that of scalarity.

When *if* combines with *even*, it introduces the two features that are always a part of its characterization: non-assertiveness of the clause in its scope, and the assumption that there is a conditional relation in some cognitive domain which relates the *if*-clause to its apodosis. As a result, the clauses of a construction with *even if* are not considered factual (according to Haiman 1974 they are "potential"), and in this respect *even if* contrasts with *although*. Furthermore, the scale implied by *even* is understood as a scale of possible conditions, one of which appears in the protasis, as in (1):

(1)   Even if it rains, the match will not be canceled.

But *even* also contributes to the interpretation of (1) the assumption that the structure in the scope of *even if* ranks high on the scale of "negative expectation." As Haiman (1974) puts it, an *even if* clause specifies a condition not relevant to the result – as is the case with *although*. Yamaguchi (1989), on the other hand, accounts for this by saying that *even if* sentences are simply not conditional. It seems, however, that the "negative expectation" relates specifically to the second contribution that *if* makes to the overall interpretation – the p/q relation. In the case of (1) the relation is predictive (and thus causal); it would normally be expected that rain will result in the cancelation of the game. This expectation, however, is viewed negatively, and contrary to it the match will not be canceled.

Thus the lack of connection between the clauses noted by Haiman and by Yamaguchi is perhaps more accurately accounted for in terms of implausibility of an expected causal link. No causal connection between p and q is in fact asserted, and the only link between p and q is the negatively viewed but expected causal link which underlies the interpretation of (1). In other words, it is not the case that rain will cause non-cancelation, but that it will fail to cause cancelation. The protasis in an *even if* construction is not a condition of q, but it is an expected condition of **not** q. A conditional interpretation is thus involved in these cases, but not in the same way as in ordinary conditionals.

Another aspect of the interpretation of *even if* sentences is discussed by König (1986). He recalls the observation made by Geis and Zwicky (1971) that an ordinary conditional of the form **if p then q** invites an inference that **if not p**

then not q (this is called conditional perfection), and notes that such an inference cannot arise in *even if* sentences. His explanation is that *even* presents the condition ***p*** as an extreme of the scale and admits the possibility for other values on the scale to hold with the same result (though not to bring it about). Thus values other than ***p*** are also admitted and conditional perfection is excluded.

Not all non-concessive conditionals invite conditional perfection as their inference. The predictive ones apparently do: if one says *If it rains, the match will be canceled*, one usually implies that the match will not be canceled in sunny weather.[1] But in non-predictive conditionals, the inference of conditional perfection is not invited so readily. For example, *If she's giving the baby a bath, I'll call back later* does not imply *If she's not giving the baby a bath, I won't call back later*. All conversational conditionals have to be excluded too, for we do not interpret *There are biscuits on the sideboard, if you're hungry* as *There are no biscuits on the sideboard if you're not hungry*. There is also some confusion among inferential conditionals, as some seem to pass the test, while others do not. Thus if the protasis is accepted (even though only tentatively) as the only premise licensing the conclusion, perfection is applicable, as in the case of *If he was wearing a purple jacket, then it was him I saw at the party*. If other premises might lead to the same conclusion, perfection does not apply, as in: *If he bought the old model for the price of a new one, he is a fool*.

Possibly, then, conditional perfection is most typically found in causal conditionals, that is, predictive conditionals which assert a causal relation between ***p*** and ***q***. As we have seen, this is not a characterization we can give to concessive conditionals in a straightforward manner. Perhaps, then, the fact that concessive conditionals do not invite conditional perfection is at least partially connected to their not being causal in the way other predictives are.

What I am claiming, then, is that the negative part of the meaning of *even if* does not apply to any of the clauses in question, but to the relation between them. That is, *even if* sentences are always related to the speaker's beliefs about

---

[1] The problem with conditionals is that they in fact consider causal links "one at a time." That is, the speaker may be aware that the match will also be canceled if it snows, but for reasons independent of the sentence itself the question of snow does not arise. So conditional perfection does not in fact exclude the possibility that other causes may bring about the same result, but this belongs to the knowledge of the world, not to the interpretation of the sentence. On the other hand, the so-called conditional perfection inference is in fact more restricted than the literature suggests. That is, as is argued by Dancygier and Sweetser (1996, 1997), it arises in the cases of a specific type of mental space construction. König's explanation quoted above is valid for concessive conditionals, but a broader view is needed to address the question of conditional perfection in other conditional constructions.

causal links which can be expected to hold. In this view, example (1) above evokes an interpretation based on a belief which might be formulated as (2):

(2)   If it rains, the match will be canceled.

A somewhat more complex causal link is background to a sentence like *Even if it doesn't rain, the match will be canceled*. Indirectly, it refers to (2) as well, but its direct source is *If it doesn't rain, the match will not be canceled* – the "conditional perfection" converse of (2). Both of these *even if* sentences seem to be implicitly negating the same thing – not *p* alone and not *q* alone, but the causal relation between them. This seems to explain why it is not possible to form a concessive conditional like *Even if it rains the match will be canceled* while holding assumption (2) at the same time – one asserts the causal relation, while the other negates it. I therefore do not feel it plausible to claim, as most analyses do, that concessive conditions are still conditions – extremely unfavorable, but still considered sufficient for *q* to happen – because *q* happens *in spite of p*, not *because of p*. It is true that *q* happens whether *p* or *not p*, but this does not mean that the relation between *q* and *p* is the same as an assumed relation between *q* and *not p*.

I have only discussed causal (predictive) examples so far. There are, of course, also examples (see Dancygier 1988b, Sweetser 1990) of *even if* sentences which express epistemic or conversational relations:

(3)   It's not five yet, even if the post office is closed.
(4)   Mary is already on her way here, even if you don't want to hear about it.

Just as in the case of predictives, these sentences refer negatively to relations between *p* and *q* that might be expected to hold. Thus, (3) invalidates the conclusion about what time it is, drawn from the observation that the post office is closed. The expected inference might be formulated as *If the post office is closed, it's past five o'clock*, and what is negated here is the possibility of concluding that the time is "past five" on the basis of the premise considered. Sentence (4) invokes a rule of appropriateness under which the speaker can offer information to the hearer if the hearer is indeed interested in receiving it. But on certain occasions the speaker may go ahead and communicate an assumption even if it is not appropriately welcomed by the hearer.

We have so far considered concessives and conditional concessives. A third group of sentences, related to the former two, is that of conditionals with concessive meaning – I shall use this term to refer to *if*-constructions which can be interpreted concessively. The paradigm example here is Haiman's (1986) sentence, given below as (5):

(5)   I'll get him, if it's the last thing I do.

Haiman's characterization of such conditionals is based on the form of the construction. He notes a general tendency for concessive conditional protases (*even if*) to follow, rather than precede their apodoses. Similarly, concessive *if*-clauses are normally sentence-final; and when such an *if*-clause does precede its apodosis, its special status is marked with intonation.

König (1986) claims that a concessive interpretation of *if* can arise in favorable contexts, that is, in sentences in which conditional perfection is excluded. This may be the case – as in (5) – where the condition appears to be the extreme of a scale, so that the whole scale of conditions is considered. However, apart from containing an expression which "triggers" the scalar interpretation (such as *the last* in [5], and a number of others discussed by König), such sentences are also prone to concessive interpretations because their straightforward causal interpretation is unlikely, while at the same time the hearer may entertain causal assumptions which are their negated variants. Given the assumption that one does not hastily decide to do things if they are known to be the last ones one ever does, it is unlikely that the *p* of (5) will be interpreted as the cause of its *q*.

Sentence (5) is most readily interpreted concessively, but does not have to be given such a reading. Sweetser (1990) argues further that the choice between a conditional and a concessive interpretation is pragmatic, for it relates to the assumptions held by interlocutors. For example, the sentences given below as (6) and (7):[2]

(6)   I wouldn't marry you if you were a monster from Mars.
(7)   I would marry you if you were a monster from Mars.

will "normally" be interpreted as "conditional" and "concessive" respectively. However, with the assumption that the speaker is keen on marrying a Martian monster, (6) becomes concessive, while (7) becomes an ordinary conditional. This pragmatic choice will depend on the kinds of causal assumptions one holds to be "normal." If the hearer has beliefs which negate the kind of dependence suggested by the sentences, concessive interpretations are likely to be chosen.

A similar, pragmatically based choice seems to be possible in the case of Yes/No questions, such as:

(8)   If it rains, will the match be canceled?
(9)   If it rains, will the match take place?

---

[2] See also Haiman's (1986) comments on sentences like *I wouldn't marry you if you were the last man on earth.*

where the former appears to be an ordinary question about a conditional, while the latter seems more appropriately understood as *Will the match take place even if it rains?* The readiness of questions to be interpreted concessively has been noted by Ducrot (1972), Van der Auwera (1986), König (1986), and Sweetser (1990). The most convincing explanations offered (König 1986, Sweetser 1990) refer to background assumptions about "normal" relations between *p* and *q*. Thus, (8) would not be understood to necessarily imply any such beliefs: the question here seems to be *about* the identity of the "normal" causal relationship. In (9), on the other hand, the question does not imply that the rain might cause the match to take place; rather, the most likely interpretation goes back to an assumption such as (2), and questions whether this already established causal assumption is going to fail in this particular case.

Finally, there is another attested group of *if*-sentences whose protases can be interpreted concessively. Some examples are noted by König (1986), who sees their affinity to concessives in the form of their apodoses – which are negated and contain an anaphoric reference to *p* – and in the lack of dependence between *p* and *q*. König's examples (quoted from literature) are:

(10)   If Calvin was still holding her hand, she could not feel it.
        (L'Engle 1962: 76)
(11)   If they saw the children, they gave no sign.
        (L'Engle 1962: 110)

In chapter 4 I discussed more examples of sentences which seem to be interpreted similarly to (10) and (11). They are repeated below as (12), (13), and (14):

(12)   If she called yesterday, I was out at the time.
(13)   If Susie is listening at the door, she is breathing very quietly.
(14)   If he told you that, he was lying.

What (10)–(11) and (12)–(14) share is the possibility of a concessive interpretation. Also, as König observed, they are characterized by a lack of causal dependence between *p* and *q*. These factors do not, however, suffice to ensure an *even if* reading – as we have seen, there are several other possible non-causal interpretations. Another interesting feature of these sentences is that there is no choice between a conditional interpretation and a concessive one – there is just one interpretation.

Sentences (12)–(14) were discussed in chapter 4 as examples of epistemic conditionals whose protases mark epistemic distance more strongly than those of ordinary inferential sentences. How is this related to their concessive interpretation? Apparently, the protases of (10)–(14) describe situations, but they also create certain expectations concerning their results. One should feel it when one is held by the hand; seeing the children should have been acknowledged somehow; if the call was placed, the addressee should have received it; if somebody is at the door, we expect to be aware of that, etc. These expectations are not realized, as the apodoses indicate. The non-fulfillment of the expectations is explicitly stated in the apodoses of (10) and (11). In (12)–(14), the absence of the expected result is not explicitly stated, but must be assumed in order to interpret the conditional successfully; the apodosis offers an account of how the protases can still be interpreted as true in absence of some expected result or evidence. Thus the gloss for (10) could be something like "If Calvin was still holding her hand, she should have felt it, but she didn't, so perhaps he had stopped." The gloss for (13), on the other hand, is more complex: "If Susie is listening at the door (as is suggested), I should be able to hear something. I can't hear anything, so maybe she isn't listening after all. Or perhaps she is, but is breathing so quietly that I can't hear." Thus in both cases, as in other concessively interpreted examples we have examined, the main source of a concessive interpretation is non-occurrence or negation of an expected result.

6.2   *If* and *unless*

Complex sentences involving subordinate clauses introduced with *if* represent conditionality in the widest range of uses. More restricted conjunctions, such as *provided that*, which Comrie (1986) describes as biconditional, or *supposing that*, will not be given specific attention here. There is just one other conditional conjunction in English which requires separate treatment, because it seems to compete with *if* in some cases and complement its range of uses in others – the conjunction is *unless*.

In most grammars of English, *unless* is analyzed as equivalent to *if not*. Quirk, Greenbaum, Leech, and Svartvik (1972) give the example:

(15)   Unless the strike has been called off, there will be no trains tomorrow.

as meaning roughly the same as (16):

(16)   If the strike has not been called off, there will be no trains tomorrow.

However, since the work of Geis (1961, 1973), it is recognized more and more commonly that *unless* does not in fact equal *if not*. This can be seen in the full acceptability of a sentence like *I'll be glad if she doesn't go to hospital*, and the bizarreness of a parallel example with *unless* under an attempted similar reading:

(17)   *I'll be glad unless she goes to hospital.

There are several points to be made here. First, the negative meaning of *unless* is not strong enough to prevent sentences in its scope from being negative and does not require the use of suppletive forms. Thus sentences like (18) and (19) are both acceptable:

(18)   You'd better keep silent unless you have something to say.
(19)   I won't open my mouth unless nobody else agrees to speak.

while (20) is not:

(20)   *You'd better keep silent unless you have anything to say.[3]

Second, as has been noted by Swan (1980), *unless* sentences cannot be causal. There has been no convincing explanation of this restriction, and I will go back to the question later in the section.

The next observation, confirmed in all analyses of *unless*, is that its conditionality should be represented with *only if*, rather than just *if*. Hence, Geis's analysis of *unless* (1973) relies on his proposals concerning *only if*, which require a brief comment.

Logicians' traditional claim (e.g. Quine 1962: 41) is that *only if* is a converse of *if*, that is, that **p only if q** means **if p then q**, and not **p if q**. The "converse analysis" seems to be unacceptable for a number of sentences, as was noted e.g. by McCawley (1974, 1981), and, besides, it carries a hidden assumption that *only if* is a kind of idiom – a view which most linguists find untenable. The belief that *if* and *only* require separate treatment is implied in all presuppositional analyses of *only* since Horn (1969), and is overtly advocated in works such as McCawley (1974, 1981) and Van der Auwera (1985).

Geis's proposals are based on the gloss he offers for *if* – "in cases in which." The gloss for *only if* is thus "only in cases in which," which, as Smith and Smith (1988) argue, leaves *only* unanalyzed. Smith and Smith's solution presents *only* as functioning to delimit the context of the utterance. In a context where the hearer of an utterance might readily access more than one assumption to interpret it, the function of *only* is to limit the range of such assumptions. This interpretation can be applied to conditionals in a rather straightforward way: in the context in which the hearer might consider other conditions as relevant to a given consequent, *only* limits the choice to just one. This is the understanding of *only if* which will be assumed in our further discussion of *unless*.

The "*only if*" interpretation of the clause in the scope of *unless* is now gener-

---

[3] It was pointed out to me that (20) may in fact be acceptable, if the speaker assumes that the hearer has nothing to say.

ally accepted. It is also common to treat *unless* as involving negation in some way. It is thus interesting to note that some sentences using both *only if* and negation, like (21), become rather odd when paraphrased with *unless*:

(21)   It'll be dark tomorrow only if the sun doesn't rise.
(22)   ?It'll be dark tomorrow unless the sun rises.

The explanation for this contrast seems to be that the apodoses of *unless* sentences have an added special status. They are in fact not presented conditionally, but as independent assertions, and only then commented upon in the subordinate clause, which is very much like an afterthought. In (22) it is actually stated that it will be dark tomorrow: an exceptional state of affairs, in our experience, but here asserted. The following *unless*-clause states that a possible exception to the assertion is the circumstance of the sun rising – which is normally taken to be the rule rather than the exception. The sentence is bizarre because it presents an odd (or exceptional) claim as its basic assertion, and a normal situation as the "exception" to that background. The fact that its bizarreness is purely pragmatic is shown by the appropriateness of the same utterance in some imagined context where the sun only comes up at infrequent or irregular intervals. (21) requires no such contextualizing, because it does not assert that it will be dark tomorrow, but presents that information only conditionally – and it presents the sun's rising as the single, but not exceptional or odd condition for non-darkness.

The fact that the assumption in the scope of *unless* is presented as a unique or exceptional circumstance seems to account for other restrictions in the use of the conjunction. As von Fintel (1991, 1994) notices, *unless*-clauses cannot be conjoined. It seems indeed bizarre to say *John will come unless he is busy and unless Mary invites him as well*, apparently because there can be only one exceptional circumstance which may prevent John's coming. The requirement that the *unless*-clause presents a unique situation preventing *q* from happening may also be a partial explanation of the unacceptability of (17) – the state of "being glad" can be inspired by situations other than "her not going to hospital," even though this is the situation the speaker chooses to mention.

I have suggested above that *unless* does not really behave as if negation were a part of its meaning. It has been shown by Traugott (1997) that the etymology of *unless* is not negative (and not strictly conditional either): the *un-* part is a distant relative of *on*, not a negative prefix as in *unhappy*. And yet *unless* is often interpretable similarly to *if not*. We need an explanation for the negation involved in the interpretation of a sentence with *unless*, if (as seems to be the case) this negative interpretation is not in the semantics of the conjunction. The actual place of negation is thus an important question in an analysis of *unless*.

Various glosses and interpretations of *unless* have been suggested. Geis (1973) proposed *except if p, q*, with no overt negative element. This "exceptive" interpretation was recently developed by von Fintel (1991, 1994), whose framework presents *unless* as an "exceptive operator on quantifier domains." Under von Fintel's interpretation a sentence such as *I will leave unless Bill calls soon* means "All of the situations in the contextual domain except the ones in which Bill calls soon are such that I leave" (von Fintel 1994: 119).

Some analysts have offered interpretations which involve negation placed before *p*, while others have placed the negation before *q*. The gloss offered by Clark and Clark (1977) contains the negation of *p* (*only if not p, q*), and Comrie's suggestion (1986) is quite similar: *if and only if not p, q*. The variant advocated by Fillenbaum (1976) differs from others in that it assumes the negation of *q* (*only if p, not q*). The version I have offered in earlier work (Dancygier 1985, 1987) also argues for the negation of *q*, but at the same time for its status of an independent statement: (*q; only if p, not q*). Under such an interpretation a sentence with *unless* will be understood as claiming that *q*, and then considering the unique circumstances (*p*) under which *not q* might occur.

The negation of *q* (rather than *p*) in the interpretation of sentences with *unless* seems to be supported by analysis of the data. In his 1986 paper Fillenbaum takes up this problem for the second time in his analysis of conditional deterrents and inducements. He suggests that the two groups of acts be distinguished with a "+" or "−" sign on the *q* clause: deterrents are *q−*, for the hearer does not want *q* to happen, while inducements are *q+*, for *q* is desirable to the hearer. Fillenbaum then tests the two groups of acts with respect to their paraphrasability with *unless*. Deterrents such as:

(23)   If you don't give me your money, I'll kill you.

are claimed by up to 90 per cent of his subjects to be equivalent to a parallel sentence with *unless*. The plausibility of such a paraphrase seems to support an analysis of *unless* involving *not q*, since this corresponds to the *q−* interpretation of (23) and explains the similarity between the two versions. Inducements, such as (24), on the other hand, are commonly judged by subjects not to be equivalent to parallel *unless*-sentences. Fillenbaum concludes that the choice between a *not p* and a *not q* rendering of *unless* must be left unresolved.

(24)   If you don't give me a ticket, I'll give you $20.

However, a more conclusive explanation might be motivated by further examination of the *p* clauses of inducements and deterrents, as well as their *q* clauses. Even though the protases of (23) and (24) are both negative, their messages are different. The message of (23) is *Give me your money*, without negation, while that of (24) is *Don't give me a ticket* – with the negation still there. Thus the former sentence can be paraphrased as *Give me your money. If you don't do as I say, I'll kill you*. But a parallel paraphrase of (24) is odd: *?Don't give me a ticket. If you don't do as I say, I'll give you $20*. In the former case, *do as I say* means (positive) *give me your money*; in the latter case it means (negative) *don't give me a ticket*.

Furthermore, paraphrases of (23) and (24) according to the ***only if p, not q*** gloss suggested for *unless* confirm the subjects' judgments concerning the plausibility of paraphrases with *unless*. Thus (25) gives the same message as (23), while (24) and (26) cannot be interpreted along the same lines. Finally, (27) is an acceptable paraphrase of (24):

(25)   I won't kill you only if you give me your money.
(26)   ?I won't give you $20 only if you give me a ticket.
(27)   I'll give you $20 only if you don't give me a ticket.

To sum up, a deterrent like (23) has to be glossed with ***only if p, not q*** and can be paraphrased with *unless*, for which the same gloss can be postulated. An inducement like (24), on the other hand, has to be glossed as ***only if not p, q***, and is thus not paraphrasable with *unless*, since *unless* lacks the reading involving the negation of *p*. Evidently, then, *if not* sentences can have more than one interpretation with respect to the place of negation, while *unless* sentences only have one – that which involves the negation of *q*.

There seem, then, to be sound arguments for assigning negation to *q*, rather than to *p*, in the gloss for *unless*. There seem also to be some arguments for treating *q* as an independent assertion, which is then restricted by specifying the unique circumstances under which it might not occur.

One argument for the independent asserted status of *q* in *unless*-sentences arises from the observation that *unless*-clauses do not often combine with questions. Geis (1973) first noted this; Brée (1985) quotes some *unless*-questions from the Brown Corpus, and observes that they are in fact rhetorical questions:

(28)   How can we have a good city unless we respect morality?
(29)   Unless God expected a man to believe the Holy scriptures, why has he given them to him?

Von Fintel (1991) argues that the explanation relies on the uniqueness condition claimed for *unless*-constructions. Under his interpretation *unless*, as an exceptive, combines only with universal quantifiers, which means that the number of potential answers to a question qualified by an *unless*-clause is very limited. Rhetorical questions are characterized precisely by extreme contextual limitation of the expected response. As von Fintel also notes, the expected answers to rhetorical questions are usually negative.

Thus what von Fintel seems to be saying is that the type of quantification involved in *unless* has the effect of limiting the number of possible answers to a question and thus strongly tends to evoke a rhetorical interpretation. This is the first part of the explanation we need – now we know why questions in the context of exceptives are prone to rhetorical interpretations. The next question is exactly how questions qualified by *unless*-clauses are interpreted. I would like to propose an interpretation of such questions on the basis of the formula advocated above, in which the assertion of q precedes the stating of the unique circumstance invalidating q. I will also, with von Fintel, assume the expected answers to rhetorical questions to be negative.

My main proposal concerning examples like (28)–(29) is that the real q's of such sentences are not the questions they contain, but the negative answers they presuppose. This seems to be a justified assumption in the case of rhetorical questions – they do not in fact offer a genuine choice between "yes" and "no," their function is rather to display how the (presumably negative) answer is reached. Thus the question part of (28) suggests that there is no way to have a good city, but the *unless* part proposes a unique condition under which the goal can be achieved. The whole reasoning can thus be paraphrased as "We cannot really have a good city (under the circumstances that there are, possibly including lack of respect for morality); we can have it only if we respect morality." But the communicated q still says that it is not possible (or not ordinarily possible) to have a good city in the way we have been acting so far – the purported rhetorical effect is thus achieved.

A similar interpretation can be offered for (29), even though the interpretation of this example is further complicated by the fact that *why* (in the same way as *because*) presupposes the factuality of the assumption in its scope. Thus the rhetorical question "why" is presented initially as having no plausible answer. Then it is suggested that there is just one, unique reason, such that "God expected a man to believe the Holy scriptures he has given him."

The communicative effect of (28) and (29) is thus to offer just one positive solution to an otherwise negatively evaluated question. We should note that the effect is different from the one a speaker could achieve with a parallel rhetorical question with *if*. For example, saying *How can we have a good city if we don't respect morality?* suggests, also rhetorically, that we cannot have a good city because we have no respect for morality – it is thus an explanation of a failure to have a good city. Sentence (28) does not state the causality that way, or even explicitly; it says, instead, that even if we do not have a good city right now, we can still have one if we change.

The interpretation suggested here seems to be supported by examples like (30), which I found in Philip Kerr's novel *March Violets* (1993:132):

(30)   Now why would a fellow like that want to kill you? Unless maybe you've
        turned critic and gave him a few bad notices.

Here the rhetorical question and its *unless* continuation are separated in discourse. So the effect is that it is first suggested that there is no obvious reason for the attempted killing, and then the *unless*-clause/sentence brings up the circumstance under which the question could be answered.

Finally, let me note that *unless*-clauses can be added to other utterances in the form of questions, provided, again, that their force is not that of a genuine question, where both "yes" and "no" are legitimate answers. In another example from *March Violets* an appointment is being made: *Here is the address. Shall we say eight o'clock? Unless you hear from me before then?* (1993: 214). The *unless*-sentence here is again an afterthought – but an afterthought to a suggestion, which happens to take the form of a question. So the message is that "the suggested time is eight o'clock, but I may suggest another time before then." *Unless* thus seems to have its usual function here, the only difference being that it comments on the speech act in *q*, rather than on an assumption asserted there.

It seems, then, that the case of rhetorical questions with *unless* offers some support to the idea that we can represent constructions involving *unless* as first communicating *q*, and then adding a condition for ***not q***. As Traugott (1997), has observed, this idea also finds some support in the dominant clause order of *unless* constructions. As has often been noted, *unless*-clauses, unlike *if*-clauses, are more often found in a sentence-final position. There has been no thorough corpus-based study of clause order here, but looking at attested data quoted for other purposes certainly confirms that the preferred placement of *unless*-clauses is sentence-final. For example, Sarah Taub (in an unpublished manuscript) quotes twenty-eight sentences with *unless*, mostly from *The Wall Street Journal*, twenty-seven of which have their *unless*-clauses in the final position. This observed order preference seems to be in keeping with the "afterthought"-like function of *unless*-clauses.[4]

There are, of course, instances where *unless*-clauses are preposed. The most common situation for preposing is that the *unless*-clause has a function similar to that of a conversational protasis; that is, it is a hedge on the appropriateness of

---

[4] Interestingly enough, in some languages (e.g. Polish) *unless*-clauses are obligatorily sentence-final.

the main clause. As we have seen, such clauses are quite free in their sentential position, because they comment on the main clauses rather than completing main-clause content. So a sentence like *Unless I am very much mistaken, you have just two more days to go* is very similar in its function to *If I'm not mistaken, you have just two more days to go*. But the sentence with *unless* still communicates the content of the main clause with a higher degree of conviction than its rather tentative *if not* counterpart. We should note, though, that *unless* clauses do not have to be strictly conversational to be preposed. Example (15) above is not conversational in the sense of expressing a speech act relation, but it still comunicates some kind of reservation on the plausibility of saying that there will be no trains the next day. Evidently, an *unless*-clause can be preposed without restrictions, if it comments on the assertability of the main clause, rather than predicating a relation between two clauses which sets up a link between two events in the real world (what Sweetser 1990 refers to as a "content-domain relation"). This is not surprising, as such comments on unassertability are usually more loosely connected with the main message, and can thus be found in various positions in the sentence.

The final problem to be considered is the use of hypothetical forms in sentences with *unless*. It has often been noted that *unless* rejects "counterfactual" forms, but examples of such uses are occasionally found. The question has so far been unresolved.

Throughout this book, hypothetical forms are taken as signaling a predictive interpretation of the whole sentence. In other words, in the *if*-conditionals considered so far, hypothetical sentences are interpreted as distanced predictions, distinguished by the choice of verb morphology from their non-distanced counterparts (which would use Present in the protasis and *will* in the apodosis). It is certainly possible to find *unless*-sentences which employ regular non-distanced predictive verb forms, as in *I will leave unless Bill calls soon*. It is thus puzzling to discover that distanced predictions with *unless* are hard to find.

It seems to me that there are two sources of this unacceptability. One consideration is the potential confusion brought about by various negative implicatures. For example, as Smith (1983) observes, a sentence like *Kangaroos would topple over if they did not have tails* is acceptable because it correctly suggests that kangaroos have tails. A similar sentence with *unless*, *Kangaroos would topple over unless they had tails*, on the other hand, suggests that kangaroos do not have tails, which contradicts our knowledge.

However, such an interpretation considers only the contribution of distanced forms, while *unless* itself also carries a negative meaning. What the so-called counterfactual forms contribute to the interpretation (as in Smith's example above) is a kind of implicature whereby both clauses may receive an interpretation as "contrary to the speaker's beliefs"; and if this is paired with the negative implicature of *unless*, confusion is likely. For example, it is not clear whether Smith's "kangaroo" example above should be read to mean what the clause itself suggests (that kangaroos have no tails), or whether *unless* changes the interpretation in such a way that kangaroos are claimed to have tails.

Further confusion is created by the fact that it is not necessarily the clause preceded by *unless* which receives the negated interpretation. As I have argued, the "layer" of negative meaning brought about by *unless* implies the negation of *q*, and the assumption in the scope of *unless* licenses the prediction of *not q*, rather than of *q*. In other words, *unless* is markedly different from *if* in that an *if*-conditional such as *I won't be able to finish on time if you don't help me* predicts *q* ("won't finish") from *p* ("no help"). This interpretation can be taken further to imply that *not q* ("finishing on time") will follow from *not p* ("your help"). Thus the relation between the clauses is assumed to be straightforward, as there is no extra implied negation in any of the clauses. An *unless*-sentence, such as *I won't be able to finish on time unless you help me*, in fact does not communicate any relation between the clauses as they stand ("your help" and "my **not being** able to finish"), but rather between "your help" and "my **being** able to finish" – with the implicated negation of *q*.

In a distanced variant this is not clear at all, as we can see in the analysis of (31) and (32), first considered by von Fintel (1991):

(31)   If you hadn't helped me, I would never have been able to finish on time.
(32)   *Unless you had helped me, I would never have been able to finish on time.

In (31) the "contrary to fact" interpretation again affects both clauses in the same manner, so the sentence is processed in terms of roughly the same causal relations as its non-distanced counterpart. But (32), according to the interpretation advocated here, would have to be glossed as follows: "I **would never** have been able to finish on time; I **would** have been able to finish on time only if you had helped me." This is hard to process for several reasons, at least if we want to come up with an interpretation parallel to that of (31). First, *I would never have been able to finish on time* is hard to maintain as an independent assertion; it requires that the hearer contextualize it with some unstated assumption which justifies the use of distanced forms. In (31), this function is naturally performed by the *if*-clause, but in its absence the hearer needs an explanation of the implicated meaning whereby the speaker could be expected not to finish, but eventually did. So we can more readily imagine the speaker saying *Without your help, I would have never been able to finish on time*, or *In weather like this, I would* *have never been able to finish on time*, to justify the use of distanced forms, something that could have stopped the speaker from finishing when she did needs to be mentioned. But if such a phrase is present, then the second part of the gloss cannot count as an afterthought or comment on the unique reasons for **not q**. Having said "I did finish on time, but I would not have been able to do it without your help (or in this weather)" already considers both **q** and reasons for **not q**. Thus the conditional clause in the second part of the gloss represents an independent conditional, because the first part of the gloss (**q**) has to be presented conditionally anyway.

This raises another interesting question which seems relevant to the non-acceptability of counterfactual *unless*-sentences – when is it at all legitimate to put both **q** and **not q** on the conversational table? As Taub has observed (unpublished manuscript), *unless*-sentences with **q**'s in the past tense which refer to specific past events are both hard to find and difficult to process: *?He fell off the cliff unless he has a good rope*. The difficulty in processing this seems to derive precisely from the fact that it is awkward for the speaker to assert something about the past (*he fell*) and then look for the unique circumstances which might have prevented it in the present. In a different way, this is also the problem of (31) and (32). The former communicates that "you helped me" and "I finished," while the latter says "I finished" as well as "I *did not* finish only if you *did not* help me." When we are talking about the past, such reasonings are bizarre.

The story becomes yet more complex when we observe that some *unless* sentences can apparently be distanced. Von Fintel (1991) quotes a sentence from Agatha Christie's story *The Hound of Death* after Fujita (1987):

(33)   Unless you had been told to the contrary, you would in all probability have considered her to be in poor circumstances – at any rate to begin with. Who was it exactly who told you that she was well off?
        (Christie 1982: 91)

How is this sentence different from (32)? The main difference, it seems to me, is that, roughly speaking, (32) is about past facts, while (33) is about alternative beliefs. While (32) straightforwardly implicates "I finished" and "you helped," (33) does not really lead the reader to a decision about "her" being rich or poor. All it does is make it clear that there were reasons for the addressee to believe her to be poor, but that he was told (and that was the unique circumstance that could change his view) that "she" was rich. But the review of available evidence of "her" financial situation does not lead to an assertion of "her" being either rich or poor. The fact that the actual point of the conversation is embedded in verbs describing communication and entertainment of beliefs (*tell* and *consider*) makes it possible for the hearer to still consider both **q** and **not q**.

Also, the sentence indicates the past act of telling, but it does not indicate that either of the alternative beliefs is definitely no longer tenable.

Perhaps, then, *unless* requires a context where q is the preferred assertion, but where there is still room for an exceptional alternative. Straightforward statements about the past, as well as those that implicate an irreversible past situation, are thus less likely to appear in a structure with *unless*. Most of the so-called "counterfactual" sentences will fall into these categories. As I argued in chapter 2, strong hypothetical forms specialize in presenting irreversible situations. Interestingly enough, this does not mean that we can never have "exceptive" construals of past situations. Above, I quoted Taub's example *?He fell off the cliff unless he has a good rope*,[5] where the situation in the present cannot describe an "exceptive" circumstance that would alter the past. But this is also because in such a sentence the past is treated as not only "knowable," but also known – there is nothing in the sentence to indicate the speaker's lack of certainty about the past events. Another example Taub gives is *He fell off the cliff unless he anchored himself well*. This one is clearly acceptable, and it is apparently because of the uncertainty involved: to the best of our knowledge, he fell (there was an earthquake, the rope broke, etc.), but we do not know whether he anchored himself well, and that could have saved him. Given uncertainty about some past events, we cannot treat statements about other related past events as irreversibly true; hence the use of *unless* is allowed. The next example Taub gives is even more interesting: *Unless he dies in the next hour, I gave him the right medicine*, which is like *?He fell off the cliff unless he has a good rope* in that only the apodosis is past. But the uncertainty here is not about whether he was given the medicine or not, but whether he was given the right one; this will be decided when the effects of the medicine become visible. So the q and ***not q*** in this sentence are "the right medicine" and "the wrong medicine" respectively. This shows, in turn, that the assumptions that enter the gloss for *unless* as p and q are not necessarily whole assertions. Apparently, this was also the case in (33).

To sum up, sentences with *unless* are unacceptable when the main clause presents the situation as irreversibly certain. This derives in a straightforward manner from the "unique circumstance" or "exceptive" meaning of the *unless*-clause. It is thus not surprising that *unless*-sentences are unacceptable in those

---

[5] Speakers vary in their judgments as to how (un)acceptable this sentence really is. It is certainly acceptable with the Present Perfect form instead of the Past if the intended meaning is inferential (*He has fallen of the cliff unless he has a good rope*), but in such a case *unless* is naturally acceptable because the overall interpretation concerns the present, rather than past events (via "present relevance" use of Present Perfect).

cases where past situations are presented as known and beyond repair. This is typically the case for so-called "counterfactual" sentences, the majority of whose uses signal the speaker's knowledge about non-irreversible past events. But in sentences which deal with beliefs and which leave room for different construals of the situations considered, *unless* can potentially be used with both Simple Past and strong hypothetical verb forms.

6.3   *Then* – a resumptive pronoun or a marker of sequentiality?

A conditional construction is composed of two clauses. The conditional clause is introduced by *if*, while the main clause may be introduced by *then*. *Then* is not obligatory in conditional sentences, but can be used in a number of cases; hence, especially when viewed as a logical connective, *if* is often seen as a short form for *if . . . then*. The meaning of *then* and its role in the interpretation is rarely brought up, for, as Haiman puts it, "there is no reason to believe that the pronominal *then* constitutes a necessary part of the meaning of the logicians' hook, or of ordinary language conditionals" (1978: 576).

Haiman (1978) offers a very convincing argument for analyzing *then* as an anaphoric pronoun referring back to the whole of the *if*-clause. In other words, in the structure of the main clause *then* replaces *if p*. The argument should further be supported with examples of conversations such as (34), where conditionality is implied solely by virtue of *then* being used anaphorically:

(34)   A: I would be afraid to leave the luggage in the car.
        B: Take it along, then.

There remains the rather puzzling question of why a conditional clause should be replaced with a pronoun which is transparently temporal. Also, on the assumption underlying both this work and Haiman's paper, the fact that one form has two different uses should be taken as a signal that these uses may well be related. An interesting suggestion in that direction can be found in sentences given by Schmerling (1975) and Wilson (1990). Wilson's examples are quoted here as (35) and (36):

(35)   I spoke to John and discovered that he was charming.
(36)   I spoke to John and then discovered that he was charming.

The sentences differ with respect to the time when the speaker discovered John's charms: while speaking to John, as in (35), or after speaking to him, as in (36). The presence of *then* is thus interpreted to mean that the temporal relation between the sentences conjoined with *and* is sequential rather than cotemporal;

the activity described in the first conjunct not only takes place, but is completed, before that of the second conjunct begins.

If these features were to be transposed onto the interpretation of conditionals, we might suggest that *then* has the role of "factualizing" the assumption in the *if*-clause. In other words, *then* re-introduces the assumption put forward in *p*, but presents it as necessarily factual relative to the ensuing prediction or communication of *q*. Recall that *if* has been claimed here to signal unassertability of the protasis *p*; what *then* seems to be doing is signaling that the assumption *p* has to be factual before *q* can be asserted.

Some such interpretation seems to emerge from a review of (un)acceptability of *then* in conditionals of various types. First of all, there are apparently no restrictions on using *then* in predictive conditionals, distanced or not (consider *If my old computer breaks down/broke down, then I'll/I would buy a new one*). And there seems to be no reason why any restrictions should apply, since predictive sentences are interpreted in terms of a sequence of events, and thus fulfill the requirements for the use of *then*. In inferential sentences, *then* is very common: examples such as *If 2 and 2 make 4, then 2 is an even number* are readily acceptable. *Then* is especially welcome in such reasonings, signaling that the premise has to hold before the conclusion can be drawn. The sequence of the steps in the reasoning from *p* to *q* is thus additionally reinforced.

Then appears to be especially common in inferential conditionals where the plausible conclusion *q* is arrived at via elimination of implausible ones. There are many examples of this use in the attested sentences I examined. Sentences (37) and (38) are among them (the former is quoted from *Operation Shylock* [by Philip Roth], the latter from *March Violets*):

(37)   In other words, if it's not Halcion and it's no dream, then it's got to be literature. (Roth 1994: 34)
(38)   If he's broke he'll be somewhere like X Bar, or the Rucker. If he's got any mouse in his pocket he'll be trying to . . . And if he's not at any of those places then he'll be at the racetrack. (Kerr 1993: 98)

Both sentences present a "review" of a set of possible patterns of reasoning. Since the first two hypotheses are rejected, together with conclusions that follow from them, the third option is put forward. The use of *then* seems to emphasize the fact that the validity of the third options is conditioned by the previous rejection of other options, and that there are possibly no more options to consider.

In speech act conditionals, the acceptability of *then* depends on the type of protasis. With classical, conversational protases *then* is usually not possible, as in **If you are hungry, then there are biscuits on the sideboard*, or **If I may say* *so, then you look great tonight,* or **If I may ask you to, then take out the garbage.* These restrictions are motivated by the semantic analysis of *then* which was proposed above. It does not have to be true that the addressee is hungry before biscuits appear on the sideboard. Perhaps more importantly, it should not be expected that "I may say that you look great" is true *before* I say that you look great, because I'm already saying it. The same seems to be the case for typical metatextual protases: we do not say **If I can still call him that, then my husband hates onion soup,* because the apodosis calls him "my husband" whether it is all right to do so or not.

At the same time, conditionals with contextually bound, hearer-perspective protases accept *then* in a number of cases, whether the relation between *p* and *q* is a speech act relation, as in example (39), or a more inferential one, as in (40) and (41) (all examples from *March Violets*):

(39)   You've seen the letter. If you think it's a fake, then check it out.
        (Kerr 1993: 95)
(40)   If it was Manstein, then I was going to have to make a run for it.
        (the speaker has just heard the door opening) *(Kerr 1993: 102)*
(41)   I had to admit one thing. If Haupthandler had killed the Pfarrs then he was as cool as a treasure chest in fifty fathoms of water.
        (Kerr 1993: 107)

In (39)–(41) *p* indeed has to hold before *q* does. The protases in all three examples are not assertable for the speaker at the moment of speech, since they concern the hearer's thoughts, or assumptions not known by the speaker to be true. They are therefore first "factualized" by *then*, and only then are the apodoses communicated.

What the above examples seem to suggest is that the clauses of conversational conditional constructions cannot be connected with *then* for two reasons. One is that they are not in any way sequential – either in the sense of events following other events, or assumptions following from other assumptions. They are comments on their apodoses, bearing no temporal relation to their content. Second, they do not describe states of affairs which have to be assertable prior to the assertion of the assumptions in main clauses. Consequently, *then* can be seen as a pronoun which "factualizes" the assumption to which it anaphorically refers, and which also marks a sequential relation between that assumption and *q*.[6]

There is yet another argument in favor of this interpretation of *then* as having a more complex meaning than pure resumptive anaphora. Haiman notes that *it*

---

[6] In Dancygier and Sweetser 1997 this interpretation is broadened and revised in terms of a specific type of mental space construction involved.

and *that* can also be used as resumptive pronouns in sentences like *If you tidied up your things, it would make me very happy, If you could bring a ball, that would be good.* It is possible, then, that the resumptiveness of personal and demonstrative pronouns fills a different function from that of *then.* Furthermore, it seems possible to have two resumptive pronouns in one construction, as in paraphrases of epistemic sentences we discussed in chapter 3, such as (42):

(42)   If her car is in the parking lot, then it means she eventually got the brakes
        fixed.

Interestingly enough, too, *then* is not obligatory in the structure of *q*, while resumptive *it* or *that* are necessary in (42), because they are subjects. Such examples seem to suggest that *then* and *it* have two different functions here, apart from perhaps both being in some sense resumptive.

Some aspects of the interpretation of *then* can perhaps be explained through the relation of *then* to *when.* *When* itself carries no assumptions of non-factuality; and its asserted, factual interpretation is even more strongly evident for its anaphoric counterpart. *When* is similar to *if* in many respects (as we have seen in chapters 2 and 3), but it is not tentative; that is, it lacks the non-assertive meaning which is crucial for *if*, even though in relation to the future it also intro-duces non-predicted assumptions. But both *when* and *if* can lead to similar statements when their *p*'s are imagined to be facts. So *then* is a natural resump-tive pronoun for both: it factualizes the content of a preceding *if*-clause, and confirms the factuality of the content of a preceding *when*-clause. The overall frame of a conditional construction with *then* is therefore to first introduce an assumption as a non-asserted, non-factual one (whether supposed, imagined, acquired indirectly, or the like), and then resume considering it, now as a factual, or true statement. This can tentatively be glossed as *Suppose that p. When p is true, q.*

An interesting fact about *then* is that it is usually optional in a conditional construction – it may be used, but does not have to be. Also, its presence does not usually alter the interpretation of the sentence in any very obvious way, though there are some differences. For example, Davis (1983), considers the following pair of examples:

(43)   If it is humid, the TV will work.
(44)   If it is humid, then the TV will work.

His comment is: "[(43)] is equivalent to an affirmative answer to the ques-tion, 'Will the TV work if it is humid?' which can be justified by observing that the TV works just fine and that humidity has no effect on it. [(44)] implies, in contrast, that there is some strange connection between humidity and the TV" (Davis 1983: 58).

The effect of *then* in such sentences is that it strengthens the dependence between the assumptions of *p* and *q*. This observation seems to be compatible with the rough interpretation offered above, according to which *then* imposes factuality on *p* and strict sequentiality on *p* and *q*. Another interesting observation has been made by Iatridou (1991, 1994). She argues that a conditional with *then* (*if p, then q*) carries the presupposition that *in some case where not p, not q*. Thus a sentence like (45) carries the presuppositions which can be rendered as (46) and (47):

(45)   If it's sunny, then Michael takes the dog to Pastorius Park.
(46)   In some cases in which it isn't sunny, Michael doesn't take the dog to Pastorius Park.
(47)   There are some cases in which it isn't sunny and in which Michael doesn't take the dog to Pastorius Park.
        (Iatridou 1994: 172)

Such presuppositions mean that the use of *then* brings situations alternative to *p* into consideration; and, more specifically, it allows the speaker to entertain the negative alternative, ***not p***, and its consequence, ***not q***. The existence of this presupposition, as Iatridou points out, explains a number of restrictions on the use of *then*. Among other constraints, *then* will not be acceptable in the cases where *p* exhausts all relevant possibilities. For example, *then* cannot be used after some disjunctive protases (e.g. **If John is dead or alive, then Bill will find him*), or after *even if* and other conditional-concessive protases (e.g. **If he were the last man on earth, then she wouldn't marry him*). *Then* is also excluded when the antecedent is a presupposition of the consequent (e.g. **If he smiles at her, then Mary likes it*), and does not appear in *only if* sentences. The presuppositional account advocated by Iatridou seems compatible with the "factualizing" and "sequentializing" functions I have attributed to *then*. Clearly, disjunctive pairs of assumptions and scales of assumptions invoked by concessive uses are not subject to "factualization," because in these cases there are multiple conflicting assumptions at stake. In the cases of the consequent presupposing the antecedent, two factors seem to be at work: first, the antecedent (or some part of it) is already represented in the consequent, and *then* would thus make the second reference to it; and second, it is difficult to clearly envisage how such sentences would be sequentially related.

Finally, there is the question of *only if* sentences. Iatridou (1991, 1994) considers several possible explanations for the restriction on the occurrence of *then* with *only if*, none of which seems to be fully satisfactory. A fact which may be relevant is that the discourse role of *only-if*-clauses is usually different from that of ordinary *if*-clauses (setting aside other differences in the interpretation). *Only-if*-clauses are more likely to follow the main clauses than ordinary protases; and when they are used sentence-finally they require an inverted construction in the following apodosis, as in: *Only if they ask me nicely will I agree to do it again.* This reminds one of the "highlighting" inversion of sentences like *Never have I seen a city as ugly as this one.* If, as Iatridou and von Fintel propose, *then* involves a dislocation structure, then perhaps the discourse role and typical sentential position of *only-if*-clauses is in conflict with such a syntactic mechanism. But, of course, this is just an informal suggestion and, obviously, more research needs to be done on this problem.

The question that remains difficult to answer is how much of the meaning involved is brought into the interpretation of the construction by the lexeme *then* itself. Von Fintel (1994) argues, for instance, that much of what we see in the use of *then* results from its syntax. Following Iatridou's suggestion (1991), von Fintel describes *then* not as a resumptive pronoun (as it fails some crucial tests here), but as a "correlative dislocation structure," similar to dislocation constructions found in Dutch and German (such as *In Hamburg, da bin ich gestern gewesen [in Hamburg, there am I yesterday been]*). Such a construction confers topic status on the dislocated element. As von Fintel puts it: "choosing the correlative dislocation structure *if . . . then* confers topic status on the *if*-clause, which means that alternatives to the antecedent must be under consideration, or at least conceivable" (von Fintel 1994: 98). This, in von Fintel's view, is all we need to say about *then*, including our concern with the contrast between (43) and (44); for the topic status, along with syntactic constraints, sufficiently accounts for the implied meaning that a different alternative will bring about a different result.

Perhaps this is indeed a sufficient explanation. But it calls for some more specific account of the difference between the topicality of *if* when accompanied by *then*, and its "garden variety" topicality without *then*. As has been noted repeatedly, initial *if* clauses tend to have topic status even without *then*, and much remains to be said with respect to the type of topic involved (see Haiman 1978, Akatsuka 1986, Schiffrin 1992). Thus von Fintel's solution, though intuitively appealing, will only be properly evaluated against a better understanding of topicality in general, and topicality in conditionals in particular. For the time being, I will finish with the observation that Iatridou's and von Fintel's analyses and my own intuitions about the use of *then* all seem to at least point in the same direction.

7 Conclusion: prototypical conditionality and related constructions

7.1 Predictiveness and a prototypical conditional

Recent typological work has expressed an understanding of linguistic categorial universals of cognitive structure. Researchers such as Kemmer (1988/1993) and Pederson (1991) have examined the way in which similar meaning categories are encoded again and again, in unrelated languages' "middle" and "reflexive" markers. Even more interestingly, not only are certain meanings cross-linguistically more likely to be encoded than others, but there seem to be a range of more or less closely related meanings which are likely to share a marker cross-linguistically. The same seems to be true of conditional constructions. When we identify a construction as "conditional" in some previously undescribed language, we do so on the basis of its meaning, and, I would claim, predictive conditional relations at the level of content are the meaning most likely to be identified as centrally "conditional" by most analysts. Yet we have an intuitive understanding that the expression of conditional relations in other domains may well share at least some aspects of formal expression with content-level prediction, in other languages as well as English.

Within English, evidence for the centrality of the predictive function to the definition of conditionality comes from several sources – beginning with the observation that native grammarians and teachers invariably light on these cases first. Most importantly, however, the expression of this kind of conditional meaning involves the tightest complex of entrenched, grammaticized constructional relation of form to meaning. As we have seen, predictive conditionals are formally distinguished from all other constructions by a consistent pattern of verb forms; as was shown above, this pattern is a characteristic of the construction as a whole, not of the protasis or apodosis in isolation. That is, whole conditionals, rather than individual clauses, are to be characterized as predictive or hypothetical. Predictives, unlike other classes of conditionals, which may derive their verb form usage from broader generalizations about

184

English grammar, depend on a specific backshifting rule for (conditional and non-conditional) predictive constructions. Non-predictive conditionals, on the other hand, make use of neutral verb forms which do not indicate predictiveness or even explicitly mark conditionality. One may of course note that the back-shifted forms used in predictive sentences are also used elsewhere with a similar interpretation (temporal adverbial clauses, constructions like *I wish . . .,* *I'd rather . . .,* reported past statements, etc.), but the range of patterns of modal-less and modally marked clauses found in (1) through (3) is at any rate (as a paradigm) characteristic of predictive conditional constructions.

(1)   If it rains, the match will be canceled.
(2)   If it rained, the match would be canceled.
(3)   If it had rained, the match would have been canceled.

Second, predictive conditionals are the only class in which the use of hypothetical forms (as in [2] and [3]) is possible without any restrictions. As we have observed, non-predictive conditionals are not used with such forms – if distanced forms appear in them, it is to signal some other kind of distance (e.g. to mark politeness), and they appear in just one of the clauses, not in a biclausal conditional pattern, as in: *I **would** like to leave now, if that's all right, And finish this letter, if you **would**,* etc.

Third, there is evidence that in a number of cases (cf., e.g. Traugott 1982, 1989, Sweetser 1990), meaning is extended from concrete relations such as real-world causality to more abstract and "subjective" relations such as logical and speech act interactional ones. This suggests the plausibility of content-level, i.e., causal predictive conditionality as a center from which semantic extension occurs to epistemic, speech act, and metatextual domains. The content domain, as understood by Sweetser (1990), is the source domain in terms of the mind-as-body metaphor of which conditionals, along with numerous other linguistic phenomena, are representative. If this is so, then the uses of conditional constructions to mark the inferential, speech act, and metatextual relations which are expressed by non-predictive constructions are instances of metaphorical use. As such, they are extensions of the more "literal" conditional meaning, and may be taken to be less central by definition. The fact that the inferential constructions, not the predictive ones, have been central to analyses of conditionals based on material implication should not be surprising if we consider the nature of epistemic conditionals. They are iconic of inferential processes, which, presumably, can be guided by logic alone. In predicting events, different processes are involved, including most centrally those connected with the only experientially based knowledge of cause–effect chains.

Fourth, predictive conditionals are found in all possible clause order configurations: their protases can be sentence-initial or sentence-final, and when they are sentence-final they can be pronounced either with or without a "comma" pause between the clauses. A further observation is that one of the clause order patterns is clearly open *only* to predictive, causal conditionals. The *if p, q* pattern is the most frequent one, and may be used in all types of conditionals. There is also the *q, if p* pattern, with an intonational pause between the clauses, in which many conditional sentences (though not inferential ones) can appear. This is the pattern which presents *p* as an afterthought, or additional information, and we should note that not only conditional protases, but also other linguistic expressions can be communicated in the same position in the sentence, with the same intonation and the same discourse function (consider *And finish this letter, while you're still here*, *And finish this letter, as soon as you can*, *And finish this letter, right now*, etc.). However, the third pattern, *q if p*, requires that the relation between *p* and *q* be predictive (causal). Other interpretations seem to be excluded because in this pattern *p* is no longer a (possibly topical) background to *q* and is at the same time incorporated into the meaning of *q*. In a sense, this pattern binds *p* and *q* together to the greatest degree – and this requires the interpretation to be predictive.

The type of non-assertiveness involved in the protases of predictive conditionals like (1) also seems to be more basic. Full assertions cannot be made about future situations, so there is a very concrete motivation for the marking of non-asserted status on these protases. What is more, these are descriptions of situations which, unlike ordinary future predictions, cannot be arrived at on the basis of the speaker's knowledge of the present and of the typical cause–effect links. They are thus not only "not known," but as "unknowable" as possible. Furthermore, the unassertability of such assumptions is motivated solely by their content-domain characteristics. That is, their status is not presented as being influenced by contextual clues, information acquired in the course of interaction, or conversational conventions. Even though all of these factors may exist in the context of the utterance, the speaker presents the assumption as solely dependent on her knowledge of possible events in the real world. Finally, in the case of hypothetical predictions the speaker is obliged to signal to the hearer (through distanced verb forms) that the situation described is not merely not known or unknowable, but indeed is very likely false – or at least the speaker has some "knowledge to the contrary."

In the most common type of non-predictive protasis, the non-assertiveness expressed is motivated, in a number of ways, by what is available in the context. The assumption brought up in the protasis may simply be observable in the immediate environment; it may have been communicated by another participant; or it may be implied by what has been said in the history of the exchange. Also, the degree of unassertability of such a protasis varies from total rejection to tentative acceptance, though some form of evidential distance (if only a shift of perspective to that of the hearer) is always present. Thus these assumptions are, in general, not fully assertable, although this unassertability is motivated not at the level of events, but at the level of beliefs. There is no implication that the assumptions themselves are for whatever reason unassertable, but that they are unassertable for the speaker at this point in the exchange. The belief-based, rather than event-based type of unassertability presents the differences among protases as similar to the differences we found among types of relations between protases and apodoses (which range from causal through epistemic to speech act and metatextual ones). And indeed, there are also non-predictive protases of the conversational type, which refer not to events, and not to beliefs, but to conventions of appropriateness, on the speech act or metatextual level.

Finally, predictive conditionals as whole sentences appear to involve more basic iconic motivation. They are iconic of a sequence of events; the event occurring earlier, and mentioned earlier, is understood to be the cause of the event occurring later, and mentioned later. In spite of other possible clause-order configurations, this is the typical frame of a piece of predictive reasoning. Other varieties of conditionals do also involve iconicity: the protasis–apodosis order in epistemic conditionals is iconic for the temporal sequence of premise and conclusion in inferential reasonings. What is more, the premise–conclusion sequence cannot be reversed. In conversational cases the sequentiality requirement is loosened: metatextual and speech act conditionals make their assertions not conditionally, but against the background of appropriateness rules. Since there is no sequential chain involved in the interpretation of these examples, clause order is quite free in these cases.

It appears, then, that prototypical conditionality involves three aspects of the construction: "sequence of events" iconicity, non-assertiveness of the protasis, and causal relation between the protasis and the apodosis. All of these are characteristic of predictive conditionals. Furthermore, by extension from this richly specified central conditional construction, we can give a satisfying synchronic account of the relationships which link together the wide-ranging class of "conditional" constructions in English, both constructions involving *if* and ones which do not.

7.2   Conditionality without *if*?

In chapter 1 I restricted this book's scope to the analysis of sentences which do have a form of a conditional construction: *if p, q*, with the protasis and the apodosis and with *if* marking the former. However, it has not been uncommon in literature to treat constructions other than *if*-conditionals as related to conditionals, provided that the constructions in question displayed meanings similar to those of conditionals. In the present section I will try to show how conditional meanings arise in constructions which do not have *if*, and I will use the account offered to support the view that "true" conditionals have the *if p, q* structure.

The constructions which are most commonly claimed to derive from conditionals are so-called pseudo-imperatives, such as (4) and (5):

(4)   Open the window and I'll kill you/I'll kiss you.
(5)   Open the window or I'll kill you/*I'll kiss you.

The imperatives in such sentences have been noted to function differently from other, independent imperatives. And it is indeed possible to paraphrase both (4) and (5) as conditionals: *If you open the window, I'll kill you/kiss you*, and *If you don't open the window, I'll kill you*, which has led to some derivational accounts linking the two constructions (see Lakoff 1966, 1972, Fraser 1969, 1971, Lawler 1975, Bolinger 1977).

However, Davies (1986), reviews the existing accounts against new data to conclude that sentences like (4) and (5) should be interpreted along with imperatives, not with conditionals, and, what is more, that they each represent a different use of the imperative.

In her account of the sentences like (4), which she calls Imperative-like Conditionals (ILCs), Davies considers the question of "intrinsic consequence," which has been suggested by Bolinger (1977) to be their necessary characteristic. Having reviewed a number of examples she concludes that the relation between the two clauses of an ILC "holds not at the semantic level of truth values, but at a pragmatic level . . . The requirement is such that, if the second conjunct functions as a prediction, it must be a prediction of the consequences fulfilling the condition; if it constitutes an enquiry, it must enquire as to what these consequences will be; if it conveys a directive, it must be a directive indicating what is to be done if the condition is fulfilled; and so on" (Davies 1986: 178).

The next observation Davies makes is about the first conjunct of an ILC. Various attempts have been made to characterize these clauses (Bolinger claims that they require stative verbs, Ibañez 1976 uses generic subjects as a criterion),

but Davies presents an argument that these clauses are sufficiently characterized as expressing "potential," "not real" situations. Finally, Davies concludes
that ILCs should not be identified with conditionals, because not all conditionals fulfill the requirements of "consequence" and "potentiality." On the other
hand, ILCs can be treated in a straightforward manner as coordinate structures
with imperatives as first conjuncts, because there is a feature which such imperatives share with other imperatives – that of describing a "potential" situation.
The difference between ILCs and other imperatives is that the latter, but not the
former also express "the speaker's acceptance of the realization of this
potentiality" (Davies 1986: 194). What the second conjunct adds to the imperative is the expression of the speaker's attitude to the potential act described,
hence the different interpretations given to (4) depending on whether *kill* or *kiss*
is used.

   In spite of terminological differences, it should be clear that the conditional
interpretations of the sentences like (4) rely on aspects of the construction's
meaning which correspond to the features of prototypical conditionality. There
is non-assertiveness (or potentiality), here introduced by the meaning of the
imperative form, rather than by *if*; there is a content–domain relation between
the conjuncts (Davies explicitly says that there are no ILCs of the "background"
or "speech act" type); and the form of the construction is iconic of the sequence
of events involved. We can thus conclude that the relation between ILCs and
conditionals is not in any sense derivational, but that the shared features of the
constructions result in similar, pragmatically motivated interpretations.

   Let us now look briefly at sentences like (5) (Imperative-like Ultimatums, or
ILUs, as Davies calls them). On the one hand, such constructions were traditionally treated along with ILCs, on the other hand, they impose some restrictions on the second conjunct, as we can see in the oddness of the interpretation
of (5) with *kiss*. Davies explains the asymmetry against her interpretation of the
imperative and argues that, unlike ILCs, ILUs have imperatives which fully
conform to the the standard use of the construction, that is, they express the
speaker's acceptance of the potentiality becoming reality. I will thus interpret
the emerging conditional meaning of ILUs in the following way: "An imperative is uttered with its usual force (potentiality and acceptance); then *or* brings
up an alternative. The alternative is also potential, but not accepted, and it will
result in the state of affairs described in the second conjunct. Because the 'cause'
event in the alternative construal is not desired, the 'result' event is also presented as not desired." Thus what we get is an interpretation very similar to that
of an ILC, but presented as an alternative, rather than as the message proper.
The conditional interpretation of the "alternative" construal arises in exactly the

same way as the conditional interpretation of an ILC – on the basis of causal connection between an unasserted antecedent and its consequence; the same kind of connection is involved in the prototypical cases of conditionality.

To summarize, both of the constructions considered above (ILCs and ILUs) can indeed receive interpretations similar to conditionals, and specifically to prototypical, predictive conditionals. The presence of the imperative introduces the feature that Davies calls "potentiality," which is also descriptive of protases of predictive conditionals. Then, if the conjoined clauses represent a sequential chain and can be interpreted as causally related, all the basic features of predictive conditionality are already part of the interpretation of these imperative constructions.

ILCs and ILUs are not the only coordinate constructions which have been noted to receive conditional interpretations. For example, Haiman (1983) makes similar observations concerning non-imperative paratactic constructions, such as (6):

(6)   You so much as touch alcohol, and your boss will fire you.

which can be paraphrased as "If you touch alcohol, your boss will fire you." On the other hand, there seem to be many coordinate sentences which do not invite the conditional interpretation, as in (7) (example from Davies 1986):

(7)   It just doesn't make sense! You buy an expensive lighter and you can't afford to smoke.

Example (7) implies contrast rather than consequence. But we can also note other important differences. While (6) is easily construed as being iconic of a sequence of events in the real world and thus inviting the reading-in of the causal interpretation, (7) is not easily read that way, partly because the events described in the conjuncts are less naturally interpretable as cause and effect. Thus the interpretation of (6), but not of (7), can give rise to the causal interpretation which constitutes the core of conditionality. What seems to be crucial, however, is the presence or absence of the second feature – "potentiality" (or "non-assertiveness"). As Haiman (1983) observes, paratactic constructions like (6) require, as Haiman calls it, "a potential interpretation of the verb" (this is similar enough to the potential interpretation of Davies's imperatives). Such an interpretation, says Haiman, can arise through the use of various expressions, including the meaning or form of the verb itself, modals, adverbs, etc. In the case of (6), the potentiality is introduced into the first conjunct by the expression *so much as*. In (7), on the other hand, there is nothing that would suggest a potential interpretation, thus the conditional meaning does not arise.

The choice of verb form in the second conjunct also seems to contribute in important ways to the interpretation, both in Davies's imperatives and in Haiman's paratactic constructions. In (4), (5), and (6) the speaker has used a predictive *will*, in a manner quite parallel to the use of *will* in the apodoses of predictive *if*-backshifted conditionals. In (7), on the other hand, the reference in the second conjunct is clearly to the present situation. Thus (6) is naturally open to a predictive interpretation, while (7) is not. In fact, the use of verb forms in (6) is *identical* to the use of verb forms in the prototypical, non-hypothetical predictive conditional: a Present tense verb form (with future/potential interpretation) in the first clause, and predictive *will* in the second. This familiar pattern recurs in a number of coordinate sentences with possible conditional interpretations. Consider (8), another example from Davies (1986):

(8)   He makes one mistake and he'll be out.

Just as in (6), all the components of conditional predictive reasoning are here. The verb (supported by the use of *one*, which is perhaps understood as "one more") carries the "potential" interpretation; there is sequential iconicity, additionally reinforced with the use of verb forms; and, consequently, there is also a causal interpretation of the relationship between the contents of the clauses. The form of (8) in various ways motivates an interpretation involving all the features of prototypical conditional meaning; and, not surprisingly, a conditional interpretation indeed arises naturally.

Apart from providing support for the account of prototypical conditionality proposed above, examples like (6) and (8) are also interesting from the point of view of their verb forms alone. The use of the present in their first conjuncts, for example, is exactly parallel to the use of the present in the protases of predictive conditionals. Thus, the backshift signaling non-predicted and "not knowable" status of an assumption used in arriving at a tentative prediction is also possible outside of *if* and *when* sentences. Just as in the subordinate clauses of conditionals and temporals, the use of *will* in the first conjunct of (8) would evoke a very different interpretation. In saying *He will make one mistake and he will be out* (if this is indeed an acceptable sentence) the speaker would communicate two possibly unrelated predictions, while the sequential and causal interpretation would be less likely. There is thus a clear correlation between the use of particular verb forms and the plausibility of some meanings, such as predictiveness, arising on the level of the construction as a whole.

We may also note that the form we traditionally call "an imperative" is another example of the verb's base form being used to refer to a futurate (or potential) situation, and in this case as well the speaker does not refer to any knowledge base which would justify a prediction. The potential occurrence of the event described hinges on the speaker's desire for the event to occur, not on the cause–effect links which will bring it about. Thus it is yet another instance of a non-predictive assumption about the future expressed through a modal-less verb form. At the same time, it is an assumption which, as in the other instances, can make further predictions possible. Many ILCs exemplify this possibility, for their second conjuncts commonly use the verb *will* in a predictive sense.

Evidently, then, a sequence of clauses which is iconic of a sequence of events is readily interpretable in terms of a causal relation between the states of affairs represented by the clauses. Furthermore, a non-assertive interpretation of the assumption describing the state of affairs which is temporally earlier can give rise to a conditional interpretation of the two-clause construction as a whole. Finally, in absence of other explicit signals of conditionality, verb forms can be an important indicator of predictive meaning. Consequently, non-assertiveness and causality, elements of prototypical conditionality, are naturally to be expected in the interpretations of constructions like ILCs, ILUs, and paratactic constructions (as represented here by [4], [5], and [6]), whose conditional interpretations thus emerge as normal and unmysterious.

7.3   Conditionality and inversion

There is yet another set of examples to be considered, where non-assertiveness is expressed in a way different from what we usually find in *if . . . (then)* constructions. There are sentences, typically considered to be variants of conditional constructions, which are conjunction-less. Instead, their protases are marked with subject–verb inversion. This appears to be possible with only three types of protases: those of strong hypothetical sentences like (3) (as in [10]), and those using modal verbs *should* and *were to*:

(9)   Should you change your mind, let us know.
(10)   Had the children been with us, they wouldn't have slept a wink.

Inversion is standardly used elsewhere in English to mark interrogative mood, which is certainly unassertive. Thus one possible explanation (suggested e.g. by Smith and Smith 1988) is that inversion plays a role similar to *if* here. It is interesting, however, that the possibility of applying inversion is open only for highly restricted cases. *Should* (in the sense of conditionally backshifted *shall*, not *ought to*, in either epistemic or deontic sense) and *were to* are practically not used outside conditionals, and the modality they introduce increases unassertability (they are usually claimed to express strong unlikelihood). Also, backshifted *should*, like hypothetical *had* or *were to*, is nearly unusable in questions: so such forms are almost automatically associated specifically with conditionality. As for sentences like (10), their conditional interpretation is also very salient, as Past Perfect is rarely a discourse starter, and when it is followed by *would have V-en* in the ensuing clause, there can hardly be any doubt as to what interpretation is meant by the speaker.

The case of *should* seems to be especially interesting here. As Nieuwint (1989) points out, *should* in conditionals is rather restricted in use (it is basically limited to speech act, non-predictive conditionals) and has a highly specialized meaning, that of "complete uncertainty." As Nieuwint argues very convincingly, a sentence with *if* is more readily interpretable as a question than the one with *should* and inversion. This is because *should* implicates that the problem in question cannot be resolved at the moment of speech – the uncertainty is complete. *If*, on the other hand, can have a force of a question which can be answered right away. Thus beginning a sentence with *Should you see John . . .* expresses no assumption to the effect that the hearer expects (or does not expect) to see John, while *If you see John . . .* may be used in a situation when the hearer can possibly resolve the uncertainty (in my terms, the speaker cannot predict that the hearer will see John). The example of *should* may be very specific, but it shows that inversion does not necessarily imply a question-like interpretation in all cases.

Finally, we should note that inversion is not only a question-forming syntactic structure. It is often treated on a par with other so-called non-canonical syntactic constructions (e.g. Green 1980, Prince 1985) and analyzed with respect to its pragmatic or discourse functions, entirely independent of interrogatives. In such analyses inversion appears to have a number of subtypes and to serve a variety of functions, but in each case the essential thing is that a word or phrase is preposed to draw the hearer's attention to some aspect of the interpretation (not necessarily to front old information).

Green (1980) notes that conditional constructions with inversion are capable of serving the same functions as their counterparts with *if*. In other words, inversion does not noticeably introduce anything new into the pragmatics of the construction. It may, then, be possible to interpret inversion in conditionals in terms of what is preposed and thus highlighted. The preposed element, in all cases where inversion is possible as an alternative construction, is the modal or auxiliary verb (*should, had, were to*) in a form characteristic for conditionals. The conditional-specific verb form is what is highlighted and put in the position normally occupied by *if*, which makes factual interpretation of the verb (and the whole assumption) rather unlikely. In other words, the clause begins with a sufficiently salient expression of non-assertiveness for *if* to be no longer necessary and for the whole construction to be interpreted conditionally.

To summarize, inverted conditional constructions seem to be motivated by a number of possibly independent, but interlocking factors. For one, as it was suggested by Smith and Smith (1988), inversion, being primarily associated with questions, may signal non-assertiveness in lieu of *if*. At the same time, inversion may have an effect of fronting and thus highlighting the modal verbs which are characteristic of conditional (that is, non-assertive) interpretations, either because they are themselves always interpreted non-assertively (*should* and *were to*), or because, at least within conditional constructions, they are associated with meanings which have broadly been termed "counterfactual" and are undoubtedly unassertive too. Finally, it also seems relevant that the three modal expressions in question (and these happen to be the only ones used in inverted conditional constructions) are not commonly found in genuine Yes/No questions, where inversion would be required. It would seem, then, that the function of inversion in English conditionals should be seen as related to the more general functions of inversion (including its discourse function), and to the semantics and pragmatics of relevant modal verbs.

7.4   *If* without conditionality?

A final question is whether the non-assertive *if* of conditionals is in any way related to the *if* of so-called embedded questions. In embedded questions, another conjunction, *whether*, can also be used. I will assume, with Bolinger (1978), that there is a difference between *if* and *whether* in such cases: *whether* reports an alternative question (that is, *whether p* necessarily invokes both *p* and *not p*), while *if* reports a simple question, positive or negative. Under such an interpretation, the conditional *if* and the embedded question *if* both qualify the assumption in their scope as it stands: it is marked as non-assertive, but its positive or negative status is unchanged.

Bolinger also postulates an affinity of the two *if*'s, such that they are both hypotheses, to be confirmed, amended, or disconfirmed by the hearer. I do not think, however, that the reaction of the hearer is in any way implied here. *If* in embedded questions, like its conditional counterpart, expresses the speaker's lack of certainty towards an assumption. The typical case is reporting a question the speaker or somebody else asked (*He asked her if . . ., I was wondering if . . .*), when the speaker is clearly quoting an assumption the author of the question could not assert (otherwise, why would the question be asked?). In a wide range of indirect questions, the central feature seems to be that the speaker expresses her own evaluation of the assumption as unassertable to her at the moment of speech: *I wonder if . . ., I don't know if . . ., I'd like to know if . . ., I doubt if . . .*, etc. Such sentences clearly do not directly involve the hearer (although they may invite the hearer's opinion). The embedding verbs in all of them, however, are "verbs of incertitude" followed by *if*. The presence of *if* seems to be required to mark the non-assertiveness of the embedded clause. Thus, the *if* of embedded questions is clearly related to the *if* of conditional constructions.

This is not to say that embedded questions and conditionals have anything in common as constructions. *If*-clauses of embedded questions never appear sentence-initially (see Luelsdorff and Norrick 1979), and there is no expectation of sequential ordering or of any kind of relation between the clauses. This is because a sequential interpretation tends to arise when the order of two clauses, in a relatively paratactic construction, is interpreted as iconic of the sequence of the events expressed by the clauses. Also, as I argued above, although *p*-clauses of conditional constructions do not have to precede *q*'s syntactically, they are prior to their apodoses in information structure. Reported questions, on the other hand, are truly embedded, and thus such interpretations are ruled out. The only link between the "embedder" and the "embedded" is that the embedding verb introduces the speaker's lack of certainty concerning the proposition in the embedded clause. That is why the role played by *if* seems to be largely similar to the one observed in conditionals – expression of unassertability.

7.5   Conclusions

This book has been an attempt to offer a general account of conditional constructions. In order to establish basic features of conditionality I have reviewed form–meaning correlations which are characteristic for conditionals and have tried to specify conventional meanings of all the formal aspects of conditional constructions. I have suggested that conditional verb forms are the best indicators of crucial aspects of interpretation such as the type of reasoning the speaker is involved in and the speaker's knowledge (as it is used in building conditional mental spaces). Other features, such as clause order, intonation, use of *then, even if*, and *unless*, also help distinguish among types of conditional constructions. Among the types of constructions which emerged from this classification, predictive constructions seem to represent prototypical conditionality; in these constructions the form–interpretation pairings are the most transparent and most conventionalized. Other, non-predictive, constructions are at the same time less conventionalized (though each type has its specific characteristics) and the role of contextual and inferential factors is greater there.

I hope to have shown that the framework adopted for this project is helpful in revealing facts about language use which cannot be formulated in more restrictive theories. Conditional sentences can be understood only in a framework which invites claims about what it is to think conditionally. Without the opportunity to include some understanding of the conceptual structure involved, we could not really say why conditionals are so different from ordinary sentences which purport to describe the speaker's conceived reality. It is important to equip one's framework with some way of describing the relationship between conceptual structure and language, especially in the cases where such relationships are a matter of conventional use. Moreover, we have to assume that not all of the conceptual structure involved in language use is *a priori* present in the participants' minds. Much of what is used in interpreting utterances is dynamically built as discourse progresses and is inherent in a particular interaction, rather than being brought into it ready-made. Conditionals are a perfect testing ground for this type of approach because they are primarily used to talk about things one does not really know about, but they also show us that there are (conceptually as well as linguistically) impressively many ways to envisage something beyond crude reality or immediately accessible knowledge.

Bibliography

References

Adams, E. (1970) "Subjunctive and indicative conditionals." *Foundations of Language* 6: 89–94.

Akatsuka, N. (1985) "Conditionals and epistemic scale." *Language* 61: 625–39.

(1986) "Conditionals are context-bound." In E. C. Traugott, A. ter Meulen, J. Snitzer Reilly, and C. A. Ferguson (eds.), 333–52.

(1992) "Japanese modals are conditionals." In D. Brentari, G. N. Larson, and L. A. MacLeod (eds.), *The Joy of Grammar: a Festschrift in Honor of James D. McCawley*. Amsterdam/Philadelphia: John Benjamins, 1–10.

Anderson, A. F. (1951) "A note on the subjunctive and counterfactual conditionals." *Analysis* 12(2): 35–38.

Atlas, J. (1974) "Presupposition, ambiguity, and generality: a coda to the Russell–Strawson debate on referring." Unpublished. Pomona College, California.

Austin, J. L. (1961) *"Ifs and cans."* In J. O. Urmson and G. J. Warnock (eds.), *Philosophical Papers*. Oxford: Oxford University Press, 153–80.

Bar-Hillel, Y. (ed.) (1971) *Pragmatics of Natural Languages*. Dordrecht: Reidel.

Barwise, J. (1986) "Conditionals and conditional information." In E. C. Traugott, A. ter Meulen, J. Snitzer Reilly, and C. A. Ferguson (eds.), 21–54.

Berlin, B., and P. Kay (1969) *Basic Color Terms: Their Universality and Evolution*. Berkeley: University of California Press.

Blakemore, D. (1987) *Semantic Constraints on Relevance*. Oxford/New York: Blackwell.

Bolinger, D. (1977) *Meaning and Form*. London: Longman.

(1978) "Yes–no questions are not alternative questions." In H. Hiż (ed.).

Brée, D. (1985) "On the semantics of *Unless*." In G. A. J. Hoppenbrouers, P. A. M. Seuren, and A. J. M. Weijters (eds.), *Meaning and the Lexicon*. Dordrecht: Foris, 309–16.

Bybee, J., R. Perkins, and W. Pagliuca. (1994) *The Evolution of Grammar: Tense, Aspect, and Modality in the Languages of the World*. Chicago: University of Chicago Press.

Carston, R. (1993) "Conjunction, explanation and relevance." *Lingua* 90: 27–48.

Chafe, W. (1972) "Discourse structure and human knowledge." In R. Freedle and J. Carroll (eds.), 41–69.

(1976) "Givenness, contrastiveness, definiteness, subjects, and topics." In C. N. Li (ed.), 25–56.

197

(1984) "How people use adverbial clauses." *Proceedings of the 10th Annual Meeting of the Berkeley Linguistics Society.* Berkeley, Calif.: Berkeley Linguistics Society, 437–49.

Chisholm, R. M. (1949) "The contrary to fact conditional." In H. Feigl and W. Sellars (eds.), 482–97.

Clark, H. H., and E. V. Clark (1977) *Psychology and Language.* New York: Harcourt Brace Jovanovich.

Close, R. A. (1980) *"Will* in *if*-clauses." In S. Greenbaum, G. Leech, and J. Svartvik (eds.), 100–09.

Cohen, L. J. (1971) "Some remarks on Grice's views about the logical particles of natural languages." In Y. Bar-Hillel (ed.), 51–67.

Cole, P., and J. Morgan (eds.) (1975) *Syntax and Semantics. Vol. 3: Speech Acts.* New York: Academic Press.

Comrie, B. (1982) "Future time reference in the conditional protasis." *Australian Journal of Linguistics* 2: 143–52.

(1986) "Conditionals: a typology." In E. C. Traugott, A. ter Meulen, J. Snitzer Reilly, and C. A. Ferguson (eds.), 77–99.

Dancy, J., J. Moravcsik, and C. Taylor (eds.) (1988) *Human Agency: Language, Duty and Value.* California: Stanford University Press.

Dancygier, B. (1985) *"If, unless,* and their Polish equivalents." *Papers and Studies in Contrastive Linguistics* 22: 65–72.

(1986) "Two metalinguistic operators in English and Polish." Paper delivered at LARS 86 Conference in Utrecht, The Netherlands.

(1987) *"If, if not* and *unless." Proceedings of the XIVth International Congress of Linguists,* Berlin/GDR, August 1987, Vol. 1, 912–15.

(1988a) "A note on the so-called indicative conditionals." *Papers and Studies in Contrastive Linguistics* 24: 123–32.

(1988b) "Conditionals and concessives." *Papers and Studies in Contrastive Linguistics* 24: 111–21.

(1990) "Conditionals: sequence of events and sequence of clauses." In J. Fisiak, (ed.), 357–73.

(1992) "Two metatextual operators: negation and conditionality in English and Polish." In L. A. Buszard-Welcher, L. Wee, and W. Weigel (eds.), *Proceedings of the 18th Annual Meeting of the Berkeley Linguistics Society.* Berkeley, Calif.: Berkeley Linguistics Society, 61–75.

(1993) "Interpreting conditionals: time, knowledge and causation." *Journal of Pragmatics* 19: 403–34.

Dancygier, B., and E. Mioduszewska (1984) "Semanto-pragmatic classification of conditionals." *Studia Anglica Posnaniensia* 17: 121–34.

Dancygier, B., and E. Sweetser (1996) "Conditionals, distancing, and alternative spaces." In Adele Goldberg (ed.), *Conceptual Structure, Discourse and Language.* Stanford, Calif.: CSLI Publications, 83–98.

(1997) *"Then* in conditional constructions." *Cognitive Linguistics* 8(2): 1–28.

Daneš, F. (ed.) (1974) *Papers on Functional Sentence Perspective.* The Hague: Mouton.

Davies, E. (1986) *The English Imperative.* London: Croom Helm.

Davis, W. (1983) "Weak and strong conditionals." *Pacific Philosophical Quarterly* 64: 57–71.

Davison, A. (1973) *Performative Verbs, Adverbs and Felicity Conditions: an Inquiry into the Nature of Performative Verbs.* Ph.D. dissertation, University of Chicago.

Donnellan, K. (1966) "Reference and definite descriptions." *Philosophical Review* 75: 281–304.

Downing, P. B. (1959) "Subjunctive conditionals, time order and causation." *Proceedings of the Aristotelian Society* 59: 125–40.

Dressler, W. (1974) "Funktionelle Satzperspektive und texttheorie." In F. Daneš, (ed.), 87–105.

Ducrot, O. (1972) *Dire et ne pas dire: Principes de sémantique linguistique.* Paris: Hermann.

Dudman, V. H. (1984) "Conditional interpretations of *if*-sentences." *Australian Journal of Linguistics* 4: 143–204.

Dummett, M. (1973) *Frege: Philosophy of Language.* London: Duckworth.

Eckersley, C. E., and J. M. Eckersley (1960) *A Comprehensive English Grammar for Foreign Students.* London: Longman.

Ellis, B. F. (1984) "Two theories of indicative conditionals." *Australasian Journal of Philosophy* 62: 50–66.

Fasold, R. W., and R. W. Shuy (eds.) (1977) *Studies in Language Variation.* Washington, D.C.: Georgetown University Press.

Fauconnier, G. (1975a) "Pragmatic scales and logical structures." *Linguistic Inquiry* 6: 353–75.

(1975b) "Polarity and the scale principle." *CLS* 11: 188–99.

(1985) *Mental Spaces: Aspects of Meaning Construction in Natural Language.* Cambridge, Mass.: MIT Press. (2nd edn. 1994, Cambridge: Cambridge University Press.)

(1996) "Analogical counterfactuals." In G. Fauconnier and E. Sweetser (eds.), 57–90.

Fauconnier, G., and E. Sweetser (eds.) (1996) *Spaces, Worlds, and Grammar.* Chicago: University of Chicago Press.

Feigl, H., and W. Sellars (eds.) (1949) *Readings in Philosophical Analysis.* New York: Appelton-Century Crofts.

Fillenbaum, S. (1976) "Inducements: on the phrasing and logic of conditional promises, threats, and warnings." *Psychological Research* 38: 231–50.

(1986) "The use of conditionals in inducements and deterrents." In E. C. Traugott, A. ter Meulen, J. Snitzer Reilly, and C. A. Ferguson (eds.), 179–95.

Fillmore, Ch. (1977) "Topics in lexical semantics." In R. W. Cole (ed.), *Current Issues in Linguistic Theory.* Bloomington: Indiana University Press, 76–138.

(1982) "Frame semantics." In Linguistic Society of Korea (ed.), *Linguistics in the Morning Calm.* Seoul: Hanshin, 111–38.

(1985) "Frames and the semantics of understanding." *Quaderni di Semantica* 6 (2): 222–54.

(1986) "Varieties of conditional sentences." *ESCOL* 3 (Eastern States Conference on Linguistics): 163–82.

(1988) "The mechanisms of 'Construction Grammar.'" In S. Axmaker, A. Jaisser, and H. Singmaster (eds.), *Proceedings of the 14th Annual Meeting of the Berkeley Linguistics Society*. Berkeley: Berkeley Linguistics Society, 35–55.

(1990a). "Epistemic stance and grammatical form in English conditional sentences." In M. Ziolkowski, M. Noske, and K. Deaton (eds.), *Papers from the 26th Regional Meeting of the Chicago Linguistic Society*. Chicago: Chicago Linguistic Society, 137–62.

(1990b). "The contribution of linguistics to language understanding." In A. Bocaz (ed.), *Proceedings of the 1st Symposium on Cognition, Language, and Culture*. Universidad de Chile, 109–28.

Fillmore, Ch., and P. Kay (1994) "Grammatical constructions and linguistic generalizations: the *What's X doing Y?* construction." Unpublished manuscript.

Fillmore, Ch., P. Kay, and M. C. O'Connor (1988) "Regularity and idiomaticity in grammatical constructions: the case of 'let alone.'" Language 63(3): 501–38.

von Fintel, K. (1991) "Exceptive conditionals: the meaning of *Unless*." *North Eastern Linguistics Society* 22: 135–48.

(1994). Restrictions on Quantifier Domains. Ph.D. dissertation, University of Massachusetts at Amherst.

Firbas, J. (1964) "On defining the theme in functional sentence analysis." *Travaux Linguistiques de Prague* 1: 267–80.

Fisiak, J. (ed.) (1990) *Further Insights into Contrastive Analysis*. Amsterdam: John Benjamins.

Fleischman, S. (1989) "Temporal distance: a basic linguistic metaphor." *Studies in Language* 13(1): 1–50.

Ford, C. E. (1993) *Grammar in Interaction: Adverbial Clauses in American English Conversations*. Cambridge: Cambridge University Press.

Ford, C. E., and S. A. Thompson (1986) "Conditionals in discourse: a text based study from English." In E. C. Traugott, A. ter Meulen, J. Snitzer Reilly, and C. A. Ferguson (eds.), 353–72.

Fraser, B. (1969) "An analysis of concessive conditionals." *CLS* 5: 66–73.

(1971) "An analysis of *Even* in English." In Ch. Fillmore and T. Langendoen (eds.), *Studies in Linguistic Semantics*. New York: Holt, Rinehart, and Winston.

Freedle, R., and J. Carroll (eds.) (1972) *Language Comprehension and the Acquisition of Knowledge*. New York: Holt, Rinehart, and Winston.

Fujita, T. (1987) "Counterfactual *Unless*." *English Linguistics* 4: 342–46.

Funk, W.-P. (1985) "On a semantic typology of conditional sentences." *Folia Linguistica* 19 (3/4): 365–414.

Gazdar, G. (1979) *Pragmatics: Implicature, Presupposition, and Logical Form*. New York: Academic Press.

Geis, M. L. (1961) *Adverbial Subordinate Clauses*. Ph.D. dissertation, The M.I.T.

(1973) "*If* and *unless*." In B. Kachru, R. Lees, Y. Malkiel, A. Pietrangeli, and S. Saporta (eds.), 231–53.

Geis, M. L., and A. M. Zwicky (1971) "On invited inferences." *Linguistic Inquiry* 2: 561–66.

Givon, T. (1990) *Syntax: a Functional-Typological Introduction*. Vol. II. Amsterdam: John Benjamins Publishing Company.

(1993) *English Grammar: a Function-based Introduction.* Vols. I and II. Amsterdam: John Benjamins.

Goldberg, A. (1994) *Constructions: a Construction Grammar Approach to Argument Structure.* Chicago: University of Chicago Press.

Graver, B. D. (1971) *Advanced English Practice.* 2nd edn. Oxford: Oxford University Press.

Green, G. M. (1980) "Some wherefores of inversion." *Language* 56: 582–602.

Greenbaum, S., G. Leech, and J. Svartvik (eds.) (1980) *Studies in English Linguistics for Randolf Quirk.* London: Longman.

Greenberg, J. H. (1963) "Some universals of grammar with particular reference to the order of meaningful elements." In J. H. Greenberg (ed.), 73–113.

(ed.) (1963) *Universals of Language.* Cambridge, Mass.: MIT Press.

(1966) *Language Universals.* The Hague: Mouton.

Grice, H. P. (1967) *Logic and Conversation.* Unpublished. William James lectures at Harvard University.

(1975) "Logic and conversation." In P. Cole and J. Morgan (eds.), 41–58.

Haegeman, L. (1984) "Pragmatic conditionals in English." *Folia Linguistica* 18 (3/4): 485–502.

Haegeman, L., and H. Wekker (1984) "The syntax and interpretation of futurate conditionals in English." *Journal of Linguistics* 20: 45–55.

Haiman, J. (1974) "Concessives, conditionals and verbs of volition." *Foundations of Language* 11: 342–60.

(1978) "Conditionals are topics." *Language* 54: 512–40.

(1980) "The iconicity of grammar: isomorphism and motivation." *Language* 56: 515–40.

(1983) "Paratactic *if*-clauses." *Journal of Pragmatics* 7: 263–81.

(ed.) (1985) *Iconicity in Syntax.* Amsterdam: John Benjamins.

(1986) "Constraints on the form and meaning of the protasis." In E. C. Traugott, A. ter Meulen, J. Snitzer Reilly, and C. A. Ferguson (eds.), 215–27.

Harper, W. L., R. Stalnaker, and G. Pearce (eds.) (1981) *Ifs: Conditionals, Belief, Decision, Chance and Time.* The University of Western Ontario Series in Philosophy of Science, 15. Dordrecht: Reidel.

Heringer, J. T. (1971) *Some Grammatical Correlates of Felicity Conditions and Presuppositions.* Ph.D. dissertation, Ohio State University.

Hiż, H. (ed.) (1978) *Questions.* Dordrecht: Reidel.

Holdcroft, D. (1971) "Conditional assertion." *Proceedings of the Aristotelian Society.* Supplementary Vol. 45, 123–39.

Holland, D., and N. Quinn (eds.) (1987) *Cultural Models in Language and Thought.* Cambridge: Cambridge University Press.

Horn, L. R. (1969) "A presuppositional analysis of *only* and *even*." *CLS* 5: 98–107.

(1984) "Toward a new taxonomy for pragmatic inference: Q-based and R-based implicature." In D. Schiffrin (ed.), *Meaning, Form and Use in Context: Linguistic Applications.* (Georgetown University Round Table 1984.) Washington, D.C.: Georgetown University Press, 11–42.

(1985) "Metalinguistic negation and pragmatic ambiguity." *Language* 61: 121–74.

(1989) *A Natural History of Negation.* Chicago: University of Chicago Press.

Hornstein, N. (1990) *As Time Goes By: Tense and Universal Grammar.* Cambridge, Mass.: The MIT Press.

Huddleston, R. (1984) *Introduction to the Grammar of English.* Cambridge: Cambridge University Press.

Hyman, L., and C. Li (eds.) (1988) *Language, Speech and Mind: Studies in Honour of Victoria A. Fromkin.* London: Routledge.

Iatridou, S. (1991) "If *Then*, then what?" *North Eastern Linguistics Society* 22: 211–25.

(1994) "On the contribution of conditional *Then.*" *Natural Language Semantics* 2: 171–99.

Ibañez, R. (1976) "Über die Beziehungen zwischen Grammatik und Pragmatik: Konversationspostulate auf dem Gebiet der Konditionalität und Imperativität." *Folia Linguistica* 10: 223–48.

Jackendoff, R. (1975) "On belief contexts." *Linguistic Inquiry* 6: 53–93.

Jackson, F. (1987) *Conditionals.* Oxford: Blackwell.

(ed.) (1991) *Conditionals.* Oxford: Oxford University Press.

Jacobsen, W. (1992) "Are conditionals topics? The Japanese case." In D. Brentari, G. N. Larson, and L. A. MacLeod (eds.), *The Joy of Grammar: a Festschrift in Honor of James D. McCawley.* Amsterdam/Philadelphia: John Benjamins. 131–59.

James, D. (1982) "Past tense and the hypothetical: a cross-linguistic study." *Studies in Language* 6(3): 375–403.

Jespersen, O. (1940) *A Modern English Grammar on Historical Principles.* Vol. 5: *Syntax.* London: George Allen and Unwin.

Joos, M. (1964) *The English Verb: Form and Meanings.* Madison/Milwaukee: University of Wisconsin Press.

Kachru, B., R. Lees, Y. Malkiel, A. Pietrangeli, and S. Saporta (eds.) (1973) *Issues in Linguistics: Papers in Honor of Henry and Renee Kahane.* Urbana, Ill.: University of Illinois Press.

Kartunnen, L., and S. Peters (1979) "Conventional implicature." In C.-K. Oh, and D. Dinneen (eds.), 1–56.

Kay, P. (1990) "Even." *Linguistics and Philosophy* 13: 59–111.

Kemmer, S. (1988/1993) *The Middle Voice.* Amsterdam: John Benjamins.

Kempson, R. (1975) *Presupposition and the Delimitation of Semantics.* Cambridge: Cambridge University Press.

Kjëllmer, G. (1975) "'The weather was fine, if not glorious': on the ambiguity of concessive *if not.*" *English Studies* 56: 140–46.

König, E. (1986) "Conditionals, concessive conditionals and concessives: areas of contrast, overlap and neutralization." In E. C. Traugott, A. ter Meulen, J. Snitzer Reilly, and C. A. Ferguson (eds.), 229–46.

Köpcke, K., and K. Panther (1989) "On correlations between word order and pragmatic function of conditional sentences in German." *Journal of Pragmatics* 13: 685–711.

Lakoff, G. (1966) "Stative adjectives and verbs in English." MLAT Report No. NSF-17. Harvard University Computation Laboratory. Cambridge, Mass.

(1972a) "Linguistics and natural logic." In D. Davidson and G. Harman (eds.), *Semantics of Natural Language.* Dordrecht: Reidel.

(1972b) "Hedges: a study in meaning criteria and the logic of fuzzy concepts." *CLS* 8: 183–228.

(1987) *Women, Fire, and Dangerous Things: What Categories Reveal About the Mind.* Chicago: University of Chicago Press.

Lakoff, G., and M. Johnson (1980) *Metaphors We Live By.* Chicago: University of Chicago Press.

Lakoff, R. T. (1973) "The logic of politeness, or minding your p's and q's." *CLS* 9: 292–305.

Langacker, R. (1987) *Foundations of Cognitive Grammar.* Vol. 1: *Theoretical Prerequisites.* Stanford, Calif.: Stanford University Press.

(1991a) *Foundations of Cognitive Grammar.* Vol. 2: *Descriptive Application.* Stanford, Calif.: Stanford University Press.

(1991b) *Concept, Image, and Symbol: the Cognitive Basis of Grammar.* Berlin/New York: Mouton de Gruyter.

Lawler, J. M. (1975) "Elliptical conditionals and/or hyperbolic imperatives: some remarks on the inherent inadequacy of derivations." *CLS* 11: 371–81.

Leech, G. (1971) *Meaning and the English Verb.* London: Longman.

Leech, G., and J. Svartvik (1975/1994) *A Communicative Grammar of English.* London/New York: Longman.

Lehmann, Ch. (1974) "Prinzipien für 'Universal 14.'" In H. Seiler (ed.), 69–97.

Lewis, D. (1973) *Counterfactuals.* Oxford: Blackwell.

(1976) "Probabilities of conditionals and conditional probablilities." *Philosophical Review* 85: 297–315.

(1979) "Counterfactual dependence and time's arrow." *Nous* 13: 455–76.

(1981) "Counterfactuals and comparative possibility." In W. L. Harper, R. Stalnaker, and G. Pearce (eds.), 57–86.

Li, C. N. (ed.) (1976) *Subject and Topic.* New York: Academic Press.

Lightbown, P. M., and N. Spada (1993) *How Languages are Learned.* Oxford: Oxford University Press.

Linde, Ch. (1976) "Constraints on the ordering of *if*-clauses." *Proceedings of the 2nd Annual Meeting of the Berkeley Linguistics Society.* Berkeley: Berkeley Linguistics Society, 280–85.

Luelsdorff, P. A., and N. R. Norrick (1979) "On *If* and *Whether* complementation." *Linguistische Berichte* 62: 25–47.

Lyons, J. (1977) *Semantics.* Cambridge: Cambridge University Press.

McCawley, J. D. (1974) "*If* and *only if*." *Linguistic Inquiry* 5: 632–35.

(1981) *Everything that Linguists Have Always Wanted to Know About Logic – but Were Ashamed to Ask.* Chicago: University of Chicago Press.

Mitchell, K. (1990) "On comparisons in a notional grammar." *Applied Linguistics* 11(1): 52–72.

Nieuwint, P. (1986) "Present and future in conditional protases." *Linguistics* 24: 371–92.

(1989) "*Should* in conditional protases." *Linguistics* 27: 305–18.

Oh, C.-K., and D. Dinneen (eds.) (1979) *Syntax and Semantics 11: Presupposition.* New York: Academic Press.

Palmer, F. R. (1965) *A Linguistic Study of the English Verb.* London: Longman.

(1974) *The English Verb.* London: Longman.

(1979) *Modality and the English Modals.* London: Longman.

(1983) "Future time reference in the conditional protasis: a comment on Comrie." *Australian Journal of Linguistics* 3(2): 241–43.

Pederson, E. (1991) *Subtle Semantics: Universals in the Polysemy of Reflexive and Causative Constructions*. Ph.D. dissertation, University of California at Berkeley.

Prince, E. F. (1985) "Fancy syntax and 'shared knowledge.'" *Journal of Pragmatics* 9: 65–81.

Quine, W. V. O. (1962) *Methods of Logic*. London: Routledge and Kegan Paul.

Quirk, R., S. Greenbaum, G. Leech, and J. Svartvik (1972) *A Grammar of Contemporary English*. London: Longman.

(1985) *A Comprehensive Grammar of the English Language*. London: Longman.

Ramsey, F. (1931) "General propositions and causality." In *Foundations of Mathematics*. London: Kegan Paul, 237–55.

Reichenbach, H. (1947) *Elements of Symbolic Logic*. New York: Macmillan. Reprinted in 1966. New York Free Press.

Rescher, N. (ed.) (1968) *Studies in Logical Theory*. Oxford: Blackwell.

Rosch, E. (1977) "Human categorization." In N. Warren (ed.), *Studies in Cross-cultural Psychology*. Vol. 1. London: Academic Press, 3–49.

(1978) "Principles of categorization." In E. Rosch and B. Lloyd (eds.), *Cognition and Categorization*. Hillsdale, N.J.: Lawrence Erlbaum Associates, 27–48.

Schiffrin, D. (1992) "Conditionals as topics in discourse." *Linguistics* 30: 165–97.

Schmerling, S. (1975) "Assymetric conjunction and rules of conversation." In P. Cole, and J. Morgan (eds.).

Searle, J. R. (1969) *Speech Acts: an Essay in the Philosophy of Language*. Cambridge: Cambridge University Press.

(1979) *Expression and Meaning*. Cambridge: Cambridge University Press.

Seiler, H. (ed.) (1974) *Linguistic Workshop II*. Munich: Wilhelm Fink Verlag.

Shibatani, M., and S. A. Thompson (eds.) (1996) *Grammatical Constructions: Their Form and Meaning*. Oxford: Oxford University Press.

Smith, N. (1983) "On interpreting conditionals." *Australian Journal of Linguistics* 3(1): 1–24.

Smith, N., and A. Smith (1988) "A relevance-theoretic account of conditionals." In L. Hyman and C. Li (eds.), 322–52.

Sperber, D., and D. Wilson (1981) "Irony and the use-mention distinction." In P. Cole (ed.), *Radical Pragmatics*. New York: Academic Press, 295–318.

(1986) *Relevance: Communication and Cognition*. Oxford: Blackwell.

(1993) "Linguistic form and relevance." *Lingua* 90: 1–25.

Stalnaker, R. C. (1968) "A theory of conditionals." In N. Rescher (ed.), 98–112. Reprinted in W. L. Harper, R. Stalnaker, and G. Pearce (eds.), 41–55.

Swan, M. (1980) *Practical English Usage*. Oxford: Oxford University Press.

Sweetser, E. (1984) *From Etymology to Pragmatics*. Ph.D. dissertation, University of California at Berkeley.

(1987) "The definition of 'lie': an examination of the folk theories underlying a semantic prototype." In D. Holland and N. Quinn (eds.), *Cultural Models in Language and Thought*. Cambridge: Cambridge University Press, 43–66.

(1990) *From Etymology to Pragmatics*. Cambridge: Cambridge University Press.

(1996a) "Reasoning, mappings, and meta-metaphorical conditionals." In M. Shibatani and S. Thompson (eds.), 221–34.

(1996b) "Mental spaces and the grammar of conditional constructions." In G. Fauconnier and E. Sweetser (eds.), 318–33.

Taub, S. (1991) "Constructions with *Unless.*" Unpublished manuscript.
Tedeschi, P. J. (1977) "Some aspects of conditional sentence pragmatics." In R. W. Fasold and R. W. Shuy (eds.), 136–51.
Traugott, E. C. (1982) "From propositional to textual and expressive meanings: some semantic-pragmatic aspects of grammaticalization." In W. Lehmann and Y. Malkiel (eds.), *Perspectives on Historical Linguistics.* Amsterdam: John Benjamins, 245–71.
(1985) "Conditional markers." In J. Haiman (ed.), 289–307.
(1987) "UNLESS and BUT conditionals: a historical perspective." In A. Athanasiadou and R. Dirven (eds.), *On Conditionals Again.* Amsterdam/ Philadelphia: John Benjamins, 145–67.
(1989) "On the rise of epistemic meanings in English: an example of subjectification in semantic change." *Language* 65 (1): 31–55.
Traugott, E. C., A. ter Meulen, J. Snitzer Reilly, and C. A. Ferguson (eds.) (1986) *On Conditionals.* Cambridge: Cambridge University Press.
Van der Auwera, J. (1985) *"Only if." Logique et Analyse* 109: 61–74.
(1986) "Conditionals and speech acts." In E. C. Traugott, A. ter Meulen, J. Snitzer Reilly, and C. A. Ferguson (eds.), 197–214.
Ward, J. M. (1954) *The Use of Tenses in English.* London: Longman.
Wertheimer, R. (1972) *The Significance of Sense: Meaning, Modality, and Morality.* Ithaca, N.Y.: Cornell University Press.
Wilson, D. (1975) *Presupposition and Non-Truth-Conditional Semantics.* New York: Academic Press.
(1990) "Pragmatics and time." Paper delivered at MIT Conference on Time in Language.
Wilson, D., and D. Sperber (1988) "Mood and the analysis of non-declarative sentences." In J. Dancy, J. Moravcsik, and C. Taylor (eds.).
Yamaguchi, S. F. (1989) "Concessive conditionals in Japanese: a pragmatic analysis of the S1–TEMO S2 construction." *Proceedings of the 15th Annual Meeting of the Berkeley Linguistics Society.* Berkeley, Calif.: Berkeley Linguistics Society, 1–12.
Zandvoort, R. W. (1962) *A Handbook of English Grammar.* 2nd edn. London: Longman.

Literary works quoted

Christie, A. (1982) *The Hound of Death.* Fontana Paperbacks.
Kerr, P. (1993) *March Violets.* In *Berlin Noir.* Harmondsworth/New York: Penguin Books, 1–248.
L'Engle, M. (1962) *A Wrinkle in Time.* New York: Dell.
Roth, P. (1994) *Operation Shylock.* New York: Vintage Books.
Vonnegut, K. (1990) *Hocus Pocus.* New York: Berkley Books.

Index of names

Adams, E. 16
Akatsuka, N. 4, 17–18, 68, 111, 113, 116, 135–6, 183
Anderson, A. F. 29, 34
Atlas, J. 93
Austin, J. L. 90, 103–5, 124, 160

Barwise, J. 35
Berlin, B. 24
Blakemore, D. 81
Bolinger, D. 11, 188, 194
Brée, D. 171
Bybee, J. 73

Carston, R. 75
Chafe, W. 135, 148
Chisholm, R. M. 29, 34
Christie, A. 176
Clark, E. V. 170
Clark, H. 170
Close, R. A. 26, 117, 118
Cohen, L. 74
Comrie, B. 4, 10–12, 26, 35, 78, 117–18, 135, 146, 151, 167

Dancygier, B. 6, 13, 17, 23, 31, 78, 84, 86, 94, 118–19, 133, 161, 163–4, 170, 180
Davies, E. 141, 188–91
Davis, W. 181–2
Davison, A. 89
Donnellan, K. 94
Downing, P. B. 29
Dressler, W. 135
Ducrot, O. 108, 133, 166
Dudman, V. H. 30, 36, 39–44, 46, 52–3, 55, 69
Dummett, M. 19, 94

Eckersley, C .E. 3, 26, 36
Eckersley, J. M. 3, 26, 36
Ellis, B. F. 29

Fauconnier, G. 20–3, 42, 54–5, 111–12, 161
Fillenbaum, S. 4, 17, 170

Fillmore, Ch. 1, 5, 7–10, 22, 31–2, 34, 51, 117
von Fintel, K. 169–72, 175, 183
Firbas, J. 135
Fleischman, S. 38, 49
Ford, C. E. 12, 84, 145–7, 153, 159
Fraser, B. 11, 161, 188
Fujita, T. 176
Funk, W.-P. 4, 36–7

Gazdar, G. 93
Geis, M. L. 162, 167–8, 170–1
Givon, T. 73, 75
Goldberg, A. 5
Goodman, N. 3
Graver, B. D. 3, 26
Green, G. M. 193
Greenbaum, S. 4, 26–8, 30, 39, 44–5, 116, 167
Greenberg, J. H. 12, 73, 146
Grice, H. P. 8, 19, 90, 94

Haegeman, L. 4, 26, 117
Haiman, J. 4, 73–4, 108, 135–6, 143, 161–2, 164–5, 178, 180, 183, 190–1
Harper, W. L. 29
Herforth, D. 47
Heringer, J. T. 89
Holdcroft, D. 124–6
Holland, D. 22
Horn, L. R. 7, 9, 19, 93–6, 98–100, 103–8, 161, 168
Hornstein, N. 3, 52–4
Huddleston, R. 30, 44
Hume, D. 78

Iatridou, S. 182–3
Ibañez, R. 188

Jackendoff, R. 22
Jackson, F. 14, 29
Jacobsen, W. 135
James, D. 38

206

Subject index